GLOBAL MARKETING
AND ADVERTISING

*To Anne, my husband
and best friend*

GLOBAL MARKETING
AND ADVERTISING
Understanding
Cultural Paradoxes

Marieke de Mooij

SAGE Publications
International Educational and Professional Publisher
Thousand Oaks London New Delhi

For information:

SAGE Publications, Inc.
2455 Teller Road
Thousand Oaks, California 91320
E-mail: order@sagepub.com

SAGE Publications Ltd.
6 Bonhill Street
London EC2A 4PU
United Kingdom

SAGE Publications India Pvt. Ltd.
M-32 Market
Greater Kailash I
New Delhi 110 048 India

Printed in the United States of America

Library of Congress Cataloging-in-Publication Data

Mooij, Marieke K. de, 1943-
    Global marketing and advertising: Understanding cultural
paradoxes / Marieke de Mooij.
        p. cm.
    Includes bibliographical references and index.
    ISBN 0-8039-5969-9 (acid-free paper). — ISBN 0-8039-5970-2 (pbk.:
acid-free paper)
    1. Target marketing—Cross-cultural studies. 2. Advertising—
Cross-cultural studies. 3. Consumer behavior—Cross-cultural
studies. I. Title.
    HF5415.127.M66 1997
    658.8'02—dc21   97-4800

This book is printed on acid-free paper.

98 99 00 01 02 10 9 8 7 6 5 4 3 2

Acquiring Editor:	Harry Briggs
Editorial Assistant:	Jessica Crawford
Production Editor:	Astrid Virding
Production Assistant:	Karen Wiley
Typesetter/Designer:	Rebecca Evans
Cover Designer:	Ravi Balasuriya

Contents

98 0939

Foreword

Geert Hofstede

A naïve set of assumptions, quite common in both business and academia up to the present day, is that people are rational in trying to maximize their income, but irrational in spending it. Producers are supposed to be rational; consumers irrational. And inside the business organization managers are supposed to be rational; subordinates irrational.

There is something fishy in this reasoning, because producers are consumers to other producers, and managers are subordinates to other managers. The aforementioned assumptions do not reflect observable reality, but a perception process in which those in control define rationality in their way. The rationality described in the policies and textbooks is usually the rationality of the producers and managers.

More fundamentally, there is no such thing as a universal rationality—a discovery that, for example, economists applying a "rational choice" model have to make. What is rational or irrational to a person depends on that person's value system, which in turn is part of the culture that person has acquired in her or his lifetime. What people around the world value varies enormously: They include poverty next to maximizing income, togetherness next to individuality, cooperation next to competition, modesty next to assertiveness, saving next to spending, chastity next to sexual fulfillment, self-effacement next to self-actualization. Downsizing personnel in order to maximize a company's profits may be rational in one society—say, the United States of America—but not in another—say, Japan—in which the commitment of permanent employees is the company's main capital.

Marketing and advertising are basically about consumers, not about producers. Marketing and advertising theories based on producers' logic but missing consumers' logic are useless. Market research agencies try to bridge the gap between the two kinds of logic, and their excellence depends on their ability to make the producer think in consumers' terms. Even within one country this is not easy; it becomes extremely difficult if consumers are children of other countries' cultures.

In the broader area of management, ethnocentric approaches over the past 30 years have gradually lost support, if only because they proved ineffective, even fatal. International or comparative management has become a recognized subdiscipline of management education; no current management text or handbook can do without it, even if the treatment of the subject often betrays hidden ethnocentrism.

It is a paradox that in the areas of marketing and advertising theories, ethnocentrism has survived longer than in (general) management. A paradox, because if there is one aspect of the business that is culture dependent it is consumer behavior. As Marieke de Mooij writes, there may be global products but there are no global people. The success of a business depends in the end on how well its products reach customers whose behavior is affected by values that may vary in all kinds of unexpected ways from those of the business' managers.

One reason for the relative backlog of culture-conscious theorizing in marketing is undoubtedly the complexity of the field. There is so much variance among consumers worldwide that it is tempting to believe prophets who assure us that we are basically all the same; for one thing, it enables marketing managers to sleep in peace, even if one day they will wake up to disaster.

Marieke de Mooij has grown to become one of the world's pioneers in the field of culture and marketing. She brought along a thorough experience base in advertising, a sound knowledge of foreign languages, extensive travel experience, and the ability to empathize with people in different parts of the world. In this book she applies her insights into marketing and into culture, using state-of-the-art literature for both, and her direct hands-on research into advertising practices in different countries. Her comparison of TV commercials from different countries is a contribution to anthropology as much as to marketing. TV commercials may well be to people of the late 20th century what folk myths were in the past.

This is a landmark book, and I wish it a broad readership. Reading it will be a culture shock to many; things that we always took for granted "ain't necessarily so" (Gershwin). For those who read and understand Marieke de Mooij, the field of international advertising will never be the same.

—*Geert Hofstede*
Velp, the Netherlands

Preface

My interest in international advertising and marketing was raised in the late 1970s, when, as an advertising educator, I became involved in the Education Program of the International Advertising Association. I found a lack of theory on how to develop successful international advertising.

Increased globalization was leading international companies to think that marketing and advertising strategies should be standardized in order to reap the benefits of economies of scale. Academic discussions about the influence of globalization on marketing and advertising increased, not in the least affected by Ted Levitt's article "The Globalization of Markets," published in *Harvard Business Review* in 1983. In Europe, expectations of a single market after 1992 added to the wish to develop standardized products, marketing strategies, and advertising for what was expected to become one homogeneous market. The argument was that people's wants, needs, and motives would become so similar that that would justify targeting uniform products and advertising campaigns to consumers across cultures.

Having lived my life in Europe and having taught in various places around the world, I could not believe that one uniform approach could be equally effective everywhere. I felt that replacing successful multi-domestic campaigns by standardized advertising would lead instead to alienation of consumers and would result in decreased market shares.

Another observation was that advertising and marketing curricula of universities worldwide reflect mainly American theories and philosophies of marketing and advertising, but are used to teach students in cultures that are very different from American culture.

At the same time, brands were increasingly seen as assets of a company, and branding strategies became a top management concern. CEOs of large companies became involved in advertising, because it became understood that advertising is a means to create and sell brands by adding value to products. Enchanted by the "big is beautiful" adage, they reinforced the call for standardization of communications. When subsidiaries or local agencies of global advertisers advise against using a standardized concept, their ideas often are too easily discarded with the diagnosis of suffering from the "Not-Invented-Here Syndrome." But local marketing and advertising people may be right: If motives, concepts, and messages developed in one culture are transported to another culture, they lose meaning and are less effective. They know that standardized advertising, which ignores local culture, is not an effective means to build powerful brands.

Cultural diversity influences marketing and advertising at all levels: consumer behavior, research methods, philosophies of how advertising works, advertising strategy, concept, and execution. They are the cause of different advertising styles in different countries. Why do the British use so much humor? Why so much nature in Asian advertising? Why are the cola wars so effective in the United States and not tolerated in many Asian countries, nor much appreciated in Holland, Scandinavia, or Spain? It's not a matter of law, it has to do with culture. A concept may be very effective in one culture, but not effective elsewhere.

Few understand or recognize the structure of cultural diversity; too many keep relying on their gut feeling. What has been lacking is a knowledge base of cultural differences and similarities that can be used for developing global strategies and meaningful local adaptations or for deciding that acting local, not global, will be more effective. This book presents such a knowledge base, a structure for understanding the consequences of culture for marketing and advertising. It is based on the model developed by Geert Hofstede, which has proved its use for understanding work-related values. I have applied it to consumer values and motivations, found that it can explain culture's influence on marketing and advertising, and that it can help to develop successful global strategies. One of my core findings is how, in each culture, two opposing human concepts appear to be very effective elements to use in advertising: the contrast of the desirable and the desired in each consumer's life. This contrast is meaningful and also varies by culture. I have called it the value paradox.

This is what this book is all about. It will describe the characteristics of a global brand, the standardization versus differentiation discussion, and how advertising adds value to brands; the concept of culture, culture's consequences for values and motivations in advertising, and how culture influences perception of advertising. Focus is on the 5-D model of Professor Geert Hofstede. The application of this model to marketing and advertising is an essential part of this book.

What I have written down is based on my experience, on literature, on research, on many confrontations with people of other cultures involved in marketing, advertising practice, and theory, on in-depth analysis of an enormous amount of advertising, and on work for clients. It does not provide a single truth; it is meant to provide food for thought. There are plenty of hypotheses and assumptions to keep academics and researchers busy for the next couple of years.

—Marieke de Mooij
Badhoevedorp
mdemooij@knoware.nl

Acknowledgments

This book could not have been written without the support of Geert Hofstede, whose 5-D model I have applied to marketing and advertising. From the start, he believed in my work and supported me hands-on. At ITIM, Bob Waisfisz, Huib Wursten, and Loes Cornelissen taught me to understand the Hofstede model in depth, which enabled me to develop the application to marketing and advertising. Giep Franzen, Professor of Advertising at Amsterdam University and former President of BBDO Netherlands, taught me the importance of values in advertising. Clary Veenstra, librarian at FHV/BBDO, helped me with collecting the necessary literature. Marion Appel of Inter/View provided data for the validation. Peter Kersten of Canon Europa was my launching client and stimulated me in the practical application of the model to develop a pan-European advertising strategy. Majorie Dijkstal, advertising researcher at FHV/BBDO, read and commented on the first manuscript. John-Philip Jones, Professor of Advertising at Syracuse University, reviewed the manuscript and gave valuable advice for improvement. Advice was also given by my fellow Associate Professor at the University of Navarre, Juan de los Angeles, and by Sandra Moriarty, Professor at the University of Colorado at Boulder. Ir Heleen van Lohuizen advised me on statistics. A word of thanks goes to all fellow teachers at educational institutions, to colleagues at ITIM who discussed and commented on my views on the consequences of culture on communications, and to students who helped me with coding commercials. These were Sonja Kleijne, Hogeschool van Utrecht, the Netherlands and her students; Dr. Pavla Kruzela at Lund University, Sweden and students Eva Larsson, Nina Söderström-Thoor, and Carin Wilkås. Theunis Pelser, Lecturer at Potchefstroomse Universiteit, South Africa, approached me for an advertising project that was very helpful. Professor Gordon Miracle, with Seth Romine, at Michigan State University, helped me with coding commercials and kept me on my toes with his critical comments. I am grateful to Hiroe Suzuki, Deputy Director Information Technology Center, Dentsu, Tokyo, Japan and Carlo Praet, doctoral candidate at Kobe University, Japan who helped me with coding Japanese commercials. In Japan, thanks also go to Hiroo Komaki of the IAA Japan Chapter, the late Kazuaki Ushikubo, R&D Japan, Hidekazu Aizawa, Dentsu Inc., Hidehiko Sekizawa of the Hakuhodo Institute of Life & Living, Hakuhodo's Hideo Ishikawa, Koshiro Fukuda of Toyota Motor Corporation, Chris Beaumont of Infoplan, and all others who helped me to understand Japanese advertising. Thanks also go to Paul Grol, Senior Consultant at ITIM, who helped me collect French and Belgian television commercials, to Anna Simonetti of ISR, Milan who collected Italian television commercials, and to all at Sage Publications who taped advertising for me. Finally, my thanks go to Marquita Flemming and Harry Briggs of Sage Publications. Marquita and I negotiated the contract entirely via the Internet, a novelty for both of us. Harry provided much-needed support during the final stages of preparing the manuscript, and his persistence helped me to continue to refine the manuscript. Last, but not least, I want to thank my husband Anne van 't Haaff for his continuing support.

The Paradoxes in Global Marketing Communications

In a meeting between the Duke of Wellington and Napoleon after the battle of Waterloo, Wellington is said to have reproached Napoleon with the words, "You fight for power, we fight for honor," and Napoleon is said to have answered: "Yes, one always fights for what one does not have."

One tends to fight for what one does not have; one needs to learn skills one does not have. What seems paradoxical is that skills that come automatically in one part of the world have to be learned in another part of the world. Although teamwork training is big business in the United States, there is hardly a market for it in Japan. Individualistic behavior comes spontaneously to Americans, but the Japanese have to learn it. The Japanese are learning to be more self-reliant and to take greater responsibility for their own actions. Group values remain important, but in education, more emphasis must be on allowing the individual to develop.[1]

Leadership is a concept that comes automatically to the French: You have it or you don't. There is no proper word for leadership in either the French or the Spanish languages. In the United States,[2] leadership is an integral part of primary education; children in elementary schools take turns being class leader for the day and may be publicly honored for it. American leaders are the heroes of capitalism; they are admired and applauded, whether they succeed or fail. Japanese leaders are faceless. Leadership is like air, necessary for life but impossible to see or touch.[3] American leaders exist to make decisions; Japanese leaders are there to let decisions happen.

Chaos is said to be a key ingredient of Silicon Valley's success. But chaos management has not been accepted as a management style in all of corporate America, because it conflicts with the desire for control. It is paradoxical to suggest that the Germans would benefit by a bit more chaos instead of rules.[4] The Germans cannot thrive on chaos: On the contrary, German life is highly structured.

Tradition and modernity are seen as contradictions in the West; in Japan they go side by side. The Japanese can be passionately conservative and yet be attracted by new ways.[5] While in the West the old must be discarded and the new must be embraced, in much of Asia, the traditional is exploited, recycled into modern ways of life.

The Value Paradox

Paradoxical values are found within cultures and between cultures. Every culture has its opposing values. Equality is an American core value, yet there is also inequality. In the United States in particular, the gap between rich and poor is widening. What is confusing in the global marketplace is that certain opposing values of one culture also exist in other cultures, but in reverse. An example is the paradox individual freedom/belonging. Individualism is a strong element of American society, and so is belonging. It seems paradoxical that both freedom and belonging are strong values of a single culture. The explanation is that in an individualistic society where people want to "do things their own way," "go it alone," people tend to become lonely if they don't make an effort to belong. The reverse is found in Japan where belonging is an integral part of society and it takes an effort to behave in an individualistic way. According to the American Society of Association Executives in Washington, D.C., in 1995 there were some 100,000 associations and clubs in America. Seven out of every 10 Americans belong to at least one such club.[6] There is no such phenomenon in Japan.

This is what I call a *value paradox*. Paradoxes are statements that seem contradictory but are actually true. Value paradoxes are found in the opposing values in value systems such as freedom/belonging, tradition/innovation, order/chaos. Value paradoxes are part of people's systems; they reflect the desirable versus the desired in life. On the one hand, one should not sin; on the other hand, most of us do sin now and again. We don't want to be fat, we should eat healthy food, yet we do eat chocolate or drink beer and we do get fat. Value paradoxes reflect the contradictory and meaningful things in life. A value paradox reflects a dilemma, it includes choice—preferring the thing one ought to do over what one wants to do or the other way around. Value paradoxes reflect people's motives and include the elements that trigger people's feelings and emotions. And thus, they are used in marketing and advertising. Because the important value paradoxes vary by culture, value-adding advertising cannot be exported from one culture to another.

The value "belonging" is frequently found in American advertising, particularly in the sentimental, emotional form. But appeals to individualism, such as "go your own way," "made for the individual," and egoism are found next to the quintessential American homecoming feelings. Both go together. For the Japanese, belonging is such an implicit part of life that it is not a value to be used as an appeal in Japanese advertising. The opposite will be of greater importance: individuality or independence, which expresses the desire to be oneself, to be able to succeed.

Those who do not understand the value paradoxes in global cultures may easily delude themselves and think that the world is becoming one global culture with similar values. There may be similar values, but one culture's values may be the reverse of those in another culture.

It is the complexity of multiple paradoxes that makes communication in the global marketplace so difficult. Not all paradoxes are as obvious as the individual freedom/belonging paradox. The West-East paradoxes are strongest and seemingly obvious, but there is also a variety of paradoxes within regions. Within Europe, value paradoxes vary from freedom/order in Germany to freedom/affiliation in the Netherlands and freedom/dependence in France. The Germans cherish individual freedom, but too much freedom leads to disorder. The Dutch value individual freedom, but affiliation needs are sometimes stronger. For the French, individual freedom goes along with dependence on power holders.

People's value paradoxes are part of the culture of the country in which they grow up. It takes some reflection to discover one's own value paradoxes, and it is much more difficult to find the value paradoxes in other cultures. A handicap is that perception of the phenomena of other cultures is from the framework of one's own culture.

Markets are people, not products. There may be global products, but there are no global people. There may be global brands but there are no global motivations for buying those brands. The Sony Walkman is often used as an example of a global product, developed for global consumers with global needs, who would use it with similar motives. That is not true: There are two distinctly different motives for using that product. In the Western world, the motive is that of enjoyment of music without being disturbed by others. This was not the motive for Masaru Ibuka, Akio Morita's cofounder of the Sony Corporation, for inventing the Walkman. He wanted to listen to music without disturbing others.[7]

The Global-Local Paradox

"Think global, act local" is a paradox. Thinking and behavior are equally influenced by culture. Someone who thinks globally is still a product of his or her own culture. Global thinking by a person of one culture may easily result in what is perceived as cultural imperialism by people of another culture. The way people think and perceive is guided by the framework of their own culture. One is inclined to see similarities from the framework of one's own culture. These similarities are often pseudo-similarities. They are based on what one wants to see, not on what is actually there. Perception of the phenomenon of Japanese individuality as a sign of Westernization of the Japanese is an example of such misperception.

The Technology Paradox

The argument is that technological development has led toward similar needs for similar products. That may be true for a small part of the world, the developed West, but not for the developing part of the world or the developed East. Developed Japan could be expected to have as many home PCs per capita as the United States but it does not. In 1995, Japan had 14 computers per 100 people, as compared with 35 in the United States, 27 in Australia, 25 in Canada, 20 in Britain and the Netherlands, 16 in France, and 12 in Italy.[8] Also, growth of expenditure on information technology equipment such as computers and telecom varies enormously, from 8.1% in the United States, to 7.1% in France, 7.8% in Japan, and only 4.1% in Italy.[9]

The Media Paradox

The growing number of satellites is supposed to create a global village in which anybody can receive any TV channel. This is theory; in reality there is no viewer freedom. Increasingly, local cable companies are deciding what local viewers will see: usually local programs. A Direct-To-Home (DTH) dish is no solution, as a variety of techniques and coding systems across countries makes it virtually impossible to receive what is available. In some ways, in the less technologically advanced, noncommercialized Europe of the past, when the airwaves were government controlled, there was more freedom to receive television programs from other countries.

The Culture-Free Versus Culture-Bound Paradox

Some product categories are perceived as culture-free and others as culture-bound. This is a matter of perception. Products are not culture-free, nor are the motivations of people to buy them. So-called culture-free products reflect the culture of the manufacturer. Certain brands of global companies have become so ubiquitous that they are perceived as universal.

A closer look reveals the culture of the company's home country. Coca-Cola, Marlboro, and McDonald's, ubiquitous global brands, reflect American culture. Gucci carefully keeps reflecting Italian culture. There are very few truly global brands.

There is ample evidence that to consumers the local is more meaningful than the global, the particular is more meaningful than the universal. Increasingly, people prefer local music, which is becoming more sophisticated, and the large music companies are decreasingly promoting global stars. To find talent "these days, talent scouts are fanning out to coffee houses in Latin America, karaoke clubs in Asia and even school dances in Central Europe."[10]

Local Markets Are People, Global Markets Are Products

Advertisers take great pains to try to understand certain subcultures, such as youth culture, knowing that they can appeal to the young only if they address them in the right way. When it comes to addressing adult women or men of different national cultures with very different value systems, many advertisers suddenly think one standard message is sufficient. This is paradoxical behavior.

The decision to standardize has more to do with corporate culture than with the culture of markets and nations. Many global advertisers are not market oriented, they are product oriented. They keep searching for that one global great idea or platform to sell their one standard product to seemingly universal global consumers. This is demonstrated by the fact that economies of scale are most often mentioned as cost-saving arguments for standardization. In reality, the cost of developing one standardized platform that truly crosses borders is very high. What seems to be efficient with respect to the production of the "hardware" of advertising is actually increasingly inefficient with respect to the "software." In order to get consensus over a "great idea" or "global platform," product managers, marketing managers, country managers, advertising managers, account supervisors, account directors, creative directors of advertising agencies, and the like in various countries have to get together, have to organize meetings and travel. Then, in the end, it appears that many adaptations are needed. Voice-overs or subtitles have to be made, pack shots, texts have to be translated, adapted, or rewritten. Slogans developed for global use have to be translated and some translations appear to include subtle changes of meaning influenced by culture. An example is how Philips' statement "Let's make things better" was translated into Spanish as *Juntos hacemos tu vida mejor,* into Italian as

Miglioramo il tuo mondo, and into French as *Faisons toujours mieux.* A survey of two hundred companies by Eurocom shows that 60% adapt strategies.[11]

People of different countries not only speak different languages, but their languages also represent different worldviews. Translations do not uncover the different worldviews, different ways of thinking, and different intellectual styles.

The Paradoxes in Marketing

The concept of marketing and many of the theories of consumer behavior with respect to consumption, buying, and communication originated in the United States and have been copied and used by teachers in many other cultures. There is little evidence of meaningful adaptations of these theories to other cultures. As a result, numerous students of marketing and advertising have learned marketing practice and theory that reflects American values and thinking patterns that may not always fit well in their own environment.

The Universal and the Particular

Marketing textbooks generally draw from the social sciences: psychology, sociology, anthropology, and economics. In turn, theories developed by philosophers of other cultures have been adopted by Americans. For example, Freud's philosophy is found worldwide in many textbooks, without taking into consideration that a philosophy of someone of Austrian-Hungarian origin might not work as well in the Anglo-Saxon world as it did in the society in which it originated. Rarely is the culture of origin of such concepts and theories taken into account when presenting them in books on consumer behavior. Even in the 1990s, motivational segmentation methods based on Freud's theories are offered to global advertisers,[12] although these theories are valid only for a limited number of cultures. Theories developed in one particular culture are generally presented as universal and do not differentiate for the particularities of other cultures.

Focus on the Individual

Theories of buying behavior, decision making, and communication behavior focus mainly on the level of the individual. When the influence of groups on individual buying behavior is considered from the sociological perspective, the individual is observed as a member of an individualistic society. By focusing only on the individual, the group dynamics of a collectivistic society are ignored. Such concepts of consumer behavior are mainly meaningful to members of individualistic cultures, which represent only around 30% of the world's population.

Literature on values and their relationship to marketing generally follows the psychological approach, assuming that personality traits can be used to explain people's behavior. The self-concept approach, in particular, has been embraced by marketers because of the hypothesis that people will buy products that are compatible with their self-concept or that will enhance their ideal self-image. Social factors strongly influence the ideal image, however. Culture plays an important role in the perception of ideal images. An example is the ideal woman's figure. Advertising in the Western world has been accused of propagating the ideal woman's figure as slim: The figure of the Barbie doll has become a white adolescent ideal. But even within the United States, the degree to which this is perceived as ideal varies: Contrary to white teens, black teens connect a full figure, rather than a slim one, with health and fertility.[13] This difference is caused by culture. Culture also influences whether the ideal image relates to the individual or to the group. Measuring values at the individual level may deliver value items that are not applicable to individuals of other sociocultural backgrounds.

Brand Personality: A Western Concept

Metaphors such as brand identity and brand personality are used and exported to countries in which words like *identity* or *personality* do not even exist in the local language. Data resulting from interviewing people in different cultures to compare "brand personalities" are meaningless, because the concept of brand personality has different meanings in different parts of the world and little meaning in Asia, in particular.

The Paradoxes of "Marketing Trends"

The marketing and advertising profession thrives on trends, to point out what is new and fashionable. Many of what are presented as marketing trends are based on value paradoxes. The trend of cocooning—withdrawing from social life into the home—was a reaction to a too competitive and individualistic life. One ought to go out into the world all alone and succeed, but in reality one wants the protection of the home. Hedonism as a trend with respect to food can never be a global trend. It is related to what the individual should do or actually does with respect to food: eating light products, remaining slim and healthy, while many really like to splurge. What is desirable or desired with respect to food and health varies by culture. There are few countries in which such extremes are found with respect to food and health as in the United States—junk food next to a variety of low calorie products, very thin and very fat people. In France and Spain, food is more an element of social and family life.

"Trends," or temporary movements in society, may reflect a reaction to a too strong focus on the desirable. Trends or fads in business and management tend to reflect actual culture and of that culture the gap between the desirable and the desired. Chaos management may be the desired, but it conflicts with the desirable: control.

The Global Advertising Paradox

McCracken[14] points out that advertising works as a method of meaning transfer by bringing the consumer good and a representation of the culturally constituted world together within the frame of a particular advertisement. A creative director decides how the culturally constituted world is portrayed in an advertisement and the decision makers at the company decide if that view reflects their cultural framework. This begs the question of what advertising represents—the culture of the consumer or the culture of the company. To give an example: In German advertising generally, fewer humorous devices are used than in British advertising. Does this reflect that German consumers have less sense of humor? No, it does not; there is no evidence that Germans lack a sense of humor. It reflects the risk-avoiding attitude of German management.

Ideally, effective advertising means that the values in the message match the values of the receiver. It is the culture of the consumer that should be reflected in advertising. Analysis of advertisements in international media such as *Newsweek, Business Week,* CNN, and MTV shows that, in reality, international advertisers target international audiences with their home country's value system. Thus, the full potential of cross-border media is not used.

Often-found hypotheses are that cultural differences in advertising are linked to product categories. This product-oriented thinking reflects a defect of marketing. The role of advertising is often regarded as being determined more by product category than by the culture of the people for whom it is created. And indeed, some advertising styles appear to be the property of one multinational company and thus reflect the culture of that company, not the culture of the consumer.

Effective Advertising Needs a Shared Culture

Common assumptions are that an advertisement will be effective if the viewer or reader decodes the advertisement successfully, if there is a meaningful transfer of "properties." The creator of the advertisement selects the elements of the advertisement according to his or her expectations about how the audience will respond, assuming shared cultural conventions. Receivers of the message must use the same conventions to evaluate the stimulus in order to be able to formulate the response. Thus, when developing one single idea for the whole world, one global stimulus for different cultures, the assumption is that responses will be similar, too. This can only happen if sender and receiver share one culture. If there is no shared culture, the response may be different from that which is intended and expected. This does not result in effective advertising.

A growing number of products and services are consumed by global target groups. For cost-efficiency reasons, companies prefer to standardize products and advertising directed at those target groups. Products may be similar, but buying motives can vary for most products. If buying motives for standardized products vary by country or area, how can a standardized advertising campaign be equally effective in all countries? Arguments for standardized advertising are all about standardizing the stimulus without taking into consideration the response to standardized stimuli. In this age of accountability, much is written about cost-efficiency in the production of advertising, but little is written about the effectiveness of standardized advertising. The cost savings of a standardized campaign are easily offset by the loss caused by less effective advertising messages. One of the reasons may well be that there is so little fundamental research on how advertising works.

Bland Global Advertising in an
Age of Communication Overload

In a world of growing media opportunities, distinctive advertising is needed that stands out from the clutter. It is paradoxical that advertisers prefer to develop what is universal instead of what should appeal to specific people in particular. In an age of increasing communication overload, people's selective perception mechanism will work harder. Add to that an increased amount of advertising reflecting cultural values that are not theirs, and not much imagination is needed to understand why advertising effectiveness is decreasing. On the one hand, advertisers know that advertising must be understood quickly, that instant recognition is necessary because there generally is little time to convey a message. On the other hand, global advertisers think they can export messages made for their own home culture to other, very different cultures. If they travel to other countries themselves, they employ travel agencies and read detailed travel guides. Yet they think that their messages can travel without guidance.

The Research Paradox

By definition, value and lifestyle research is culture-bound, yet studies based on the value patterns of one culture are indiscriminately exported to other cultures. Value and lifestyle studies developed in the United States are used in Europe; and within Europe, French positioning models have been sold to the Netherlands even though the value systems of these markets are very different.

Although a large part of the world uses more visuals and symbols in advertising than words, the American term used for advertising research is *copy research*. This reflects a strong bias toward valuing the verbal and factual elements of advertising over the visual elements. The frameworks of researchers of one culture are systematically used to measure effectiveness in other cultures.

Much of the literature on the cross-cultural aspects of international advertising describes studies of advertising styles of different countries by comparative analysis of the content of advertising. The methods used are based on the conventions of the culture of the researcher, not on the culture of the material to be analyzed. An example of an American convention is the treatment of visuals as only a sensory stimulus, because pictures are assumed not to provide information.

General findings of cross-cultural studies are that advertising styles vary widely among nations, but very few studies explain why. What these studies usually analyze is the stimulus, the symbols that a creative director has selected from her or his cultural frame of mind. Comparisons of audiences' assumed differences are usually crude. An example is comparing the United States, Europe, and Asia, or "developed" markets and "developing" markets, assuming that these categories include cultures with similar motivations or response patterns. There are few studies that attempt to match stimulus and response across cultures. In order to do this, the cultures of both the sender and the receiver must be studied.

How Advertising Works

There are continuous heated discussions among researchers about how advertising works. Time and again new models are developed. The assumption that the way advertising works may be related to culture is rarely included.

Generally, how advertising works is studied from the psychological perspective, at the individual level. The comparison of cultures should be studied from the anthropological perspective, at the collective level. The study of how international advertising works needs the multidisciplinary perspective, using findings of effectiveness at the individual level and taking into account how culture influences the individual behavior of members of different countries.

Because the United States has a longer research history than other markets, its methods and styles are often followed. As a result, a characteristic of most studies is their "American-ness." Hypotheses are based on American assumptions, and research methodology is based on American conventions and philosophies of how advertising works. Only a few realize that this will not always work in cross-cultural research. Wells[15] points out that Western models of advertising are not sufficient for understanding Russian advertising. An example she gives is that in the former Soviet Union, the term *advertising* is frequently used to refer to many types of promotional activities, embracing aspects of both marketing and communications. This is the case not only for the former Soviet Union, but is valid for many other cultures, including "Western" cultures, such as those in culturally diverse Europe. American concepts do not necessarily explain how advertising works in other cultures.

Diverse thinking patterns make advertising people think differently about how advertising works. Defining advertising primarily as "persuasive communication," for example, is typical of the Anglo-Saxon intellectual style but it is not a universal way of thinking. I have been involved in advertising education in the Netherlands from 1971 onward, at a time when advertising theory was developed from American textbooks. The concept of "persuasive communication," ubiquitous in American textbooks, has not become a core concept in Dutch advertising theory, although it is used in advertising effectiveness research by multinationals. The persuasion and hard-sell models are specifically American. They are too often used as the basis for explaining how advertising works in other cultures.

An example of such cultural blindness is asking "How the persuasive process is supposed to work at the individual level in Japan."[16] Persuasiveness is not an ingredient of Japanese advertising, and the collectivistic nature of Japanese culture hardly includes an "effect at the individual level."

Categorizing advertising according to hard sell versus soft sell is part of the American framework, yet it is used not only by American researchers, but also by researchers in other cultures where it does not apply.

The Content-Form Paradox in Advertising

It is often stated that advertising appeals or concepts can cross borders and that it is mainly the execution that has to be adapted. However, the concept, including the basic form used, can be as much culturally defined as the execution; it is part of it. Procter & Gamble (P&G) successfully adapts the execution but uses a few very American forms: testimonials and comparative advertising. One cannot separate form and content. At each level, the elements are influenced by culture.

1. The appeal includes values and motivations. Culture has enormous consequences for values in advertising.
2. The basic advertising form involves the organization and packaging of the advertising messages.[17] A basic advertising form is a form used in different executions, reflecting a specific approach. The basic approach in some cultures is that of a lecturer teaching the public. The basic approach in others is an attempt only to please the consumer in an indirect way. There is an array of different forms preferred by different cultures.
3. Execution refers to how people behave and what people look like. How people interact reflects more than the anecdotal: Cultural values can be recognized in behavior. The variation in executional elements is enormous, as is the variation in how they reflect culture.

Conclusion

Those who believe that the future holds one global culture are deluded by value paradoxes that make the values of one culture seemingly similar to those of another, different culture. The most obvious example is that the increased focus on individuality by the Japanese means that they are Westernizing. The global-local paradigm is another paradox: One cannot think globally; every human being thinks according to his or her own culturally defined thinking pattern. One can act globally, and that is what global companies do. When they globalize, they produce and distribute globally. For global communications, however, thinking must be local, it must focus on the particular, not on the universal. That is not what is actually done.

In global marketing communications, we use the systems of one culture to develop advertising for other cultures. We use categorizations of one culture to describe others. Our worldview is changing but we do not have one adequate global language with which to reach global consumers. We find pseudo-similarities and think they are real and universal. We use one culture's motives to move people of other cultures. What we need is a new language to understand what moves people of different cultures, to develop systems to understand the differences and find the real similarities, which are few and far between. As a start, we have to learn to see the value paradoxes in the global marketplace and to understand them. This chapter has presented only a few examples. The rest of this book will focus on the value paradoxes used in marketing communications, and tools will be presented for understanding the paradoxes in order to develop effective global advertising.

Notes

1. "Reforming Japan." (1996, March 9). *The Economist,* pp. 19-24.

2. "The leadership thing." (1995, December 9). *The Economist,* p. 53.

3. "The heavier-than-air manager." (1995, December 23). *The Economist,* p. 88.

4. "Ministering the future." (1995, October 28). *The Economist,* p. 84.

5. Benedict, R. (1974). *The chrysanthemum and the sword.* Rutland, VT: Charles E. Tuttle, p. 291. (Original work published 1946)

6. "America's strange clubs: Brotherhoods of oddballs." (1995, December 23). *The Economist,* p. 63.

7. Morita, A., with Reingold, E. M. (1987). *Made in Japan.* Great Britain: William Collins.

8. "Survey of the world economy." (1996, September 28). *The Economist,* p. 4.

9. "Economics indicators: Information technology." (1996, November 23). *The Economist,* p. 130.

10. "The new music biz." (1996, January 15). *Business Week,* pp. 20-25.

11. Kapferer, J. N., & EUROCOM. (1992). "How global are global brands?" *ESOMAR Seminar on the Challenge of Global Branding Today and in the Future,* Brussels, October 28-30, p. 205.

12. Callebaut, J., et al. (1994). *The naked consumer.* Antwerp, Belgium: Censydiam Institute.

13. Springer, K., & Samuels, A. (1995, April 24). "The body of the beholder." *Newsweek,* pp. 50-51.

14. McCracken, G. (1988). *Culture and consumption: New approaches to the symbolic character of consumer goods and activities.* Bloomington: Indiana University Press, pp. 71-89.

15. Wells, L. G. (1994, March). "Western concepts, Russian perspectives: Meanings of advertising in the former Soviet Union." *Journal of Advertising, 23*(1), 83-95.

16. Johansson, J. K. (1994, March). " 'The sense of nonsense': Japanese TV advertising." *Journal of Advertising, 23*(1), 17-26.

17. Zandpour, F., Chang, C., & Catalano, J. (1992, January/February). "Stories, symbols, and straight talk: A comparative analysis of French, Taiwanese, and U.S. TV commercials." *Journal of Advertising Research,* pp. 25-38.

CHAPTER 2

The Global-Local Paradox

Worldwide advertising campaigns, such as for Coca-Cola, Marlboro, and Nike, have set a standard for global advertising. These campaigns have contributed greatly to the success of the brands. Yet, Coca-Cola is also increasingly localizing. Advertising is the most important means for developing global brands. To understand the global-local paradox in advertising, this chapter first takes a look at the global brand. Although it has often been suggested, successful global brands are not necessarily similar in all markets. There is a wide variety of successful brands that are not fully standardized, although literature suggests standardization is the only road to success.

How Standardized Is a Global Brand?

In most categories, companies do not compete with products but with brands, augmented products that are differentiated and well positioned versus other brands in the category. In order to dominate, a global brand must be a leadership brand in all important markets in the world. Coca-Cola is now sold in 195 countries with 5.2 billion people.[1] Landor Associates in 1990 compiled a list of the Top 10 most powerful brands worldwide: Coca-Cola was number one. In 1994, Young & Rubicam repeated the study, and again Coca-Cola was the number one brand worldwide. On a similar list by Interbrand, another consultancy that specializes in branding, Coca-Cola also took the number one position in 1990. In 1996, however, that place was held by McDonald's. Most brands vary widely on the criteria for comparing brands, such as a brand's market share, the variety of people (e.g., age and nationality) the brand appeals to worldwide, and the loyalty of its consumers. Over the years, brands tend to shift position. Examples are Kellogg's, which was number two on the 1990 Interbrand list and disappeared from the list in 1996. Disney, on the other hand, not on the 1990 list, appeared on the 1996 list. Eight of the Top 10 brands are American, 1 is Japanese (Sony), and 1 is European (Mercedes-Benz).[2]

In global branding, the facets of the brands referred to are usually the formal brand identity (logo, symbol, trademark, brand name, colors, shapes), its positioning, its marketing mix, distribution, strategic principles, and advertising. The assumption is that the above facets should all be identical. Yet the classic examples of global brands are rarely fully globally standardized. If a global brand is defined as a brand of which all elements are standardized (identical brand name, package, and advertising worldwide), there are hardly any global brands—even Coca-Cola.[3] What constitutes a global brand can be described as follows:

> A global brand is one which shares the same strategic principles, positioning and marketing in every market throughout the world, although the marketing mix can vary. It carries the same brand name or logo. Its values are identical in all countries, it has a substantial market share in all countries and comparable brand loyalty. The distribution channels are similar.

Marlboro is the quintessential global brand. It is positioned around the world as an urban brand appealing to the universal desire for freedom and physical space, something that urban dwellers typically lack and that are symbolized by the "Marlboro man" and "Marlboro Country." Also, everywhere, Marlboro is a premium brand. Its advertising concept is uniformly used worldwide, with only small allowances in the execution.

A global brand is positioned the same way in every market. If the brand is a premium-priced brand, it is premium-priced around the world. If it is positioned vis-à-vis an age segment of the market, the positioning must be similar in every market. This is an ideal that cannot always come true, as the competitive environment of markets may vary, causing the need for adaptations in positioning. Yet real leadership brands must aspire to being leadership brands in all markets.

For most global brands, the product mix will vary to meet local consumer needs and competitive requirements. For example, both Coca-Cola and Pepsi-Cola increased the sweetness of their drink in the Middle East, where consumers prefer a sweeter drink. The issue is not exact uniformity, but rather whether it is essentially the same product that is offered. Other elements of the marketing mix, such as price, promotion, appeal, media, distribution channels and tactics, may also vary. There are marked differences in the added values imputed to Coca-Cola by U.S. and non-U.S. consumers. In the United States, Coke is part of the social fabric of Americana, much like McDonald's. Outside the United States, Coke exemplifies the idea of "American-ness" in its own way. Non-American consumers drinking Coca-Cola outside the United States are quenching their thirst, too, but they are drinking in a little bit of Americana as well. In non-Western societies, especially, the brand helps make aspirational American lifestyles a little more approachable.[4] Procter & Gamble's Pampers brand was introduced in the United States in the late 1960s. Pampers created a disposable diaper market by providing a product that was more convenient than a cloth diaper. Pampers is now one of P&G's largest brands and is sold through a similar marketing strategy worldwide.

A global brand is available in most countries in the world. McDonald's, in 1995, offered its services via more than 18,000 distribution points in 89 countries. In January 1996, McDonald's made it known that they intended to open another 2,500 to 3,200 outlets annually from 1996 onward. Two thirds of those will be outside the United States.[5] The company has standard specifications for its technology, product, client service, hygiene, and operational systems, but its communications are localized.

The majority of brands with global availability are of U.S. origin. In 1992, few European Union (EU) companies used domination strategies. In 1992, of 46 major EU-based food companies, half were present in only one or two countries, 24% in two or three countries, 17% in three or four countries, and only 9% in five or more countries.[6] One of the reasons given for the lag in developing strong brands in Europe is the lack of opportunities in branding compared with the United States. Television commercials have been an important ingredient in the success of, for example, P&G brands, and the U.S. television networks have provided an opportunity to reach the whole country with the same message. Not only was commercial television introduced much later in Europe, but—more important—language and cultural differences have prevented this from happening in Europe.

A global brand usually originates in a particular country. In many cases, in spite of being global, it is associated with that nation.[7] This can be beneficial if the image of the country remains constant. In case of change, both upgrading (Japan from "shoddy" to "high quality") and downgrading ("American values" have become ambiguous; for some they are positive, for others negative) will influence the brand's image and acceptance. Japanese electronics companies currently gain from the label "Made in Japan," and Marlboro has gained a great deal by being American.

A global brand may be a product that is not standardized at all. An example is Knorr soups and sauces: The package with brand name and logo as found in supermarkets around the world provides the global brand image, yet the contents follow local tastes. Examples are goulash soup in Hungary and chicken noodle soup in Singapore. The logo and packages are similar worldwide, however, and can be recognized easily among competitive brands worldwide.

There are many brands that have all the characteristics of a global brand, yet they do not carry the same brand name everywhere. Sometimes the brand identity is global, but the names or symbols vary from one country to another, often for historical reasons. Examples are the different brand names of Unilever ice cream, many of which represent the names of the original companies Unilever acquired. Yet the combination with the same logo makes them recognizable worldwide. Examples of names are: Ola in the Netherlands, Olá in Portugal, Frigo in Spain, Langnese in Germany and Russia, Eskimo in Hungary, Algida in Greece and Bulgaria, Eldorado in Italy, Good Humor in the United States, Wall's in Singapore and Malaysia, and Streets in Australia. Illustrations 2.1-2.6 show examples from the United States, Hungary, Bulgaria, the Netherlands, Spain, and Russia.

Many detergent brands carry different names in different countries, although the brand identity and positioning are similar. Names of Unilever's detergents are Surf and Wisk in the United States, Omo in the Netherlands and France, Skip in Spain, Persil in the United Kingdom, and Pollena in Poland. Reasons for using different names in different countries or regions may be legal, political, historical, or cultural, or due to language differences. The most important reason may well be to keep and leverage the brand names of an acquired company after having acquired it for its well-known local brand names. Companies buy other companies because of the brand name in which that company has invested years building an association network in the minds of consumers. Change would include loss of investment in the consumers' minds.

The Global Brand: The Consumer's Viewpoint

The essence of a brand is that it is a name in the memory of consumers. It is a perceptual map of positive and negative associations, a symbolic language, a network of associations. Brands create meaning and identification. A brand's values must fit the mental mapping of people.[8] These values are conveyed by advertising. The brand owner has the opportunity to control the meaning the brand has for people. Marlboro used to be a

Illustrations 2.1-2.6 (From top left to right.)

brand for females and was turned into a male brand. Lucozade used to be an energy drink for feeble people and was repositioned as a sports drink.[9]

A universal function of a brand for customers is quality assurance. As a value, however, quality assurance is of varying importance in different cultures. In the early 1990s, consumers expressed a growing desire for well-known brands. The outcome of Frontiers, an international survey in Europe, showed that consumers in all EU countries think that "buying branded articles is best, as you can trust the quality." Yet there are differences (see Table 2.1): Consumers in the South of Europe are more brand loyal than those in the North.[10]

The Perception of Global Brands

Many successful global brands have an international image, but this is not a necessity for success. A brand may be sold worldwide and show all the characteristics of a global brand, but that does not necessarily make it a brand that is perceived as global by the consumer in all countries. There are few brands that are perceived as global by the consumer. Successful global brands can be perceived as local in certain countries: for example Nivea, a brand of Beiersdorf in Germany. A number of studies have shown that consumers do not care whether brands are domestic or imported, local or global, as long as the brands offer good value for money.[11] It may well be that part of the success of a global brand is its integration into the local culture. It is the consumer who makes a brand successful by buying it and being loyal to it. Most often the need for a global brand is in the mind of the producer, not in the mind of the consumer.

Most strong brands, even if they are distributed worldwide, still have a strong national base and a very unequal market position in other countries. Moreover, brands that are now classic examples of global brands did not become global overnight. Some brands globalize faster than others. Brands that have become strong global brands are usually very old. Consumers have good memories, even for brands that have not been advertised for some time. Once a brand is known to consumers, it cannot easily be erased from consumers' minds.[12] An interesting example is the German cigarette brand Ernte 23, which had become very weak in West Germany over the past decades. After the Berlin Wall came down, the brand became very strong in Saxony in former East Germany. People remembered the "good old days," which were expected to return after reunification.[13] Particularly in Europe, many brands have a very unequal status in countries other than their home

TABLE 2.1 *Brands as Guarantors of Quality in Europe*

	Percentage Agree	Percentage Disagree
Spain	77	9
Italy	74	19
E. Germany	66	23
France	58	20
W. Germany	55	28
The United Kingdom	47	41
The Netherlands	43	37

SOURCE: Frontiers (1991/1992), Henley Centre/Research International.

country. Danone, for example, is a prominent leader in France, but a challenger in Germany and the United Kingdom.

Increasingly, Consumers Prefer National Brands

Research confirms that the American consumer increasingly favors national brands above, for example, Japanese brands,[14] and that European consumers favor their national brands over brands from other countries. However, this depends on the product category. Global brands in soft drinks are more evident than in the automobile and cigarette categories. The French prefer their Renaults and Peugeots, and the Germans like their Volkswagens and Mercedes.[15]

The local environment plays a strong role in the perception of brands and the values consumers attach to brands. When the Berlin Wall fell in 1989, the first things Eastern Europeans wanted were Western brands. But in 1995, local brands returned as a result of growing nationalism and increasing self-awareness. Lower prices, improved quality, and nostalgia have made Eastern European consumers return to their "good old" local brands. This is a slow but steady shift in consumer behavior. For a short time, values attached to a foreign or global brand may have a very strong appeal, but as time goes by, these values may change because of changes in the local environment.

The peoples of the EU feel European to only a limited extent. Only a small part of the populations reckon that in the near future they will see themselves as purely European.[16] About one third of the European population considers its roots to be local. They may feel Bavarian, German, but a citizen of the world at the same time. These multiple belongings have an effect on brand management in the sense that global branding must pay more attention than ever to local particularities.[17] People increasingly prefer brands with a strong identity rooted in their own history. Regional loyalties may even be stronger than national loyalties, and these are historically determined. In Italy there is no such thing as an Italian restaurant. There are restaurants focusing on the regional cuisines of Tuscany, Venice, Sardinia, or Umbria. The fragmentation of the German beer market has to do with historical and cultural issues, not with differences in consumer tastes.[18]

Nationalistic feelings can prevent further expansion of import-brands with a strong nationalistic flavor. In August 1995, as a response to the very successful McDonald's in Moscow, Moscow's mayor established by decree a successful competitive fast food restaurant, called Russian Bistro, offering value-for-money typical Russian fast food dishes.[19]

Global Branding Strategies

There are different strategies global companies can follow with respect to branding. First, there is the choice between different brand types, described below.

Different Brand Types

Single-Product Brands or Monobrands. An exclusive name is assigned to only one product. The brand's main purpose is to give added value to the product. Examples are Lion, After Eight, Pepsodent, Club Med. The vast majority of existing brands were developed as single-product brands that were built to position products within national boundaries.[20]

Range Brands or Line Brands. A group of products is ranged under one name, under one promise or positioning. The purpose is to give a product a place in a range of other products. An advantage of range brands is that products can share brand awareness and meaning. Examples are: Schweppes (tonic, bitter lemon, soda water, ginger ale), Budweiser (light, dark), Mercedes (190, 300 SE).

Umbrella Brands or Corporate Brands. Different products or brands are marketed under one name. The name can be the company name or an umbrella brand name of a company. The umbrella name can be used as an endorsement, to indicate the source: Nestlé's name on the package of Nescafé, Maggi, or Dairy Crunch means it endorses the quality. GM endorses Pontiac, Buick, Oldsmobile, and Chevrolet. Examples of corporate brands are: Benetton (clothes, perfume), Mitsubishi (banks, cars, domestic appliances), Philips (hi-fi, television, light bulbs, electric razors), Braun (razors, coffee machines, kitchen machines), Sony, Nestlé (baby food, chocolate, coffee), Canon (cameras, photocopiers, office equipment). Examples of umbrella brand names are: Nivea (soap, facial products, body milk, deodorant), Cartier (watches, pens, fashion).

Strategies for International Branding

There are basically six strategies[21] companies use for internationalization:

1. Cultivate Established Local Brands. Develop a national brand into an international brand, transport brand value and strategy to more countries. New products or brands may have characteristics (real or imaginary) that also appeal to consumers of other nations. Timotei shampoo, which originated in Scandinavia, is an example: Its formula as well as its nature-based imagery seems to appeal to Asians.

2. Global Platform, Local Adaptations. Develop one global platform, a concept for the world that can carry local products with local values. With respect to the product formula, this is the strategy is followed by Coca-Cola and McDonald's. With respect to communications, the KitKat "take a break" concept is an example of this global-local approach.

3. Create New Brands. Recognize a global need or want and develop a new product for this. There are very few successful examples of truly global needs and wants, so this is a very risky strategy. An example is the Nintendo Gameboy.

4. Purchase Local Brands and Internationalize. This is a strategy used by such major packaged food companies as Unilever, Danone (BSN), Kraft, and Nestlé. The purpose of most mergers and acquisitions has been to become owners of a company's brands in order to thrive on local brands first, then add international brands or harmonize local brands with international brand portfolios.

5. Develop Line Extensions. This strategy is particularly used in global branding to reap the benefits of global promotion programs. The investment in global sports or event sponsorship is so enormous that trying to catch more products as extensions of one name is an appealing strategy. Examples are Coca-Cola Light and Pepsi Max.

6. *Employ a Multi-Local Strategy.* Different strategies are developed for different countries for local recognition. The company name is often used as endorsement for quality guarantee ("Nestlé, the best of Australia").

Since the early 1990s, there have been two main trends in international branding strategy.

1. *From monobranding to endorsement branding.* The cost of launching and developing new brands is so enormous that international companies increasingly choose endorsement strategies or line extensions.
2. *Brand rationalization or concentration on core brands.* Changing diverse multinational portfolios into a limited number of global brands. Examples are the change of the Marathon candy bar into the Snickers bar, and Treets and Bonitos being replaced by M&Ms.

Choice of Strategy

The core marketing dilemma is whether to sell an identical product (a global brand) throughout its sales area, or to make whatever modifications are needed to account for local differences (a local brand). A global brand can be a mass brand, looking to satisfy a common product need in all countries, or it can be a niche brand targeted at common niche segments in every country. Local products and brands, although different even in name, may be endowed with common values.[22] Conversely, a global product, via its advertising, can be loaded with local values to add local significance. Even if the product or brand cannot be standardized, it can be given a global image through advertising. Coca-Cola and Pepsi-Cola are beverages, a product category that is basically culture-bound. Yet they have been made into global brands by linking global values to the product in global advertising. In both global branding and global advertising, the choice has to be made between standardization or differentiation.

The Global-Local Dilemma

A growing number of products and services are consumed by global target groups. For cost-efficiency reasons, companies prefer to standardize products and advertising directed at those target groups. This section summarizes the arguments for and against the standardization approach, the factors influencing the degree of standardization, and the role of global advertising.

The Standardization Viewpoint

The ultimate form of standardization means offering identical products worldwide at identical prices via identical distribution channels, supported by identical sales and promotion programs. Assumed homogenization of needs across borders is the most frequently mentioned reason for standardization. Levitt,[23] in 1983, called it "the globalization of markets." The successful examples of fully standardized brands he mentioned were: McDonald's, Coca-Cola, Revlon Cosmetics, Sony Television, and Levi's jeans—products that Levitt said could be bought to an identical design throughout the whole world. Companies that make their profits by following this trend of globally homogenizing needs and preferences achieve, as a result of standardization, economies of scale in procurement, logistics, production, and marketing, and also in the transfer of management expertise, all of which is eventually supposed to lead to lower prices. More important is the fact that standardization is said to offer the possibility of building a uniform worldwide corporate image, a world brand or global brand with a global image. With a smaller portfolio of strong, global brands, companies expect to achieve greater marketing effectiveness. Proponents of the Levitt theory included the possibility of developing powerful advertising that crosses international boundaries, cutting across all lines of culture, nationality, race, religion, mores, values, and customs.

More than a decade later, the standardization topic is still a source of considerable debate. In the early 1990s, surveys of international agency practitioners confirmed overall optimism about the increasing expectations of standardized marketing and advertising. Since the beginning of the 1990s, Unilever, Mars, and P&G, among others, began to streamline their brand portfolios. They were seeking greater marketing effectiveness with fewer brands, moving away from complicated multinational portfolios toward what are called "harmonized global brands."[24] A *Media & Marketing Europe* (M&M) poll conducted in July 1994 of international advertisers shows that a clear majority of respondents see an international image for a brand as the principal reason for managing campaigns multinationally. Making the brand international is said to allow for cost reductions, a key factor in multinational brand management. In terms of advertising, the argument is the cost savings from production—like "sending a team to a tropical island to shoot dozens of Bounty ads at the same time."[25]

Usually, the choice is not between a fully standardized or a fully differentiated marketing strategy, but somewhere in between. Few products and brands allow for a fully standardized approach. Increasingly, advertisers and agencies are in the process of understanding that one brand with one message for the whole world will not work. Michael Perry,[26] former head of Unilever, states: "Be warned: the successful brand that assumes it can travel without assessing the cultural differences is acting arrogantly and often suffers accordingly."

The issue of standardized advertising is particularly relevant to the discussion about advertising overkill and irritation. The bland type of advertising based on the lowest common denominator is assumed to cause much irritation. Dieter Reigber of Burda says: "People don't mind advertising, provided they feel they are being spoken to appropriately."[27] This is what standardized advertising does not do: One single message cannot be appropriate for everyone.

For the producer, the desire to develop universal products for perceived universal needs seems to be overpowering, yet these universal needs are often only very superficial. Even the requirements for cars vary widely by region. Nissan produces only a few "world cars"; most of their models are tailored to local or regional needs. In the United States a sporty "Z" model as well as a four-wheel family vehicle is needed, in Europe there is a need for small city cars or family shopping "second" cars. Nissan sells about 5,000 "Z" cars a month in the United States and only 500 in Japan. Tastes vary greatly: Consumers do not like averages. When it comes to product strategy, managing in a borderless world does not mean managing by average taste. The lure of a universal product is a false allure, says Kenichi Ohmae, formerly of McKinsey.[28] Needs may be universal, but attitudes, motivations, and expressions of needs vary. Observing Japanese people drink Coca-Cola or eat at McDonald's in the Tokyo Ginza does not mean that Japanese core values are changing.

The desire of women to be beautiful is universal, but the expression of beauty varies. Perspiration is a universal condition, but attitudes toward it differ throughout Europe. Continental Europe, particularly the hotter countries, tends to see perspiration as the body's natural cooling mechanism; the United Kingdom tends to see it as an embarrassment.[29] The word *average* is probably the greatest enemy of quality. The customer wants it her or his way.

Factors Influencing the Degree of Standardization

From a marketing point of view, a number of factors influence the decision on standardization or adaptation; among others: product cate-

Illustration 2.7 Japan: McDonald's and Coca-Cola in Tokyo

gory, the company's organization and management, homogenization of consumer needs and tastes, product life cycle and brand positioning, the media, market affluence, and advertising themes and executions.

Product Category

Generally, both practitioners and academics tend to categorize products on a sliding scale of being culture-free or culture-bound. The least culture-bound products or services mentioned are cigarettes, hard liquor, industrial products and services, hi-tech products (computers, compact disc players, television) and hi-touch (fashion, perfumes, jewelry). These are said to be easier to market internationally than culture-bound products like food. Consumer tastes are said to be converging across national boundaries for a few product types with respect to affluent, style-conscious consumers for some high-tech categories and for some service categories, such as credit cards and airlines. This convergence of needs does not take place everywhere at the same pace, however,[30] or a seemingly similar product will be used in different ways. Credit cards may seem a universal product, but they are not used for the same needs. In the United States they are used to borrow money; in continental Europe they are used mainly as a means of payment, thus more as a debit card. Car makers want to reap the benefits of economies of scale of manufacturing standardized products. But distribution and marketing is often handled by local franchise holders or independent subsidiaries, and essentially identical products are sold on different key features such as safety, elegance, and speed, depending on the target market or culture.[31] Needs for business-to-business products and services are assumed to be universal because b-to-b products are used for the same purposes. However, buying motives and the decision-making process vary widely across countries.

The 1994 M&M Europe poll of international agencies and media owners suggests that airlines and tobacco manufacturers are "the most global," that is, they carry the most standardized brands and advertising. Car hire and hotels are standardized to a lesser degree. Categories like cosmetics and toiletries, clothing and footwear, and breakfast cereal are still perceived as highly local. The least global categories include dairy products, frozen foods, oils and fats, and over-the-counter (OTC) health care. Global categories are recognizable by the smaller number of companies involved in a line of business.[32] An example is the soft drinks industry, globally dominated by Coca-Cola and Pepsi-Cola.

Defining products as culture-free or culture-bound by observing the degree of standardization of advertising, as done by some academic researchers, is a dubious activity. The standardization often is more producer driven than market driven and can be a result of the company's organization. French organizations are characterized by centralized control, which often results in standardized advertising campaigns. Or the country-of-origin concept is used (perfume from Paris), which is standardized by definition. French cheese comes from France, Scotch whisky from Scotland. Finding that most advertising for French perfume is standardized should not lead to the conclusion that perfume is a culture-free product. Particularly with respect to perfume, people's tastes and motivations vary widely. Also the substance of perfume varies from oil-based to alcohol-based according to local customs.

Product Life Cycle and Brand Positioning

The product itself—the brand and its positioning, its price and other product characteristics—may influence the possibility of standardization. New products or brands are easier to standardize than mature products. Yet by introducing one single product worldwide, and not adapting to usage and attitude differences, manufacturers will run the risk of finding a mass market in one culture and a niche market in another. A product may be in different

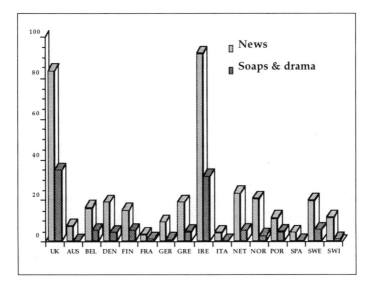

Figure 2.1 Often-Viewed TV Programs in English, Without Translation or Subtitles (EMS 1995 Data)
SOURCE: EMS 1995. Copyright © Inter/View.

phases of its life cycle in different markets, with the consequent need for different advertising approaches. Established brands in different markets may have different brand images and inconsistent positioning strategies, making it difficult to move the product to a global approach.

The Media

The availability and growing penetration of international media—especially satellite television—have led to high expectations. To use these media, an "international" campaign must be produced. But whether the media deliver to an international audience in any but a superficial sense seems highly questionable.[33] Increased availability of television due to new technologies and more permitted advertising has not resulted in more cross-border campaigns. Different cultures demand different television programming reflecting national tastes, so the scope of pan-regional television programming is limited to only a few types of program, such as sports.[34] Although young people in Europe increasingly learn to understand the English language, 1995 data from the European Media Survey show that few non-native English speakers in Europe watch English-language TV programs without translation or subtitles.

A significant difference is the degree to which countries are accustomed to dubbed television programs. In large markets such as Germany, France, and Spain, imported television programs are dubbed. In smaller markets, such as the Netherlands and Denmark, programs are subtitled. When viewers are used to dubbed programs, they will accept dubbed television commercials. Not so in countries that are used to subtitling. In these countries, consumers find dubbed commercials highly irritating.

There are very few truly international consumer magazines: Magazines such as *Elle* and *Cosmopolitan,* which used to be "exported" to other countries in the original format, have turned to local editions in most European countries, which make them local media. Using the globalization of media as a reason for a standardized advertising approach is often based merely on hype about the influence of the media on creating a global village.

Market Affluence

Standardized products are more easily accepted in less affluent markets. Conditions in less affluent markets (under-supply economies and less competitive markets) may make multinational companies less conscious of being ultra-competitive. Also, in less sophisticated markets, foreign products tend to be perceived as superior to local products.[35] But affluence is increasing worldwide, and consumers are becoming more sophisticated and governments more protective of local values. This will result in decreased acceptance of products from other countries with values that are not appreciated by indigenous populations.

Coca-Cola was one of the first brands to penetrate into developing markets. Coca-Cola is often called the definitive global brand, as it was one of the leaders in the globalization process. But its prototypical global commercial "I'd like to teach the world to sing in perfect harmony" dates from the 1970s, when it was a different world. Since then, Coke has taken consumers seriously and much of Coke's advertising has been adapted to local circumstances. One of the early examples of adaptation was the U.S. "mean Joe Green" campaign, which in other countries featured local sports heroes.

Company Organization and Management

The degree of standardization also depends on a company's corporate culture, or the vision of its management. It depends heavily on how important advertising managers think cultural differences are. The culture of a company's country of origin strongly influences the vision of its managers. Some American companies tend to reflect universalistic philosophies about people's values, assuming that their own values are valid for the whole world and should be shared by all. French companies, too, because they are used to centralized governance, may also be inclined to impose one central idea on the world.

Homogenization of Consumer Needs and Tastes

The hype about converging consumer tastes across regions reflects the high visibility of a few global brands, but there is little evidence to support the assumption that European consumers buying these brands have common goals and expectations.[36] Despite satellite TV, increased travel, the "chunnel" between France and England, and many other developments expected to change consumer habits, breakfast habits of the English and the French have not converged. How coffee is made varies, as well as where and how it is consumed. In the North of Europe, the coffee ritual takes place in the home or in the office, while in the South it takes place in the café. All over Europe, the trend is toward increased preferences for national products.

Advertising Concept and Execution

In the dialogue on the standardization of advertising, three misconceptions are common: (a) that advertising concepts based on strong image cues are able to cross borders more easily than campaigns based on copy; (b) that, if the associative values are universal, image strategies can be used cross-culturally; and (c) that advertising themes or concepts can be standardized, while only the execution may need adaptation.

Because the most described problem of international advertising is the translation problem, it is often suggested that using mainly visuals will solve the problem. However, visuals can be as strongly related to culture as language. There are few universal associative values, and the universal ones are usually not very strong. Even when an advertisement's buying proposal can be standardized because of similar expectations of products, cultural and legal differences will make it difficult to standardize an advertisement's creative execution (style). Cultural values are reflected both in the appeal and in the execution.

Can Advertising Ideas Travel?

Some advertising ideas travel, most do not. Display of pure product attributes or simple product or usage messages without reference to people's values will not pose great problems, yet pure display or product merit appeals will not position a brand well versus the competition in the global market-place with increasing numbers of parity products. Advertising concepts at the value level do not travel easily. If acceptable to all cultures, they run the risk of being bland, not very meaningful, and thus not very effective.

There are very few concepts that work equally well everywhere. An example is the country-of-origin concept: French perfume must look French. However, growing nationalism may reduce the effectiveness of this type of concept. Coca-Cola is clearly known as an American brand. But what will happen if consumers decide to support local colas? Other old, established brands such as Nivea, that have never traded on a national origin, may be fortunate enough to survive such a scenario due to consumers perceiving them as a national brand.[37]

The Local Viewpoint

Proponents of the global viewpoint prefer focusing on the similarities more than on the differences. They are inclined to put the convenience for the producer before the demands of the consumer. In 1992, Unilever's Chairman Michael Perry exposed this fallacy and said never to forget that a "global brand is merely a local brand replicated many times."[38]

The decision to direct activities locally is based on the existence of essential differences that influence marketing in different countries. Important categories of differences are: infrastructure, climate, language, traditions and habits, consumer perception, nationalism, availability of media, and economic and technological differences. Reading, viewing, and listening habits vary by country. Leisure time, spending priorities, and social needs differ. There is a variety of laws and regulations. Different customs, attitudes, and needs make many of a firm's normal procedures inapplicable or untransferable. Laws, customs, habits, and attitudes are a reflection of culture.

The Importance of Culture

In advertising and marketing literature, influences of culture on consumer behavior and perception of advertising are at most anecdotal. They focus on the expressions of culture and little on the differences in values that are the cause of behavior and communication styles. Why do the British use so much humor in advertising? Why do the French include erotics? Why does comparative advertising work well in the United States but is not accepted in Japan? Why do people prefer different types of promotions? Saving stamps, for instance, are much more accepted in the Netherlands than in the United Kingdom and Canada.

Even when products are accepted in more than one culture, advertising will have to be adapted, and that means more than translating a central message. It is often said that language difficulties can be overcome by translation and back-translation. But language reflects culture. A line that works in one market seldom works straightforwardly in another.[39] Differences among languages go far beyond mere translation problems. Some concepts are not translatable; also, between cultures that speak similar languages, cultural differences are found. The Belgians and the Dutch are said to be two countries divided by one language. Even between English-speaking countries, adaptations are often necessary, both for copy and for visuals. A simple example is that in Australia, diapers are "nappies" as they are in Britain. Yet the type of humor found in some Australian commercials might be considered in bad taste outside the Australian market.[40]

Effective Global Advertising

Much of the standardization debate has concerned itself with the issue of standardizing the advertising stimulus, the message. Yet it is the response that counts. People process advertising messages in social and cultural contexts and then respond. The individual consumer's response to an advertising message is based on executional, cultural, and sociological considerations.[41] Jeremy Bullmore, with 33 years' experience at J. Walter Thompson, writes

> that much of the world's most original and effective advertising was quite incomprehensible except to those to whom it was addressed. . . . Do not believe the old saying that good advertising speaks for itself. Good advertising speaks for itself only to those for whom it is intended. Much good advertising speaks quite deliberately in code, or uses a secret language, and excludes the rest of us. That's one of the reasons why it's good.[42]

John Philip Jones[43] states that global, standardized campaigns are usually derived from U.S. stereotypes, and the waste involved is consequently substantial. One piece of research shows that in 1976 as many as 70% of a sample of manufacturers ran "fully standardized" campaigns. By 1987, this proportion had come down to 10%. The reduction in the use of uniform campaigns is good presumptive evidence of failure, and the cost is obviously large, in terms both of the money spent and of the management time devoted to grappling with the problems.

Selecting the right balance between local and global is the trick: trying to save cost by standardizing for clusters of markets. Defining clusters based on similar language, average age, or income is not the road to success. Clusters have to be defined according to similarities with respect to consumers' responses in terms of feelings, perceived cultural and social relevance, meaningfulness, and the execution's ability to differentiate the brand clearly from its competition in the consumer's mind.[44]

Global Advertising Means
Adding Value to Global Products

Successful brands are made by adding values to products in the global marketplace, too. The next sections will deal with the value concept in marketing and advertising.

Advertising and Branding

A brand is more than a product with a name, a trademark, or a promise of performance. A brand is a network of associations in the mind of the consumer. A name that is not in one's memory is not a brand.[45] The association network notion of a brand is crucial for understanding advertising's role in developing global brands, because it so clearly shows the link between consumers and brands as a result of advertising. The associations (meanings) that we attach to the objects of the material world influence our purchasing and decision processes.[46] It is the primary task of advertising to manipulate brand meanings. Advertising tries to attach meanings to brands and these meanings are interpreted in the light of the target's motivations and aspirations. Association networks may vary across target groups, and the ultimate goal of advertisers will be to develop strong, consistent association networks for brands that fit the target's values and motivations. The core problem of global marketing is whether people of one country will form associations similar to those of people in other countries.

The associations in the consumer's mind will relate to a number of aspects of the brand (see Figure 2.2):

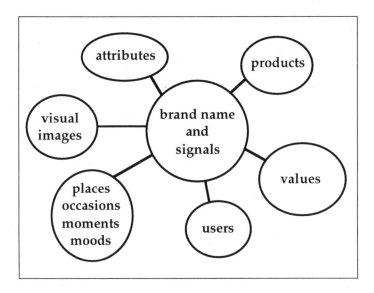

Figure 2.2 Elements of a Brand Association Network
SOURCE: Giep Franzen, BBDO College Seminar on Branding, 1992-1993.

- the brand name and the brand's visual images: the package, logo, brand properties, and other recognizable aspects
- the product or products linked with the name (one product = monobrand; a number of products or extensions = range brand)
- attributes: what the product is or has (characteristics, formula)
- benefits or consequences: rewards for the buyer or user—what the product does for the buyer
- places, occasions, moments, moods when using the product
- users: users themselves or aspiration groups
- values

Associations are structured in the human mind: Attributes and benefits will be linked with users and may be specific for the product category or for the brand. An example is a simple association network or perceptual map for Coca-Cola (Figure 2.3), I developed by conducting a number of interviews in my own environment in 1995. This association network is not representative for the Dutch and is only meant to serve as an example.

An important finding from a simple exercise like the one with Coca-Cola is the fact that associations include advertising properties of both Coca-Cola (Coca-Cola light break) and Pepsi-Cola (Michael Jackson). An explanation

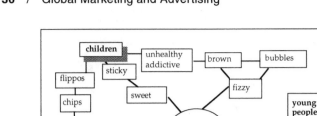

Figure 2.3 Associations With Coca-Cola

may be that both Coca-Cola and Pepsi-Cola used music marketing in the past. For the people I interviewed, the attribute "American" is indiscriminately linked with both Michael Jackson and Coca-Cola's advertising. New cola drink brands such as American Cola, introduced by the European chain store SPAR, and Virgin Cola could easily attack the positions of both Coca-Cola and Pepsi-Cola, not only by price differentiation, but also on the undifferentiated values of both market leaders (see Illustration 2.8).

In our world of abundant brands and communications, differentiating a brand at the attribute or benefit level does not make strong brands. Advertising will only work at the attribute level if a product has unique attributes that distinguish it from the competition. Such distinctions usually do not last long, as they are copied quickly by the competition. To return to our example: Coca-Cola and Pepsi-Cola have the following attributes in common: soft drink, sweet tasting, thirst quenching, cola drink, and being "an American drink." In order to differentiate them from each other, they have to add strong, meaningful values. If a brand is associated with meaningful and distinctive values, this distinctiveness can be transferred to other areas. The British brand Virgin, owned by Richard Branson, carries associations of adventure, rebellion, and nonconformism linked to the personality of its owner. These values can be used for all products of Branson's company: the airline, records, and a cola drink. However, these values may not be meaningful for the whole world.

Illustration 2.8 The Netherlands: Herschi Cola

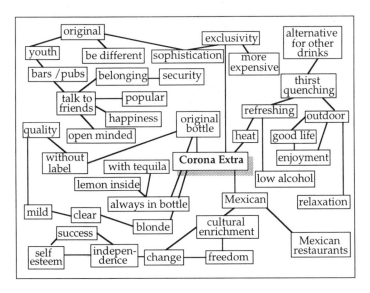

Figure 2.4 Association Network for Corona Extra

Another association network is the one for Corona Extra, a Mexican beer brand exported to many countries in the world. It distinguishes itself by its transparent white bottle with a long neck and the ritual of drinking from the bottle with a slice of lime pushed into the neck. A mixed group of Spanish and German students developed the association network presented in Figure 2.4. This association network includes attributes and benefits as well as values. Two clusters of values can be distinguished. Those of the Germans are success, self-esteem, independence, and freedom; those of the Spanish are individualism, belonging, and happiness.

The purpose of advertising is to turn products into brands by developing strong association networks in people's minds by adding value to products.

Advertising Reflects Society's Values

The values selected to differentiate brands relate to the cultural mind-set of the strategist, but should also relate to the cultural mind-sets of the target group. What makes advertising effective is the match between the values in the advertising message and the values of the receiver. The core problem in global advertising is the cultural match between the advertisement and the target groups. Although the large international companies try to measure the effectiveness of their advertising on a continuous basis, there is not much fundamental research on what makes advertising effective. There are, however, some rules of thumb.[47] Advertising, to be effective,

- must create meaningful associations
- must be relevant and meaningful
- must be linked with people's values
- must reflect the role the product or brand plays in people's lives
- must reflect people's feelings and emotions
- must be instantaneously recognized

All above mentioned elements are influenced by the culture of both the advertiser and of the audience. As a result, effective advertising reflects culture, is a mirror of culture. So, in order to use the value concept for effective global advertising, either a global set of values will have to be found or a model must be created to describe cultural differences in a meaningful and structured way.

Conclusion

In the global marketplace, international companies have tried to follow the steps of the successful global brands such as Coca-Cola, Nike, and McDonald's. The name of the game has been standardization because of assumed economies of scale. In reality, few successful global brands are fully standardized. The wish for global brands is in the mind of the producer, not in the mind of the consumer. Consumers don't care if the brand is global, and they increasingly prefer local brands or what they perceive as local brands.

In past decades, companies have learned to understand that brands are their major assets, and a variety of branding strategies has been developed. The major multinationals have at the same time learned their lessons about globalization. Many of them have restructured their organizations and harmonized their brand portfolios; others are in the process of doing so. Harmonization of brand portfolios was driven by the wish to create economies of scale in production, sales, marketing, and advertising. The core dilemma felt in this process has been the choice between a standardized product and marketing activities and a differentiated approach or any position in between. Not all arguments for standardization have been equally valid.

The role of production in the global marketplace is different from the role of advertising. Advertising adds value to products and thus makes them into brands. Advertising links products to people. Until now, too little attention has been paid to the implications of this role of advertising in the global marketplace. Effective advertising reflects the values of the audiences it targets: The values included in advertising must match consumers' values in order to make advertising effective. This begs the question of whether one standardized advertisement can include the variety of values of all world populations. The question can be ignored if one global world culture is waiting around the corner. In order to understand the unlikelihood of a global world culture, the concept of culture must be understood. That will be the topic of the next chapter.

Notes

1. Samuelson, R. J. (1995, May 29). "We aren't being taken over by the world economy." *Newsweek,* p. 7c.

2. "Assessing brands: Broad, deep, long and heavy." (1996, November 16). *The Economist,* pp. 84-85

3. De Mooij, M. (1994). *Advertising worldwide* (2nd ed.). Hemel Hempstead, Hertfordshire, UK: Prentice Hall International.

4. Banerjee, A. (1994). "Transnational advertising development and management: An account planning approach and a process framework." *International Journal of Advertising, 13,* 95-124.

5. *NRC Handelsblad,* January 18, 1996.

6. Mårtenson, R. (1994). "The role of brands in European marketing." *The Journal of Brand Management, 2*(4), 244.

7. Thomas, M. J., Bureau, J. R., & Saxena, N. (1995). "The relevance of global branding." *The Journal of Brand Management, 2*(5), 304.

8. Woesler de Panafleu, C. (1994, October). "Future identification values of brands." *ESOMAR Seminar on Building Successful Brands,* Prague, p. 1.

9. Feldwick, P., & Bonnal, F. (1994, October). "Reports of the death of brands have been greatly exaggerated." *ESOMAR Seminar on Building Successful Brands,* Prague, p. 23.

10. Barnard, P. (1993, March). "Brandscapes." *Admap,* p. 28.

11. Mårtenson, "The role of brands," p. 247.

12. Mihailovic, P., & De Chernatony, L. (1995). "The era of brand culling—Time for a global rethink?" *The Journal of Brand Management, 2*(5), 308-315.

13. This story is from Klaus Brandmeyer, at a BBDO College seminar in 1992.

14. De Mooij, M. (1994). *Advertising worldwide,* p. 99.

15. *Advertising Age International,* April 27, 1992, p. I-28

16. "More-or-less European union." (1995, August 26). *The Economist,* p. 28.

17. Woesler de Panafleu (1994), "Future identification values of brands."

18. Zambuni, R. (1993). "Developing brands across borders." *The Journal of Brand Management, 1*(1), 22-29.

19. Nijenhuis, H. (1995, August 16). "Fast food per decreet in Moskou." *NRC Handelsblad.*

20. Macrae, C. (1993). "Brand benchmarking applied to global branding processes." *The Journal of Brand Management,* pp. 289-302; see p. 291.

21. De Mooij, M. (1994). *Advertising worldwide,* pp. 81-108.

22. Wolfe, A. (1991). "The single European market: National or Euro-brands?" *International Journal of Advertising, 10,* 49-58.

23. Levitt, T. (1983, May-June). "The globalization of markets." *Harvard Business Review,* pp. 92-102.

24. Mihailovic & De Chernatony (1995), "The era of brand culling."

25. "It's their money—What do they think? Europe's top advertisers polled." (1994). *Media & Marketing Europe* in association with *Stern.*

26. Michael Perry, Former Chairman of Unilever, at the 1994 IAA World Congress, Cancun, Mexico.

27. Dieter Reigber in "Bored to tears or tears of laughter." Teillers & Tardjopawiro. *Media & Marketing Europe,* pp. 51-52.

28. Ohmae, K. (1989, May/June). "Managing in a borderless world." *Harvard Business Review,* pp. 152-161.

29. "Eurobrief." (1994, May). *Media & Marketing Europe,* p. 19.

30. Banerjee, A. (1994). "Transnational advertising development," pp. 97-99.

31. Westcott, T. (1994). "Worldly wide." In Media & Marketing in 1994 [Special Issue]. *Media & Marketing Europe,* p. 8.

32. Media & Marketing in 1994 [Special Issue], *Media & Marketing Europe.*

33. White, R. (1990, September). " 'L'Europe des patries' and pan-European advertising." *Admap,* pp. 15-17.

34. Dibb, S., Simkin, L., & Yuen, R. (1994). "Pan-European advertising: Think Europe—Act local." *International Journal of Advertising, 13,* 125-135.

35. James, W. L., & Hill, J. S. (1991, June/July). "International advertising messages: To adapt or not to adapt (that is the question)." *Journal of Advertising Research,* pp. 65-71.

36. Dibb et al. (1994), "Pan-European advertising."

37. Mihailovic & De Chernatony (1995), "The era of brand culling."

38. Michael Perry of Unilever, cited on p. 109 in Banerjee (1994), "Transnational advertising development."

39. Anholt, S. (1994, March). "The appliance of creative licence." *Media & Marketing Europe,* p. 19.

40. Agee, T. (1993). "Localization versus standardization of advertising 'down under'." Unpublished manuscript, University of Auckland, New Zealand.

41. Banerjee (1994), "Transnational advertising development," pp. 101-102.

42. Bullmore, J. (1991). *Behind the scenes in advertising.* Henley-on-Thames, Oxfordshire, UK: NTC Publications, pp. 79-82.

43. Jones, J. P. (1992). *How much is enough?* Lexington, MA: Lexington Books, pp. 8-9.

44. Banerjee (1994), "Transnational advertising development," pp. 116-117.

45. Information from Giep Franzen, former president of FHV/BBDO in the Netherlands and Professor of Advertising at the University of Amsterdam. He pioneered the thinking about the function of brands in the Netherlands.

46. Duckworth, G. (1995, January). "New angles on how advertising works." *Admap,* pp. 41-43.

47. Franzen, G. (1994). *Advertising effectiveness.* Henley-on-Thames, Oxfordshire, UK: NTC Publications.

Culture

The global-local paradox points out the need to understand the consequences of culture. In order to build relationships between consumers
and brands, advertising must reflect people's values. The basic notion that
in the global marketplace not all consumer values are similar, and that
particularly advertising cannot easily be harmonized, has been recognized
by both practitioners and academics. This acknowledgment has not
resulted in theories on how international advertising works. The first step
to take is to learn to understand culture.

Culture Defined

In the English language, as in many other languages, *culture* is a complicated word. It is used to describe high art (classical music, theater,
painting, and sculpture) and it is often used to contrast these forms with
popular art. It is used by biologists who produce cultures of bacteria, it
is used in agriculture and horticulture. In advertising, cultural differences
usually refer to the expressions of culture.

For the purpose of understanding the word for marketing, Rice[1] defines
culture as "the values, attitudes, beliefs, artefacts and other meaningful
symbols represented in the pattern of life adopted by people that help them
interpret, evaluate and communicate as members of a society." Culture both
affects and describes human behavior.

Geertz[2] states that *culture* is best seen not as complexes of concrete
behavior patterns—customs, usages, traditions, habit clusters—but as a set
of control mechanisms—plans, recipes, rules, instructions (what computer
engineers call "programs")—for the governing of behavior. Humankind is
dependent upon the control mechanisms of culture for ordering its behavior.

Hofstede[3] defines *culture* as "the collective mental programming of the
people in an environment. Culture is not a characteristic of individuals; it
encompasses a number of people who were conditioned by the same
education and life experience."

This is a concept of culture in the broad sense as opposed to the narrow meaning of culture as "civilization" or "art." Culture is learned, not inherited. It derives from one's social environment, not from one's genes. Hofstede[4] distinguishes culture from human nature and from the personality. The personality is the individual's unique personal set of mental programs that she or he does not share with any other human being. Culture is what the individual members of a group have in common. The term *culture* may apply to ethnic or national groups, or to groups within a society, at different levels: a country, an age group, a profession, or a social class. The cultural programming of an individual depends on the groups or categories to which he or she belongs. The expressions of culture belonging to a certain level of cultural programming will differ: Eating habits may differ by country, dress habits by profession, and gender roles by both country and social class. When discussing "culture," it is important to be specific about the level, whether "national culture," "corporate culture," or "age culture," in order not to create confusion. What is true at one level need not apply to another.

Culture is the glue that binds groups together. Without cultural patterns, organized systems of significant symbols, people would have difficulties in living together. Geertz[5] suggests that there is no such thing as a human nature independent of culture. Without interaction with culture, and thus the guidance provided by systems of significant symbols, our central nervous system would be incapable of directing our behavior. We are incomplete or unfinished animals who complete or finish ourselves through culture. Conclusions from psychoanalytic work in India, Japan, and the United States by the cross-cultural psychologist Roland are in accord with Geertz's statement. From Roland's[6] psychoanalytical work,

> it is apparent that the kinds of personalities persons actually develop, how they function and communicate in society, what their mode of being and experience is in the world and within themselves, and what their ideals and actualities of individuation are depend overwhelmingly on the given culture and society to which they belong.

Our ideas, our values, our acts, and our emotions are cultural products. We are individuals under the guidance of cultural patterns, historically created systems of meaning.

Advertising reflects these wider systems of meaning: It reflects the way people think, what moves them, how they relate to each other, how they live, eat, relax, and enjoy themselves. All manifestations of culture, at different levels, are reflected in advertising. In order to analyze advertising as a manifestation of culture at the broader level, it must be understood that culture is expressed in several ways.

Cultural Universals

Although people are not the same, we tend to perceive them to be the same. International marketing and advertising people, in particular, are led by wishful thinking: They want people to be the same, to have the same needs and aspirations. This leads to cultural blindness: both perceptual and conceptual blindness. As a result, many international marketers embrace the idea that there are cultural universals, modes of behavior that exist in all cultures. Textbooks on international marketing tend to mention the search for cultural universals as a valuable orientation, referring to, among others, Murdock's list of cultural universals,[7] modes of behavior existing in all cultures. Examples of universals are bodily adornment, cleanliness, training, cooking and food taboos. Indeed, a basic, universal need is eating. But it is not just to eat, it is to prefer certain foods cooked in certain ways and to follow a rigid table etiquette in consuming them.[8] It is not to talk, it is to utter the appropriate words and phrases in the appropriate social situations in the appropriate tone of voice. Religion may be perceived as a cultural universal, but the belief in one god or more, people's relationships with their gods, and the rituals of worship are all part of culture and define the artefacts developed within a culture. Why are European cathedrals of a different structure than mosques or Hindu temples, or American churches? Because they serve different religious practices. The concept of divinity is a Western concept. Ruth Benedict,[9] in her classic study on Japanese culture, describes how, after World War II, Japan was to adopt modern values in which a concept of a divine monarch—as perceived through the eyes of the Americans— did not fit, and it was suggested to the Japanese emperor that he disavow his divinity. The emperor's reaction was said to be that it would be an embarrassment to strip himself of something he did not have.

Manifestations of Culture

Hofstede[10] distinguishes four manifestations of culture: symbols, rituals, heroes, and values. In Figure 3.1, these are depicted like the layers of an onion, indicating that symbols represent the most superficial and values the deepest manifestations of culture, with heroes and rituals falling somewhere in between.

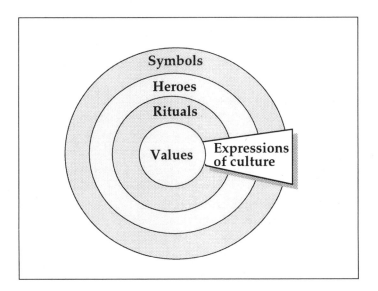

Figure 3.1 Culture as an Onion
SOURCE: Hofstede (1991).

Symbols are words, gestures, pictures, or objects that carry a particular meaning recognized only by those who share a culture. The words of a language or a particular kind of jargon belong in this category, as do dress, hairstyles, flags, status symbols, and individual commodities such as Coca-Cola. New symbols are easily developed and old ones quickly disappear; symbols from one cultural group are regularly copied by others. This is why symbols are shown in the outer, most superficial layer in Figure 3.1. Coca-Cola, Pepsi-Cola, Marlboro, and Nike are examples of brands that have become global symbols. Yet they may include different associations for Americans, the country of origin of the brands, than they do for the Chinese.

Heroes are persons, alive or dead, real or imaginary, who possess characteristics that are highly prized in a society, and thus serve as role models for behavior. Even fantasy or cartoon figures, like Batman or Charley Brown in the United States and Astérix in France, can serve as cultural heroes. In the television age, outward appearances have become more important in choosing heroes than they were before. Fantasy heroes can become globally known, but the stories in which they play a part often become local. Or, some stories "sell" better than others. Astérix behaves in a different way than Donald Duck. The educational programs of *Sesame Street* are developed locally in order to fit into a country's education system. Topics vary among

European countries. In 7-Up commercials using Fido Dido, different "acts" are used. A research method developed by Pegram Walters International shows diverse reactions by different nationalities to different parts of the same commercial, indicating that parts of Fido Dido's behavior are appreciated in a different way by different nationalities.[11]

Rituals are the collective activities considered socially essential within a culture: They are carried out for their own sake. Examples include ways of greeting, ways of paying respect to others, and social and religious ceremonies. Business and political meetings organized for seemingly rational reasons often serve mainly ritual purposes; for example, allowing the leaders to assert themselves. Sporting events are rituals for both the players and the spectators. The rituals around American football are very different from those around European football. In particular, the phenomenon of cheerleaders is nonexistent in Europe.

In Figure 3.1, symbols, heroes, and rituals are included in the term *expressions of culture.* They are visible to an outside observer. Their cultural meaning is invisible, however; it lies in the way the expressions are interpreted by the insiders of the culture. Brands are part of a ritual, and advertising helps make the ritual. Manufacturers use and create rituals around their products to differentiate them from competitive products. Sara Lee/Douwe Egberts, the Dutch coffee company, has carefully created a typical Dutch "coffee culture" by systematically showing coffee-drinking rituals. The beer brand Corona Extra distinguishes itself from others by the suggestion that it should be consumed by drinking from the bottle after having pushed a piece of lime into the long neck of the bottle. Advertising displays the rituals around products and brands. When discussing whether an advertising message can cross borders, it often is said that an idea or a concept can cross borders but that the execution will have to be adapted because many visual and verbal elements of advertising do not travel. Examples of executional aspects are how people look, the color of their skin, how they are dressed, their language, their eating habits, and what their houses look like. These elements are the expressions or artefacts of culture. This relates to the word *culture* used in the sociological sense, meaning a "way of life" adopted by groups of people: "How we do things here, how we feel and how we think."

At the core of culture lie values. Values are defined as "broad tendencies to prefer a certain state of affairs over others." Values are among the first things children learn, not consciously but implicitly. Developmental psychologists believe that by the age of 10 most children have their basic value system firmly in place and that after this age changes are difficult to obtain.

People are not consciously aware of the values they hold, so it is difficult to discuss or observe them.

Researchers try to describe values by asking people to state a preference among alternatives. One of the difficulties in researching values is interpreting what people say. There is a distinction between the desirable and the desired: how people think the world ought to be versus what people want for themselves. Language is another problem: Values don't translate easily because words expressing values have abstract meaning. They must be seen as labels of values. A word may serve as a label of a value in one culture but be the label of a different value in another culture. This explains the difficulty of translating advertising copy into languages other than the one in which it is conceived. This issue will be further discussed in Chapter 5.

The so-called global culture refers to the expressions of culture, the symbols, converging eating habits, and global heroes, particularly those who appeal to the young. Nike and Coca-Cola have become global symbols. Fast food, and particularly the Big Mac or pizzas, have become a global ritual. Michael Jordan has become a global hero. Yet the core or central values have not become global; they vary across cultures and are not likely to change during our lifetime. This stability of core values is not well understood by advertising people, who are particularly fond of "trends." Linking new products and services to "new" habits and lifestyles can be a profitable activity. Lifestyles are the expressions of culture. Trends labeled as "changing values" or "global trends" might better be scrutinised before applying them. The core values of culture are stable, and often what is presented as a new "trend" is a newly packaged core value. An example is the "cocooning" trend when introduced in the Netherlands, meaning that people were withdrawing into their homes. At all times people turn to the safety of the home to withdraw from a threatening world; and, particularly in the Netherlands, time spent at home is quality time, as expressed by the word—untranslatable into English—*gezelligheid.*

Selective Perception

Perception is the process by which each individual selects, organizes, and evaluates stimuli from the external environment to provide meaningful experiences for him- or herself.[12] Selective perception means that people focus on certain features of their environment to the exclusion of others. This phenomenon has strong consequences for advertising in an age in which the growing discrepancy between communication supply and consumption has led to the phenomenon of communication overload—

that is, the share of communication supply that is not consumed. Communication overload in developed economies such as the United States and Japan is estimated at an average of 97%.[13] The quantity of "commercial communication" to which advertising belongs is expected to grow so enormously that consumers must be increasingly selective in what receives their attention. Culture reinforces this selective process. No two national groups see the world in exactly the same way. Medical studies of blind adults given sight through corrective surgery show that we have to be taught the "rules of seeing." These rules of seeing are not universal principles, but are formed by the natural and social environments that teach us both what to look at and how to see it.[14] What people see is a function of what they have been trained or have learned to see in the course of growing up. Perceptual patterns are learned and culturally determined. Because they are culturally determined, they also are consistent. You see what you want to see and you don't see what you cannot see because it does not fit with your experience, your prior learning. Our experience makes us see the world in a certain way. Our interests, values, and culture act as filters and lead us to distort, block, and even create what we choose to see and hear. We perceive what we expect to perceive. We perceive things according to our cultural map.[15] We become confused when things appear to be different from what we expected, and we may draw the wrong conclusions. Expecting guests at eight, but having them arrive at nine will lead some of us to conclude that our guests are polite, others of us that they are impolite. Others, arriving at our house at dinner time without invitation, may expect food because of their perception of hospitality. One reaction will be sharing whatever food there is, the other is embarrassment and waiting with dinner until the visitors have left. Some people nod their heads when they say "yes," but that may mean "no" in quite a few other countries. We expect and see things from our own cultural frame of mind. We are prisoners of our own culture. Consumers are, and so are creative directors who follow their own cultural, automatic pilot when developing advertising. This phenomenon enables them to develop effective advertising for their own culture, but it limits their ability to develop effective advertising ideas, including meaningful values, for other cultures. Advertising in which the values do not match those of the culture of the receiver will be less noted or be misunderstood and thus will be less effective. Researchers encounter the same problem: Finding the values of cultures other than one's own is extremely difficult, if not impossible.

A way to reduce the extent to which our perception is blocked by our own cultural experience is the self-reference criterion, which eliminates culture blocking through learning to understand our own culture first. As no other culture is identical to our own, we judge all other cultures from that perspective, so a first step to understanding other cultures is understanding our own culture.

Stereotyping

Stereotyping means mentally placing people in categories. Stereotypes can be functional or dysfunctional. Stereotyping is functional when we accept it as a natural process to guide our expectations. Stereotyping is dysfunctional if we use it to judge individuals incorrectly, seeing them only as part of a group. An example of a functional stereotype is that the Germans are punctual, which is correct. On average, they are more punctual than many other peoples. Certainly the Italians and the Spanish have a different concept of time. For the Spanish, knowledge of this aspect of the German culture means that they can adapt their behavior: When they are expected for dinner, 8 o'clock means 8 o'clock, and not 9 or 10 as it does in Spain. An example of a dysfunctional stereotype is the British saying that the French are dirty, oversexed, and ludicrously obsessed with their culture, and the French saying that the British are cold, uncultivated, hypocritical, and unreliable.[16] Yes, the British are more reserved in the eyes of the French, the Italians generally more chaotic in the eyes of the Germans, and the Germans rigid as perceived by the British. It is important to realize that culture is relative: Stereotypes are in the eyes of the beholder's culture. Because culture is stable, stereotypes can be found in literature from early times on. An example is the way the Dutch have become part of the English language: "going Dutch," "a Dutch treat," and "a Dutch uncle" are expressions that reflect characteristics of the Dutch as observed by the English. Similar expressions do not occur in the German and French languages.

Advertising depends on the use of effective stereotypes because it must attract attention and create instant recognition. Advertising simplifies reality and thus has to use stereotypes. Advertising messages are generally short, and if audiences do not immediately recognize what the message is about, it is lost. Culture interferes. When we perceive or depict people of other cultures, we do so from the perspective of our own culture. Different cultures have different stereotypes of other cultures. What are the characteristics of the stereotyped French? The Germans think the French are resourceful, the British think they are humorless and short-tempered. The Dutch think the French are not very serious, the Spanish think they are cold and distant. The Finns think they are romantic, yet superficial. The Americans think they are pleasant and intelligent, yet pretentious. Asians think they are indiscreet.[17]

From this example, it is obvious that it is particularly dangerous to use strong national stereotypes in international advertising. The creative director's stereotyped perception may be different from the stereotyped perception of audiences in countries other than his own, resulting in misunderstanding. For a 1994 award-winning commercial for the Odéon Theatre in Paris, produced by French creative people, the objective was "to encourage Europeans to get to know each other better and to get rid of received ideas about other nationalities."[18] The commercial shows various people imitating stereotypical characters from around Europe. What it in fact does, is show stereotypes from the French perspective. Germans, as portrayed by the French, are ogres carrying backpacks, recognizable only to the Finnish as typically German. Italians could recognize neither the Germans nor themselves in this commercial.

Thinking Patterns and Intellectual Styles

There is not just one way of logical thinking. Linear, externalized logic is part of Western philosophy and science and different from other cultures' "logic," such as the more inward-looking Buddhist philosophies. Digital thinking and decision making is a characteristic of the North American communication system. The Japanese are more inclined toward the analog. The North Americans are structural and analytical; they lack the dynamics of the Chinese Yin-Yang, the European dialectic (the process aimed at abolishing differences of opinion), or the Japanese holistic pattern recognition approach that involves recognizing the feeling of the overall situation before looking at the details. The North American approach works toward extremes in order to facilitate decision making. In European culture, the emphasis is on making an analysis in order to generate ideological and theoretical arguments. Most Europeans and Latin Americans tend to attach more weight to ideas and theories than do Americans, who tend to distrust theory and generalizations, which they may label as too abstract or unrealistic.

The way in which arguments are supported also varies across cultures. Some tend to rely on facts, some on ideology or dogma, and others on tradition or emotion. For the Japanese, the *kimochi* or feeling has to be right;

logic is cold. The Saudis seem to be intuitive in approach and avoid persuasion based primarily on empirical reasoning.[19] The French have a philosophy, Americans want data and proof of hypotheses. Usunier[20] distinguishes four different intellectual styles: the "Gallic" (French), the "Teutonic" (German), the "Saxonic" (English and American), and the "Nipponic" (Japanese). Saxons prefer to look for facts and evidence. Teutonic and Gallic styles tend to place theoretical arguments at the center of their intellectual process. Data and facts are there to illustrate what is said rather than to demonstrate it. The Teutonic style includes a preference for reasoning and deduction. The Gallic style is less occupied with deduction; it is directed more toward the use of persuasive strength of words and speeches in an aesthetically perfect way. The Nipponic intellectual style favors a more modest, global, and provisional approach: Thinking and knowledge are conceived of as being in a temporary state, avoiding absolute, categorical statements.

Western culture, both European and American, categorizes virtually everything. Duality, a way of categorizing, is implicitly and explicitly part of Western culture: concrete versus abstract, present versus past, new versus old, past versus future, harmony versus conflict, inner-directed versus outer-directed. The stimulus-response concept in communication theory expresses this duality pattern, as do cause and effect, the typical dual way of thinking about how advertising works. Duality comes naturally to Americans and Europeans. What does not come naturally to them is looking for multiple causes, as people brought up in cultures with a more pluralistic view do.[21]

Japanese thought is not logical, but intuitive.[22] The Japanese are not familiar with polar thinking. Two-dimensional maps used to structure values or wants or for positioning brands are not very popular in Japan, where people are not used to responding on bi-polar scales.[23]

American and European cultures are used to thinking in single cause-and-effect terms. This is related to the way their language and time system affect their thinking, causing them to frame their thoughts in a linear, sequential manner. Synchronicity is the opposite. In synchronic thinking cultures, events are experienced simultaneously by different people in different places, so that people separated by space have been known to experience identical sensations and emotions.[24]

How people learn influences their thinking and response. "Western" learning methods are largely based on critical thinking and analysis. Asian learning systems are very much based on memorizing. Different cultures teach different ways of gathering and weighing evidence, of presenting viewpoints and reaching conclusions. Particularly in the United States, if there are no facts to support an opinion, the opinion will not be considered legitimate or valid. There is an expression in the American language that expresses this: "the point," as in "Let's get right to the point," or "What's the point of all this?" Writers and speakers are supposed to "make their points clear," meaning that they are supposed to say or write explicitly the idea or piece of information they wish to convey. The directness associated with "the point" is not part of Chinese or Japanese languages.[25]

Language

There are two ways of looking at the language-culture relationship: Language influences culture, or language is an expression of culture. Edward Sapir and Benjamin Lee Whorf hypothesized that the structure of language has a significant influence on perception and categorization.[26] This implies that the worldview of people depends on the structure and characteristics of the language they speak. Users of markedly different grammars are led by their grammars toward different types of observations and different evaluations of similar acts of observation, and thus are not equivalent observers, but must arrive at somewhat different views of the world.[27] According to this viewpoint, language is not only an instrument for describing events, it also shapes events. Observers using different languages will posit different facts under the same circumstances, or they will arrange similar facts in different ways. The other viewpoint is that language reflects culture. The approach is to realize that only the ability to speak is universal for humankind. Which language a person speaks is part of the culture in which she or he grows up. The language reflects all manifestations of culture, the expressions and the values. Language illustrates culture. Expressions of culture are particularly recognizable in the use of metaphors. Examples are expressions like "he is a team player," "he drives me up the wall," a "ballpark estimate," all derived from American baseball in the American language, whereas British English has a number of expressions relating to cricket. The elements used in metaphors will vary. In Egypt, for example, the sun is perceived as cruel, so a girl will not be described as "my sunshine," but may be compared with moonlight.[28] "Moonlighting" in English means having a second job in the evening.

It is the cultural environment that explains why some languages have more words for one thing than for others. Some languages have more different words for the different substances of ice or rain than others. The Norwegian language reflects a historic seafaring nation, having one strong word for "wind in your favor": *bør*. Some languages have words that do not exist in others. The English *pith,* the archaic word for marrow, refers to the white under the skin of oranges and other citrus fruit. This seems to be directly linked with the British "marmalade culture." There is no equivalent in the Dutch language for the English *to fudge* (empty talk, refusing to commit oneself). The Dutch are not inclined to fudge, which may explain their image of being blunt.

Some culture-specific words migrate to other languages if they express something unique. Examples of such words are *management, computer, apartheid, machismo, perestroika, geisha, sauna, Mafia, kamikaze.*[29] Often, these words reflect the specific values of a culture. They cannot easily be translated into words of other cultures, or they have been borrowed from another culture from the start. The English language does not have its own words for *cousin* and *nephew,* these were borrowed from French (*cousin* and *neveu*). This phenomenon may reflect the fact that the roots of individualism are in England. In early English society, as early as the 13th century, children at the age of 7 or 9 years, both males and females, did not grow up in an extended family but were put out to hard service in the houses of other people.[30] The way a person describes kin is closely connected with the way he or she thinks about them. In extended families, a father and a father's brother may both be termed "father." The Hungarians differentiate between a younger sister (*húg*) and an older sister (*növér*). The Russian language has different names for the four different brothers-in-law. In Indonesian, *besan* is the word for "parents of the children who are married to each other."[31]

The Dutch language shows frequent use of diminutives; so does the Czech language. Use of the diminutive suffix in Spanish reflects something positive while using the enlargement suffix turns it into something negative.

The English language reflects the way Anglo-Saxons deal with action and time. They have a rich vocabulary expressing this, such as "down to earth," "feedback," "deadline." The English word *upset* expresses the way the English handle their emotions, with self-constraint. Although it is used to express emotions of "not feeling OK" or "angry" by non-British speaking the English language, it usually does not express the same as it does when used by the British. *Upset* is not translatable into most other languages. The English concept of sharing includes more values than a translation in other European languages can include. It includes "generosity," "participating," "caring for fellow people," "not totally concerned with the self," and "communicating positive things." It includes showing "how good you are" and "achievement." It covers both the German *teilen* and *mitteilen* or the Dutch *delen* and *mededelen* and more than that.

The Dutch and the Scandinavians have words for "togetherness" that express much more than "being together" and that do not exist in the Anglo-Saxon world. The words are *gezellig* (Dutch), *hyggelig* (Danish), *mysigt* (Swedish), and *kodikas* (Finnish). The Danes use it even in combinations like *hyggetime* ("together time") and *hyggemad* ("together food").[32] It means sharing your feelings and philosophies in a very personal way while being together in a small group. An Englishman living in the Netherlands, when asked his opinion about it, will shiver and say: "It is so intrusive." The concept means preferring a dinner party for four people to a larger group, whereas a small group is not considered to be a dinner party by the British or the Americans, who tend to apologize if there are not more than two couples for dinner. For the Dutch and the Scandinavians, the concept can be used very effectively in advertising for the type of product used during such meetings, such as coffee, sweets, and drinks. The concept will not be understood by members of other cultures. The coffee company Sara Lee/Douwe Egberts has used it very effectively for advertising their coffee in Holland during the past century and has earned a substantial market share through its use.

German examples include the word *Reinheit,* which has a wider meaning than the word *purity.* The word *ergiebig* is another example, meaning delivering quality and efficiency, or more for the same money. The Spanish word *placer* means much more than the translation *pleasure.* It includes pleasure while eating, enjoyment, sharing a social event, softness, warmth, the good life, contentment, and satisfaction (see also Chapter 11, where it is discussed under "The Spanish Advertising Style"). The French notions of *savoir faire* and *savoir vivre* include a vast array of values specific to French culture and cannot be properly translated. The Japanese expression for "computer graphics" carries the meaning of a picture, a drawing, and illustration or sketch, but not of a graph. Another example is the Japanese word for "animation," which in translation carries the meaning of "comics" or "cartoons."[33] In Japan, the word for "heart" associates with "warmth," not necessarily with "love," as love is not expressed the same as in the Western world. There are no proper equivalents to the words *identity* and *personality* in the Japanese language, as the concept of identity is alien to the Japanese people.

Untranslatable concepts often are so meaningful to members of a specific culture that they are effective elements of advertising copy. This implies that words that are labels of culturally meaningful concepts are too ambiguous to use in international campaigns.

Language is much more important than many international advertisers realize. It is common knowledge among those who are bi- or trilingual that copy carrying cultural values is difficult to translate. Monolingual people generally do not understand this. If translations are needed, particularly for research purposes, the best system is translating and back-translating the questions, to be sure that at least the questions have the same meaning. Yet the values included in the words cannot be translated, and linguistic equivalence is thus not easily attained.

Signs, Symbols, and Body Language

Pierce,[34] one of the founders of semiotics as a discipline, distinguishes three basic types of sign: icon, index, and symbol. An *icon* bears a resemblance to its object. An *index* is a sign with a direct existential connection with its object—smoke is an index of fire. A *symbol* is a sign whose connection with its object is a matter of convention, agreement, or rule. Words and numbers are symbols; so is the red cross. Globalization has led to increased use of icons. Airports, stations, and other places frequented by international travelers use icons because they are not linked with language. They also help with faster information processing. Other examples are the use of diagrams such as bar or pie charts in reports and presentations. Icons, indexes, and symbols are part of the fundamental semiotic instruments used for advertising. Language codes, signs, symbols, and gestures are all rituals of culture and define cultural groups. Semiotic habits are the grammar of a culture. Culture is the shared ability to recognize, decode, and produce signs and symbols, so culture also is a combination of semiotic habits. Differences in semiotic habits delineate cultures.

Semiotics, the study of signs and symbols, is in many countries an integral part of advertising theory, although used more in some countries (France, Eastern Europe) than in others. Some cultures use more symbols in advertising than do others. This is related to writing and language. The Japanese and other Asians using the kanji script seem to have a greater ability to perceive and use symbols. Experience with Japanese students in a non-Japanese learning environment shows that they tend to be more comfortable with pictures and symbols than with language than Western students are, particularly if the language is not their native language.[35]

Signs and symbols are an important part of association networks in our memory: package, color, letters, signs. Color can have a particularly strong cultural meaning. Black is the color of mourning in the Western world. In

Illustration 3.1 555 Cigarette Brand in Cambodia

China, white symbolizes mourning. Gold has a strong symbolic meaning for the Chinese, but not combined with black, a combination used by Benson and Hedges cigarettes in their global campaign. IKEA uses the colors blue and yellow internationally, the colors of the Swedish flag, but not in Denmark—a country that in the past was occupied by the Swedes. Those colors still have too negative a connotation for the Danes. Because of this, IKEA uses the combination of red and white in Denmark, the colors of the Danish flag. For some cultures, symbolic language is much more important than verbal language. In Asia, numbers have significance unknown to Western cultures. Numbers can be particularly meaningful. An example is the 555 cigarette brand in Asia. Illustration 3.1 shows this brand in Cambodia.

Gestures are important cultural signs: Gestures that in one culture have a positive meaning can be embarrassing to members of another culture. A Russian gesture meaning "friendship" means "winning" in the United States. Germans raise their eyebrows in recognition of a clever idea. The same expression in Britain and the Netherlands is a sign of skepticism. The Hungarian gesture as shown in outdoor advertising for Pepsi in Illustration 3.2 is perceived as obscene not only in West European countries, but also in Bulgaria, so close to Hungary.

Putting your feet up on your desk may demonstrate relaxation or a "Friday feeling" in the United States, but showing the soles of your shoes or feet is offensive in the Arab world. Showing your tongue to other people in Europe is a sign of contempt, but for children is a sign of challenging other children. In Asia it is impolite, even for children. For the Maoris in New Zealand it is a sign of great respect.

Illustration 3.2 Pepsi Light Gesture in Hungary

It is easy to make mistakes, as every seasoned traveler will have discovered. What is considered polite in one culture may be considered obscene in another. What is friendly here is hostile there. A comprehensive guide to the meaning of gestures was developed by Desmond Morris,[36] who adds the note that signaling by gesture is a predominantly masculine pursuit. In some countries it is so exclusively masculine that a female researcher had to withdraw before the local men would even discuss the subject. Axtell[37] distinguishes four general categories of gestures: greetings gestures, beckoning gestures, insulting gestures, and touching gestures. There are three common and popular gestures that are often perceived as universal, but are not: the OK signal, thumbs up, and "V" for victory. The U.S. OK sign means "zero" in France and Hungary, "money" in Japan. The thumbs-up gesture is used by pilots the world over, but in some countries it is not so accepted. The "V" sign means victory for the English if the palm and fingers face outward; if the palm and fingers face inward, it means "up yours."

Proxemics, the study of people's use of space as a cultural artefact, organizing system, and communication system,[38] deals with the degree to which people want to be close to other people or to touch others. It is an aspect of body language and an expression of culture. When someone from the south of Europe makes a motion to a northern European to link arms while walking in the street, the latter may not know how to react as touching in public is not something universal in Europe. Northern Europeans don't like to be close to other people. Observance of people's behavior in elevators will show that when the crowd in an elevator dissolves, the French will stay where they are, yet the British will quickly increase space between each other.

Hall,[39] in particular, has studied differences in proxemics in various cultures. In the United States, there is a commonly accepted invisible boundary around any two or three people in conversation that separates them from others. Distance alone serves to isolate, give privacy. Someone can be in a room with other people without disturbing their "privacy." When a person stands still or sits down even in a public place, a small sphere of privacy balloons around him or her, which is considered inviolate. Anyone who enters this zone and stays there is intruding. For the Germans, there is no such thing as being in the room without being inside the zone of intrusion of the other party present, no matter how far away. When an American wants to be alone, she or he goes into a room and shuts the door. The English have internalized a set of barriers that they erect and that others are supposed to recognize. Hall[40] says that the difference between the Americans and the English is between architectural and spatial needs of privacy. For the French or the Spanish, proxemics are very different. Mediterranean use of space can be seen in the crowded trains, buses, sidewalks, and cafés. These cultures are characterized by high sensory involvement, expressed in the way they eat, entertain, and crowd together in cafés. Isolating oneself is seen as an insult to others. Anglo-Saxons tend to go into their room and shut the door when they want to be alone. The Spanish don't do this. American students, studying in Spain and living with families, tend to become confused when their families show concern every time they are alone in their rooms with the door shut. Another example is how professors and students relate. Spanish professors and students socialize outside class, they go to bars, dance, and touch. This is seen as inappropriate in the United States, where professors can even be accused of sexual harassment if the interaction is between people of different sexes. Differences between Arabs and Americans or Europeans are even stronger. Arabs do not like enclosed space. Muslims have particularly strong rules for space between men and women. In advertisements, if showing men and women together is allowed at all, the distance must be carefully observed. What is seen as a basic expression of warmth or love in the Western world may be seen as inappropriate in Muslim countries. The American home compartmentalizes the family, so children grow up leading separate lives. This has consequences for media behavior. Americans are not used to watching television in groups, as are the Spanish.

The concept of space can also be objective or relative. Space as "objective space" in the Western sense, for example, is not part of Indian culture, where one always places oneself in relationship to others. Showing directions in geometric space (first street at your right, then turn left, etc.) will not work as well as directing people by pointing out landmarks in relationship to other landmarks (after the church tower, walk beyond the mailbox, turn left at the butcher shop, etc.).[41]

When comparing cultures, it is important to learn which are the signs and symbols used by a culture and how they are recognized.

Imagery and Music

Imagery, or the use of pictures and symbols as a way of conveying meaning, is based on pictorial conventions. Pictorial conventions are not self-evident but formed for the purpose of representation. There are significant cross-cultural differences in pictorial perception. Most pictorial artefacts are conventional constructions; visual perception is profoundly influenced by learned habits of interpretation, and the assumption that a picture's purpose is to represent reality is a peculiarly Western product of the imagination.[42] The selection of style, of point of view shown in a picture, is based on the cultural learning of a photographer or creative director, with the cultural learning of the audience in mind. Audiences, consumers, use their learned vocabulary of pictorial skills in the response.

Western people also tend to think of the interpretation of pictures as a process occurring in time: the sequence of information processing as a function of visual layout. But not all cultures have a sequential thinking pattern. The concept of time varies, as well as the direction of viewing (left to right or right to left). Preferences for symbols or verbal expression and for movement or stills vary so much that art directors should think twice before developing an international campaign based on visuals. Yet the statement that visuals travel better than words is still often heard. Pictures, just like verbal language, have to be translated into the pictorial language of other cultures.

Music is another aspect of culture. Although many types of music have proved able to travel (classical music, jazz, pop music), cultures tend to have their own rhythm. A people's music is inseparable from their lives, and songs represent an important part of their identity. Music represents a sort of rhythmic consensus, a consensus of the core culture. Technically, little is known about what human synchrony is, but rhythm is basic to synchrony. Being in sync with the core culture must be more effective than being out of sync.[43] Language has a rhythm, too. Those who have learned to speak a foreign language well, according to grammar and idiom, know that they will not be understood if they have not learned the music and rhythm of that language.

Global Culture

The more superficial aspects of culture, such as symbols and rituals, can travel. This often makes people think that eventually there will be one global world culture, created by large companies such as Coca-Cola and Nike. Global communication has, indeed, influenced the relationships among people worldwide, resulting in several "global cultures," such as corporate cultures and professional cultures. These exist, however, at the level of practices and expressions of culture, the heroes and rituals. Large multinationals tend to shape a corporate culture with shared practices: ways of dressing, meeting, communicating, and presenting, all overriding the multitude of national cultures. This is useful to give cohesion to the worldwide group of employees, to give identity to the company, and to differentiate the company from competitive companies. A strong corporate identity is important for marketing and developing brand images. At product and brand level, global advertising has developed global cultures: the Pepsi Generation, Marlboro Country, the World of Peter Stuyvesant. However, they remain at the level of symbols, heroes, and rituals.

National, historically defined cultures have strong emotional connotations for those who belong to them. These connotations define their identity. *Identity* here means the subjective feelings and values of a population sharing cultural characteristics, a shared "memory," a "history." Global or cosmopolitan cultures cannot refer to such a common identity. Unlike national cultures, a global culture is essentially memoryless.[44] The countermovement is regionalization. In 1995, the global music industry discovered that global music stars were less appreciated than local or regional stars.

> Many experts think the U.S. portion of the worldwide music market will shrink to just 20% by 2000, down from a third today and 50% in 1987. After years of selling the tunes of Michael Jackson and Mariah Carey to overseas markets the five large companies that control 80% of the industry—Polygram, Warner, Sony, EMI and Bertelsmann—are pouring billions of dollars into regional studios, plants and distribution networks.[45]

Conclusion

In order to understand the global-local paradox, it is necessary to grasp the concept of culture. The often-heard argument for a standardized marketing and advertising approach is that consumers worldwide will eventually adopt similar habits, customs, and values. The examples provided usually concern the expressions of culture. The core values of culture vary greatly and it doesn't look like they are converging.

Cultural values determine the way people think or their intellectual styles. International marketing and advertising people must understand these differences in learning and thinking patterns because they influence the way people will respond to surveys, how they will process information, and how they will respond to advertising. This will influence the way we think advertising works and thus the theories of how advertising works.

Because language is the reflection of culture, words expressing people's values cannot easily be translated. This is why translating advertising messages for an international campaign to cross borders often leads to bland copy. Some words are so culturally significant that they cannot be translated. This supports the advice that it is better to have local copywriters write texts from a central brief than to translate a copywriter's text from one culture into another. This advice is of even greater importance with respect to public relations (PR) work, when often difficult messages have to be transferred from one culture into another.

The art of advertising is to develop symbols or advertising properties as part of an association network. But very often these signs or symbols have originated in one culture and cannot be decoded the same way by members of other cultures, or, when transported to other cultures, must be given another meaning relevant to that culture. The European campaign for KitKat (candy bar) is based on the concept of the "break": "take a break, take a KitKat." The break was an English institution: the eleven o'clock morning tea break, when working people had their morning tea, and brought a KitKat as a snack. KitKat in the United Kingdom was called Elevenses. This type of break did not exist in any other country, so the break concept had to be "translated" in a different way for the other countries in Europe. Continental Europeans do not have the same "break" memory as do the British.

Understanding the concept of culture and the consequences of cultural differences will make marketing and advertising people realize that one message, whether verbal or visual, can never reach one global audience, because there is not one global culture comprised of people with identical values. Worldwide, there is a great variety of values. The problem is that we have to be able to recognize and to vocalize the differences. Models for understanding this variety will be provided in Chapter 4.

Notes

1. Rice, C. (1993). *Consumer behaviour: Behavioural aspects of marketing.* Oxford, UK: Butterworth Heinemann, pp. 242-253.

2. Geertz, C. (1973). *The interpretation of cultures.* New York: Basic Books, p. 45.

3. Hofstede, G. (1991). *Cultures and organizations: Software of the mind.* New York: McGraw-Hill.

4. G. Hofstede, cited in M. De Mooij, *Advertising worldwide* (2nd ed.). Hemel Hempstead, Hertfordshire, UK: Prentice Hall International, chapter 4.

5. Geertz (1973), *The interpretation of cultures,* p. 49.

6. Roland, A. (1988). *In search of self in India and Japan.* Princeton, NJ: Princeton University Press, p. 324.

7. Murdock, G. P. (1945). "The common denominator of culture." In R. Linton (Ed.), *The science of man in the world crisis.* New York: Columbia University Press.

8. Geertz (1973), *The interpretation of cultures,* p. 53.

9. Benedict, R. (1974). *The chrysanthemum and the sword: Patterns of Japanese culture.* Rutland, VT: Charles E. Tuttle, p. 301. (Original work published 1946)

10. This draws on Hofstede, G. (1991). *Cultures and organizations: Software of the mind.* New York: McGraw-Hill, p. 9. With permission.

11. De Mooij (1994). *Advertising worldwide.*

12. Adler, N. J. (1991). *International dimensions of organizational behavior* (2nd ed.). Belmont, CA: Wadsworth, p. 63.

13. Franzen, G. (1994). *Advertising effectiveness: Findings from empirical research.* Henley-on-Thames, Oxfordshire, UK: NTC Publications, pp. 17-24.

14. Scott, L. (1994, Sept.). "Images in advertising: The need for a theory of visual rhetoric." *Journal of Consumer Research, 21,* 260.

15. Adler (1991), *International dimensions of organizational behavior.*

16. Platt, P. (1989, January). "An entente cordiale mired in stereotypes." *International Management,* p. 50.

17. Usunier, J. C. (1993). *International marketing: A cultural approach.* Englewood Cliffs, NJ: Prentice Hall.

18. *Brochure Cannes Lions '94.* (1994). Advertising Age and Creativity.

19. De Mooij (1994), *Advertising worldwide,* p. 135.

20. Usunier (1993), *International marketing,* p. 71.

21. Hall, E. T. (1984). *The dance of life.* Garden City, NY: Doubleday/Anchor, p. 135.

22. Doi, T. (1973). *The anatomy of dependence.* Tokyo: Kodansha International.

23. Information from private conversation with Kazuaki Ushikubo, November 1995.

24. Hall (1984), *The dance of life,* p. 191.

25. Althen, G. (1988). *American ways.* Yarmouth, ME: Intercultural Press, pp. 30-31.

26. Usunier (1993), *International marketing,* p. 99.

27. Feyerabend, P. (1988). *Against method: Outline of an anarchistic theory of knowledge.* New York: Verso, p. 286.

28. From a conversation with Geert Hofstede.

29. Hofstede (1991), *Cultures and organizations,* p. 213.

30. Macfarlane, A. (1978). *The origins of English individualism.* Cambridge, MA: Blackwell, pp. 146, 174.

31. Burger, P. (1996, June). "Gaten in de taal." *Onze Taal,* p. 293.

32. Burger (1996), "Gaten in de taal."

33. Miracle, G. E., Bang, H. K., & Chang, K. Y. (1992, March 20). "Achieving reliable and valid cross-cultural research results." Working paper panel of Cross-Cultural Research Design, National Conference of the American Academy of Advertising, San Antonio, TX.

34. Pierce, C. S. (1990). "Collected papers" [1931-1958]. In J. Fiske (Ed.), *Introduction to communication studies* (2nd ed.). New York: Routledge, pp. 47-48.

35. From private conversation with Mieke Vunderink, IRIC, Maastricht, on December 8, 1995.

36. Morris, D. (1994). *Bodytalk: A world guide to gestures.* London: Jonathan Cape.

37. Axtell, R. E. (1991). *Gestures: The do's and taboos of body language around the world.* New York: John Wiley.

38. Hall (1984), *The dance of life,* p. 7.

39. Hall, E. T. (1969). *The hidden dimension.* Garden City, NY: Doubleday/ Anchor, pp. 131-157.

40. Hall (1969), *The hidden dimension,* p. 140.

41. Roland (1988), *In search of self in India and Japan,* pp. 272-273.

42. Scott, L. (1994), "Images in advertising," pp. 261-263.

43. Hall (1984), *The dance of life,* pp. 190-191.

44. De Mooij (1994), *Advertising worldwide,* p. 125.

45. "The new music biz." (1996, January 15). *Business Week,* pp. 20-25.

Dimensions of Culture

Consumers and advertising professionals alike know very well when "something does not fit," when "something is not right" in international communications. But this has to be vocalized to make people of other cultures understand why the "something" does not fit; one has to be able to explain and convince.

Documenting Cultural Differences and Similarities

Without models for understanding and classifying cultural differences, objections to an imposed advertising idea from another culture can too easily be labeled with the "not-invented-here syndrome." Culture specifics have to be documented in such a way that similarities can be found by making generalizations.

The dilemma of understanding another culture is that it has to be compared with one's own culture. The assumption is that there is something to be compared, that no one culture is so unique that any parallel with other cultures is meaningless. The study of culture can be characterized by the dispute between those stressing the unique aspects of culture and those stressing the comparable aspects. Are we comparing the incomparable, or can cultures be classified according to dimensions that make them comparable?[1] Two dilemmas for the researcher are ethnocentrism and the choice between the specific and the general or the emic and the etic approach.

Ethnocentrism

Because we are all more or less prisoners of our own culture, it is difficult to exclude our own cultural value pattern from the way we perceive and classify other cultures. Perceiving other cultures only from the cultural perspective of the researcher is ethnocentric behavior. In a more extreme sense, *ethnocentrism* refers to a tendency to feel that the home-country people are superior to people of other countries; that they are more intelligent, more capable, or more reliable than people of other countries. Usually, ethnocentrism is more attributable to inexperience or lack of knowledge about foreign cultures than to prejudice.[2]

The Specific and the General, the Emic and the Etic

There are basically two approaches to comparing cultures, from the emic or from the etic point of view. The terms *emic* and *etic* are derived from the "phonemic" and "phonetic" classification in linguistics. The phonetic classification is universal and allows characterizing any sound in any language. In a particular language, however, only certain sounds are used and they are called phonemics. The phonemic is the specific, the phonetic is the general.[3] The suffixes *-etic* and *-emic* have been promoted to independent terms in anthropology for distinguishing the two approaches. The emic approach tries to describe behavior of one particular culture, the etic approach uses external criteria to describe and compare behavior of different cultures.

Dimensions of Culture

A relatively small number of models have been developed for the systematic comparison of cultures. For the purpose of global marketing and advertising, the most useful ones are those that distinguish dimensions of culture. They can be used as an instrument to make comparisons between cultures and to cluster cultures according to behavioral characteristics. Edward Hall, for some 40 years, has studied dimensions of culture. He focuses on the communication patterns found within cultures. His four dimensions are: context, space, time, and information flow. The context and time concepts will be described in the following sections. Gannon[4] identifies metaphors that members of given societies view as very important, if not critical. Hofstede distinguishes five dimensions of culture that are based on an enormous database with scores for 85 countries. The differences in advertising explained in this book are based on this model. The next sections will provide a description of the dimensions used to compare cultures.

High-Context and Low-Context Cultures

Hall[5] distinguishes cultures according to the degree of context in their communication systems. In a high-context communication or message, most of the information is either part of the context or internalized in the person; very little is made explicit as part of the message. The information in a low-context message is carried in the explicit code of the message. Twins who have grown up together are an example of high-context communication; they do not need to explain to each other why they behave in a certain way. Two lawyers in a courtroom are an example of low-context; they need the words and rhetorics of their coded, professional language. In general, high-context communication is economical, fast, and efficient. However, time must be devoted to programming. If this programming does not take place, the communication is incomplete. Generally, high-context cultures are more predictable, but only if one is familiar with the system.[6] To the observer, an unknown high-context culture can be completely mystifying, because symbols that are not known to the observer play such an important role. Low-context cultures are characterized by explicit verbal messages. Effective verbal communication is expected to be explicit, direct, and unambiguous. Low-context cultures demonstrate high value and positive attitudes toward words. The Western world has had a long tradition of rhetoric, a tradition that places central importance on the delivery of verbal messages.[7] Argumentation and rhetoric in advertising are found more in low-context cultures, whereas advertising in high-context cultures is characterized by symbolism or indirect verbal expression. For the Japanese, the verbal mode is only one aspect of communication; the nonverbal is often seen as having greater importance. Western philosophical tradition emphasizes the importance of words. In Japan, such a tradition does not exist. The Japanese have always valued reserve over eloquence.[8]

An important consequence of context is that words and sentences as well as pictures have different meanings depending on the context in which they are embedded. Hall states that one can find the degree of context of cultures in many different ways. Any of the basic cultural systems and subsystems can serve as a focus for observation. These include matters such as material culture, business institutions, marriage and the family, social organization, language, the military, sex, and the law. Hall has chosen the law to illustrate points on contexting. He observes that American lawyers see the law as something that is set apart from real life. In U.S. courts, contexting testimony, such as hearsay, is not admitted. Only established facts, stripped of context, are admissible as evidence. "Answer the question, Yes or No." Hall uses this example to reveal U.S. courts as the epitome of low-context systems. In contrast, he mentions the French courts in which great leeway in the testimony is admitted as evidence. The court wants to find out as much as possible about the circumstances. Understanding means context, people and motives, not raw facts or data. The French are as a rule more involved with their employees and with clients and customers. Hall concludes that maybe the French culture is a mixture of high- and low-context institutions and situations.[9]

Hofstede finds a correlation between collectivism and high context in cultures. In collectivistic cultures, information flows more easily between members of the group and messages are more implicit. Collectivistic cultures show more indirect communication versus more direct communication in individualistic cultures. Another explanation for the difference between cultures with respect to indirect communication and the use of symbols is given by Indrei Ratiu,[10] who has made a link between the use of symbols and the degree of homogeneity of cultures. Homogeneous cultures have more in common with respect to cultural heritage, and their members can thus rely on shared symbols more than members of heterogeneous cultures can. The relatively high use of symbols by the English and the Japanese may be understood by the fact that their countries are islands and their nations have a long history.

Cultures are on a sliding scale with respect to context. Most Asian cultures are high context, while most Western cultures are low-context cultures, extremes being Japan and China (high-context) and Germany, Switzerland, and the United States (low-context cultures). Americans, in particular, need data to evaluate things. For foreigners, the quantity of numbers and statistics encountered in the media and in daily conversations in the United States is stunning.[11] As Hall[12] says: "many Americans don't seem to be able to evaluate the performance of anything unless they can attach a number to it."

The distinction high-context/low-context communication is useful for understanding the differences between cultures with respect to verbal and nonverbal communication, direct versus indirect advertising, and the use of symbols versus facts and data. The difference between cultures relying more on visuals and symbols and those relying on facts and data is particularly interesting for advertisers. How differences in communication and advertising styles can be explained by the distinction between high- and low-context cultures will be further described in Chapter 7.

Dimensions of Time

Time is more than what the clock reads. Different cultures have different concepts of time. Western advertisers tend to use clocks in their international advertising to symbolize efficiency, which is not recognized as such in cultures where people have a different sense of time. Time is a core system of cultural, social, and personal life. Each culture has its own unique time frame. Hall's[13] important study of time as an expression of culture provides an explanation of differences in behavior and language. He distinguishes different types of time: biological time (light-dark/day-night, hot-cold/summer-winter), personal time (how time is experienced), physical time (absolute-Newtonian vs. relative-Einsteinian), metaphysical time, micro time (culture specific), sync time (each culture has its own beat), sacred time, and profane time. Hall developed his theories during his stay with Native Americans, discovering how differently they dealt with time than did Anglo Americans. Different concepts of time can explain significant differences in behavior.

Closure

Americans are driven to achieve what psychologists call "closure,"[14] meaning that a task must be completed, otherwise it is perceived as "wasted." What Hall saw, as characteristic of Hopi (Southwestern Native Americans) villages, was the proliferation of unfinished houses. The same can be seen in Turkey, in southern Europe, and in other collectivistic cultures, where additional rooms will only be built when family needs arise.

Time Heals

The cultures of the world can be divided in those in which time heals and those in which it does not.[15] In "time heals" cultures, things that happened before those now living were born are not held against the currently living. For those for whom time does not heal, the past will keep dominating the present. The culture of Bosnia is one of "time does not heal." The culture of Indonesia is one of "time heals."

Long-Term Versus Short-Term Thinking

In Western culture, one may make up one's mind quickly and think that things will happen rapidly after one has made up one's own mind. In other cultures, there are long periods during which people make up their minds or wait for a consensus to be achieved, and there can be a time lag between making up one's mind and related action. Long- versus short-term thinking is one of the cultural dimensions that will be described in more detail later in this chapter under "Long-Term Orientation (LTO)."

Time Orientation Toward the Past, Present, or Future

North Americans tend to be future oriented; the future is a guide to present action, although the time horizon is short-term. The old is easily discarded and the new embraced. Most things are disposable, from ideas, trends, and management fads to marriage partners. Even the "old" is treated as new. An example was the "back to the roots" trend. Many Europeans are past oriented; they believe in preserving history and continuing past traditions.[16] Others deal with time in a dialectical way, which means that at no given time, past, present, or future, is it possible to isolate that time from the events that led up to it and that flow from it.[17] Japan has a very long-term future time horizon, as have the Chinese, but they look to the past for inspiration. The Chinese tend to combine both the past and the future in one holistic view of life, including reverence for their forefathers and long-term responsibility for future generations, but have no respect for cultural history. African time is said to be composed of a series of events that are experienced. The future is of little meaning, because future events have not yet occurred.[18] Destiny as an aspect of time and referring to a future has not been investigated by the West.[19] It is part of the Indian magic-cosmic world that the Western world has regarded as superstition and ignorance. In the sense of destiny, time becomes extremely complicated. There are issues of premonitions as to what will happen in the future, what part one will have, and what part one can play.

Time Is Linear or Circular

Time can be conceived as a line of sequential events or as cyclical and repetitive, compressing past, present, and future by what these have in common: seasons and rhythms. The latter time orientation is linked with Asian culture, the former is the Western time orientation. The linear time concept causes people to see time as compartmentalized, schedule dominated. Americans have a linear time concept with clear structures, such as beginning, turning point, climax, and end. Time is used as a measuring instrument and a means of controlling human behavior by setting deadlines and objectives. Time is tangible, like an object; it can be saved, spent, found, lost, and wasted. Temporal terms such as *summer* and *winter* are nouns, they are treated as objects. For Native Americans, summer is a condition: hot; the term is used as an adverb, not related to time but to the senses.

In Japan, time is circular and is related to the special meaning of seasons. Japanese time thinking is not in terms of today, tomorrow, or the day after tomorrow. The seasons form an automatic, upward spiral; everything returns automatically. Saying "back to the old values" in Japan does not imply a step backward but a step forward. It means progressing through an upward spiral, using what was good in the past for progress.

Monochronic and Polychronic Time

Hall's[20] distinction of how people handle time is between monochronic (M-time) and polychronic (P-time) cultures. People from monochronic cultures tend to do one thing at a time; they are organized and methodical, and their workdays are structured to allow them to complete one task after another. Polychronic people, on the other hand, tend to do many things simultaneously. Their workday is not a chain of isolated, successive blocks; time is more like a vast, never-ending ocean extending in every direction. The Germans adhere to the more rigid and compartmentalized way of dealing with time. To people who do many things at the same time, such as the Spanish, Arabs, Pakistani, or South Americans, however, punctuality is nice, but by no means an absolute necessity in the middle of a hectic day. When two people of different time cultures meet they may easily offend each other, because they have different expectations of time. In particular, the fact that in polychronic cultures people interfere during meetings is very annoying to people of monochronic cultures. Monochronic time cultures are usually also low-context cultures, and polychronic cultures are usually high-context cultures. Not all M-time cultures are the same, however. In Japan, tight M-time is for business, and P-time is for private life.

Cause and Effect

Time also relates to the concept of cause and effect used to explain the sequence of events. The cause-effect paradigm appears particularly in North American decision-making culture. Things don't just happen, something makes them happen. Symbolic and mystical explanations of events are not accepted. Preference is given to concrete and measurable causes that precede the consequence or effect. Concepts in other cultures are very different. With the Chinese, for instance, causes and results do not have to follow each other, they often happen simultaneously. One event can be explained by another, unrelated event that is happening at the same time.[21] The American way of decision making often leads to suboptimalization due to the too simplified cause-and-effect model they use. The Japanese use a holistic cause-and-effect model that takes into account a multitude of causes that have a joint effect.[22]

Time as Symbol

Time is money and a symbol of status and responsibility. To be kept waiting is offensive in M-time cultures, it is perceived as a message. It is not in P-time cultures. Status is linked with the degree of discretion a person has in the ways she or he can schedule time in M-time cultures. Waiting one's turn is basic for M-time cultures. In P-time one does not wait one's turn. In P-time having friends, intermediaries, is more important. Friends come first, not those who have patiently waited in line. A clock used as symbol of efficiency does not have that connotation in P-time cultures.

Relationship to Nature

There are basically three types of relationships between humanity and nature: mastery-over-nature (man is to conquer nature), harmony-with-nature (man is to live in harmony with nature), and subjugation-to-nature (man is dominated by nature).[23] Harmony with versus mastery over nature and the time-related dimension of past-present-future orientation are two of five dimensions of people's value orientation as formulated by Kluckhohn and by Kluckhohn and Strodtbeck.[24]

In the Western world, humanity is viewed as separate from nature. In particular, the North American relationship to nature is that it should be conquered, controlled; nature and the physical environment can be and should be controlled for human convenience. To most North Americans, the expression "to move a mountain" is not a metaphor symbolizing the impossible, but rather an optimistic challenge based on past experience.[25] The outlook of U.S. culture is that it is the person's responsibility to overcome obstacles that may stand in his or her way. The harmony-with-nature orientation draws no distinction between or among human life, nature, and the supernatural; each is an extension of the others.[26] The Japanese experience of nature is one of communion, of exchange, characterized by a subtle intimacy. It is an experience of identification with nature. Westerners tend to explain the Asian reverence for nature as a relationship with God that involves living in harmony with the world of nature. Takeo Doi,[27] the Japanese psychologist who has published on the essence of Japanese culture, says that in Japan, God as a creator is absent and human beings therefore seek comfort by attempting to immerse themselves completely in nature. Other cultures, such as many African cultures, see people as dominated by nature, and the supernatural forces play a dominant role in religion. This subjugation-to-nature involves the belief that nothing can be done to control nature.

Gannon's Cultural Metaphors

Gannon tries to cluster cultures by identifying metaphors that members of given societies view as very important, if not critical. In addition to dimensions found by Kluckhohn, by Hall, and by Hofstede, he focuses on 23 additional aspects of culture, among others: religion, early socialization and family structure, small group behavior, public behavior, leisure pursuits and interests, greeting behavior, humor, language and body language, sports, educational system, food and eating behavior, and social class structure. All are practices or expressions of culture. Gannon provides an interesting description of 17 cultures according to the following metaphors: the traditional British house, the Italian opera, the German symphony, French wine, the Swedish *stuga,* the Russian ballet, Belgian lace, the Spanish bullfight, Irish conversations, the Turkish coffeehouse, the Israeli kibbutzim and moshavim, the Nigerian marketplace, the Japanese garden, the Shiva's dance of India, American football, and the Chinese family altar. Metaphors such as those described by Gannon are purely descriptive and provide good insight into the expressions of culture. They are less useful for analyzing cultures and predicting people's behavior.

Hofstede's Five Dimensions of Culture

To compare cultures, Hofstede[28] distinguishes among them according to five dimensions: Power Distance, Individualism versus Collectivism, Masculinity versus Femininity, Uncertainty Avoidance, and Long-Term Orientation. The dimensions are measured on a scale from 0 to 100 (index), although some countries may have a score below 0 or above 100 because they were measured after the original scale was defined. This 5-D model was developed by Geert Hofstede, who analyzed data collected by IBM to try to find an explanation for the fact that some concepts of motivation did not work in all countries in the same way. The model is based on 30 years of quantitative research. The original data were from an extensive IBM database for which—between 1967 and 1973—116,000 questionnaires were used in 72 countries and in 20 languages. Later, an additional Chinese Value Survey was conducted in 23 countries by Michael Harris Bond. Smaller surveys have been made in Central and East Europe. The results were validated against about 40 other cross-cultural studies from a variety of disciplines including sociology, market research, and medicine, initially described in Hofstede's 1984 book, *Culture's Consequences,* and later popularized and updated in his *Cultures and Organizations: Software of the Mind.* Hofstede gives scores for 56 countries; others have extended this to 85 countries. The combined scores for each country explain why people and organizations in various countries differ. As in all other cross-cultural studies, the data are comparative. Throughout the present book, countries will be compared with respect to their relative position on Hofstede's dimensions. Those who are interested in the actual score lists can find them in Hofstede's *Cultures and Organizations: Software of the Mind.*

Although the model was originally used to explain differences in work-related values, I have applied it to consumption-related values and motives. This was validated in two ways: (a) by content analysis of a large sample of television commercials and print advertisements, to determine whether and how cultural values are reflected in advertising; and (b) by linking the Hofstede data to the 1995 results of the European Media & Marketing Survey (EMS)[29] and to the Reader's Digest Eurodata—A Consumer Survey of 17 European Countries,[30] to determine whether and in what way(s) consumption behavior correlates to the Hofstede dimensions. Actual product data and data on related behavior indeed appear to correlate with culture. The correlations found were significant at different levels.[31] The Reader's Digest Survey is a study of the lifestyles, consumer spending habits, and attitudes of people of 17 European countries in 1969 and 1991. The EMS is a European "industry" survey that collects three broad types of data in 17 European countries simultaneously: (a) advertising effect data, based on corporate and brand management; (b) media data, to provide schedule reach and frequency estimates of print media exposure and TV net audience levels and profiles; and (c) classification data, covering both the respondent's business and personal environment. EMS 1995 was guaranteed by a joint-industry group of 10 companies that included advertisers, agencies, publishers, and TV networks. From 1997 onward, the Hofstede questions are included in the EMS questionnaire, which provides EMS subscribers a direct link between culture and a variety of marketing data. Data from 16 countries are used.[32] As no similar cross-country surveys are available for other regions, I could not extend the exercise to other areas in the world.

The content analysis work is reflected in Chapters 8, 9, and 10. Correlations among data from the Eurodata Survey, EMS, and Hofstede's dimensions are presented throughout the following chapters. Short descriptions of the five dimensions are given below, with a few general consequences. Specific consequences for value studies, consumer behavior, and advertising are provided in the following chapters.

Power Distance (PDI)

The power distance dimension (PDI) can be defined as *"the extent to which less powerful members of a society accept and expect that power is distributed unequally."* It is reflected in the values of both the less powerful and more powerful members of the society. It influences the way people accept and give authority. In large power distance cultures, everyone has his or her rightful place in a social hierarchy, and as a result acceptance and giving of authority is something that comes naturally. This cannot be compared with the Western concept of authoritarianism. To the Japanese, behavior that recognizes hierarchy is as natural as breathing. It means "everything in its place."[33] In cultures scoring lower on the power distance index, such as the Americans', authority has a negative connotation. Small power distance cultures stress equality in rights and opportunity in the workplace. In the United States, it is assumed that superior and subordinate are basically equal. Both have rights as well as responsibilities that are spelled out in contractual terms. Indians, members of a large power distance culture, always perceive a hierarchical order in any relationship, wherein the superior and the subordinate will be much more connected emotionally and by reciprocal responsibilities and expectations.[34]

The acceptance of hierarchy is indirectly recognizable in behavior. In Japan, every greeting, every contact must indicate the kind and degree of social distance between individuals. Generally, in large power distance cultures it is accepted that people have their fixed parking spaces, expressing the hierarchy in the organization. Another phenomenon is that people in these cultures tend to apologize when others bump into them, as opposed to small power distance cultures where the one bumping into another will apologize. They should not have been there in the first place. Koji Yanase, deputy secretary-general of the Japan Federation of Bar Associations, explaining why there are half as many lawyers in his entire country as in the greater Washington area alone, is quoted as follows: "If an American is hit on the head by a ball at the ballpark, he sues. If a Japanese person is hit on the head, he says, 'It's my honor. It's my fault. I shouldn't have been standing there.' "[35] Another reflection of the "rightful place" concept is a difference in behavior by the press. In November 1994, it become known in France that the late president François Mitterrand, married father of two sons, had kept a mistress and fathered a daughter, Mazarine, by her, because *Paris Match* published photos of father and daughter. This is something not done in France, because power holders have prerogatives. The way the British press has handled the mishaps of the British royal family is very different, to say the least.

Dependency is an element of these hierarchical relationships between people: Someone who becomes dependent immediately reinforces the other as superior in the hierarchical relationship, thus enhancing the latter's inner esteem by giving a sense of being needed and of being idealized.[36] In large power distance cultures, there are strong dependency relationships between parents and children, bosses and subordinates, professors and students, masters and learners. In small power distance cultures, children are raised to be independent at a young age. Americans will avoid becoming dependent on others and they do not want others, with the possible exception of immediate family members, to be dependent on them.

In large power distance cultures, organizations tend to be hierarchical and inequality is accepted. Status is important for showing power, and older people are important because of respect for old age. In cultures of small power distance, powerful people try to look less powerful, older people try to look younger. Malaysia scores highest on power distance and Austria lowest. Mexico and France score high, the United States relatively low, Denmark and Hungary very low.

The degree of power distance tends to decrease with increased levels of education. As a result, it is expected that improved education worldwide will lead toward decreased PDI scores, but relative differences between countries are not expected to change because of the stability of cultural values.

Individualism/Collectivism (IDV)

The contrast individualism/collectivism (IDV) can be defined as *"people looking after themselves and their immediate family only, versus people belonging to in-groups that look after them in exchange for loyalty."* In individualistic cultures, one's identity is in the person, people are "I"-conscious, express private opinions, and self-actualization is important; individual decisions are valued more highly than group decisions. In individualistic cultures, people give priority to the task; in collectivistic cultures priority is given to relationship with people. In individualistic cultures, there is more explicit, verbal communication. Individualistic cultures are low-context cultures. In collectivistic cultures, people are "we"-conscious, their identity is based on the social system to which they belong, and avoiding loss of face is important. Collectivistic cultures are "shame" societies. Having or losing "face" is the expression used by people belonging to collectivistic cultures. When one has done something wrong, it reflects not on oneself, but on the group to which one belongs and one therefore feels shame. Collectivistic cultures are high-context cultures.

Most Western countries score individualistic, Asian and Latin American countries collectivistic. Within Europe, England scores highest on the individualism dimension, Portugal lowest. Between 70% and 80% of the world's population is more or less collectivistic.

Members of collectivistic cultures emphasize goals, needs, and views of the in-group over those of the individual; the social norms of the in-group are favored over individual pleasure, and shared in-group beliefs over unique individual beliefs.[37] Collectivistic cultures vary with respect to the type and rank-order of importance of in-groups. In-groups vary from the extended family (whether members live in joint or unitary households is not relevant), with neighborhood and school friends absorbed in the extended family, to the larger community such as the Indian *jati* or Spanish *barrio,* or the occupational unit.[38] Some put kinship organizations (family) ahead of all other in-groups, whereas others put their companies ahead of other in-groups. In-group relationships in collectivistic cultures are usually limited to three groups: brother/sister (family group), co-worker and colleague (company in-group), and classmate (university in-group). Modernization in Japan has made the occupational unit more important than kinship links. Members of collectivistic cultures draw sharp distinctions between members of in-groups and out-groups. In-group relationships in collectivistic cultures are more intimate than in individualistic cultures.

Members of collectivistic cultures are born as part of a group that defines their identity. They cannot choose. Members of individualistic cultures belong to many specific in-groups that they join willingly. Because they are joined willingly, these in-groups have less influence than in-groups do in collectivistic cultures.[39] Members of the collectivistic in-group are implicitly what in individualistic cultures are called one's "friends." Members of individualistic cultures have to invest time in friendship, and they belong to many specific in-groups, which may change over time. Seven out of 10 Americans belong to at least one club or association,[40] while membership in associations is not very popular in Japan. Although many Americans have close friends to whom they feel special attachments and strong obligations, such friendships are small in number. Many other people are called "friends" but there is no element of mutual obligation, something that comes so naturally in the collectivistic in-group, which may consist of a large number of people.

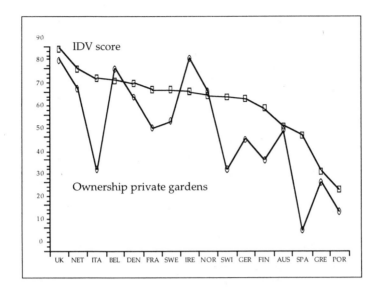

Figure 4.1 Correlation Between IDV and Ownership of Private Gardens
SOURCE: Data reproduced from Reader's Digest Eurodata—A Consumer Survey of 17 European Countries, sponsored by The Reader's Digest Association, Inc.
NOTE: rho = 0.71***

In individualistic cultures there is a strict division between private life and public life/work life, between private time and work time. In collectivistic cultures there is no such strict division. This is illustrated by the fact that in collectivistic cultures people have relatively few private gardens, as people prefer to socialize in public places, together. Within Europe there is a correlation between the IDV dimension and ownership of private gardens, as illustrated in Figure 4.1.

The merging of private and public life in collectivistic cultures explains what I call the technology paradox (see Chapter 1 under "The Technology Paradox"). The fact that a market is developed does not imply that people will use technological products such as home computers in the same way as in other countries. In collectivistic cultures, there is no incentive to take work home, and ownership of home computers appears to correlate with individualism. In Japan, one of the most developed countries, home PC ownership is relatively low. The chart in Figure 4.2 shows that also within Europe, home PC ownership correlates with individualism. In 1990, PC ownership was also related to income, but in 1995, among 12 of the wealthiest countries worldwide, the number of computers per 100 people correlated even stronger with individualism (0.90***) and there was no relationship with income.

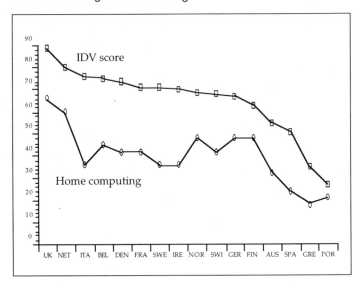

Figure 4.2 Correlation Between IDV and Ownership of Home Computers
SOURCE: Data reproduced from Reader's Digest Eurodata—A Consumer Survey of 17 European Countries, sponsored by The Reader's Digest Association, Inc.

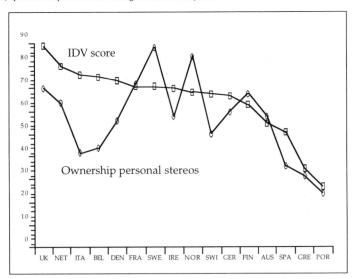

Figure 4.3 Correlation Between IDV and Ownership of a Personal Stereo
SOURCE: Data reproduced from Reader's Digest Eurodata—A Consumer Survey of 17 European Countries, sponsored by The Reader's Digest Association, Inc.

Usage of a personal stereo is a very individualistic habit. In Europe, ownership of personal stereos appears to correlate with individualism, as illustrated in Figure 4.3. 1996 sales data of personal stereos in the same countries (Euromonitor) confirm this correlation with IDV (0.49*).

In Italy, the IBM data used by Hofstede were collected in the North, where people appeared to be highly individualistic. Other studies[41] and my own observations of Italian television advertising indicate that the Italians as a whole are much more collectivistic. This is confirmed by the Eurodata survey, which shows collectivistic behavior by the Italians: relatively fewer private gardens and fewer home computers and personal stereos than would be expected from the IDV score. Further illustrations of this difference can be found in Chapter 6 under "Needs," and in Chapter 7 under "High-Context and Low-Context Communication."

Individualistic cultures are universalistic cultures, whereas collectivistic cultures are particularistic. People from individualistic cultures tend to believe that there are universal values that should be shared by all. People from collectivistic cultures, on the other hand, accept that different groups have different values. Being individualistic, most North Americans believe that democracy—especially North American democracy—should ideally be shared by all. People from collectivistic cultures find such a view hard to understand.[42] Particularly, journalists of individualistic cultures demonstrate universalistic thinking, assuming certain truths as self-evident and commenting on events in other parts of the world from their universalistic and ethnocentric point of view. Hall[43] observes, "Americans, more than most, seem dominated by the need to shape other people in their own image." This is particularly reflected in American marketing and advertising philosophies. Cristina Martinez, Latin American regional account director for Eastman Kodak at J. Walter Thompson Co., Miami, says: "we're finding that teen-agers are teen-agers everywhere and they tend to emulate U.S. teen-agers."[44] The Japanese, the Chinese, and other Asians feel so unique that they cannot and will not imagine that Westerners will ever be able to adopt their values and behavior.

Individualism is increasing worldwide because it is linked with wealth, but it remains a relative concept. If it is said that Japanese society is individualizing, that does not mean Japanese values will come close to American values. Americans are much more individualistic than the Japanese. That relative difference is expected to remain. Japanese words with respect to individualism carry different meanings. If the Japanese say they individualize, they mean a change from focus on the needs of the company to a focus on the needs of the individual, that is, having more time for hobbies, not spending all one's time with work and the company. What the Japanese call collectivism is conformance to the group. Activities not related to the group are seen as individualistic. Because individualism goes against conformance to the group, or consensus, individualism to the Japanese means rebellion, assertiveness. This is a reaction against the "old" collectivism of being part of the company so strongly that there was nothing else in life than being only one little wheel in the organization. So, the Japanese are redefining their style of collectivism. What they call individuality is a way to rebel against overly strong conformance to the group, which limits their competitiveness. The observation that Asian countries and their values are Westernizing, a conclusion based on this new focus on individuality, is an example of universalistic thinking. The expectation that Japan will eventually "converge" toward an Anglo-Saxon model is based on wishful thinking.

Masculinity/Femininity (MAS)

The masculinity (MAS) dimension can be defined as follows: *"the dominant values in a masculine society are achievement and success, the dominant values in a feminine society are caring for others and quality of life."* In masculine societies, performance and achievement are important. Status is important to show success. There is a tendency to polarize: Big and fast are beautiful. Feminine societies, those scoring low on the masculinity index, are more service-oriented, have a people orientation: Small is beautiful. There is a tendency to strive for consensus. Quality of life is more important than winning. Status is less important for showing success, or success is not demonstrated at all. Being a "winner" is positive in masculine societies and is negative in feminine societies. In masculine cultures, children learn to admire the strong. In feminine cultures, children learn sympathy for the underdog, the loser.

Sweden is lowest on the masculinity dimension, Japan highest. All Anglo-Saxon countries score high on masculinity; the Scandinavian countries and the Netherlands score low. Countries in Central America score lower on masculinity than those in South America and North America.

In feminine cultures such as the Scandinavian and the Dutch, you are not supposed to hurt other people's feelings, not supposed to win, but rather to have more respect for the loser, the underdog. The Dutch are said to be blunt or, to put it softly, straightforward. This is explained by not wanting to hurt other people's feelings: Not being straightforward is seen as devious, thus as hurting people.

Result-, winning- and success-orientations are characteristic of American, English, and German cultures and recognized in advertising. Aggressive behavior related to an explicit winning mentality is stronger in masculine cultures than in more feminine cultures such as the Scandinavian, Dutch, French, and Spanish cultures. A core value of feminine cultures is modesty, not showing off. So, if one excels, it should not be shown. This is illustrated by a quote from the 19th-century Dano-Norwegian author Anders Sande-mose, who called this value *Janteloven* (Jante's law),[45] saying:

> *Du skal ikke tro* . . . (You should not "feel" that . . .)
> > *du er noget* (you are anything)
> > *du er lige så meget som os* (you are equal to us, i.e, at our level)
> > *du er klogere end os* (you are more clever than we are)
> > *du er bedre end os* (you are better than we are)
> > *ved mere end os* (you know more than we do)
> > *er mere end os* (you are more than we are)
> > *at du du'r til noget* (you are good at anything)
> *Du skal ikke le ad os* (you must not make fun of us)
> *Du skal ikke tro* . . . (you should not think . . .)
> > *nogen bryder sig om dig* (that anybody likes you)
> > *at du kan lære os noget* (or that you can teach us anything).

This attitude is confirmed by the answers to the following statement in EMS 95: "I like to stand out in a crowd," to which respondents could answer on a 4-point scale: strongly agree, tend to agree, tend to disagree, and strongly disagree. The correlation of the response "strongly agree with 'I like to stand out in a crowd,' " with the MAS dimension is illustrated in Figure 4.4.

A consequence of this dimension is role differentiation: small in femi-nine societies, large in masculine societies. In feminine cultures, males can take typically female jobs without being seen as "sissy." In Germany (high on masculinity), household work is less shared between husband and wife than in the Netherlands (low on masculinity).[46] Masculinity versus femininity of cultures is recognized in many expressions. Americans call a problem a challenge. Their society is an opportunity society, as opposed to a welfare state.

Japan is a very masculine society with strong role differentiation. This, combined with collectivism, can explain the way men and women relate. There is no such thing as the Western love-relationship between men and women in marriage. "You are there, exist together, and you take each other for granted." Literally: You are like air for each other. The way Americans describe and express love is not accepted, as speaking out is not good. Kumiko Hashimoto, the wife of the Japanese Prime Minister Ryutaro Hashimoto, was quoted as saying the following about her relationship with

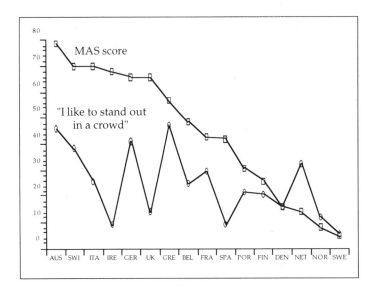

Figure 4.4 Correlation Between MAS and Strongly Agreeing With "I Like to Stand Out in a Crowd"
SOURCE: Data EMS (1995). Copyright © Inter/View.

her husband: "I give way to him almost as if he were a feudal lord, with everything done as he wishes."[47]

The masculine/feminine dimension discriminates between cultures particularly with respect to values related to winning, success, and status, which are much used in advertising appeals. It is therefore an important dimension for marketing and selling. It reflects the division between countries in which hype and the hard sell prevail and countries with a soft-sell, more modest approach. Related to this is thinking in comparisons. In the United States, a very masculine culture, students know their rank in class based on their test results. Such a system does not exist in the Netherlands.

In comparative cross-cultural studies, researchers tend to distinguish between the Anglo-Saxon world and continental Europe, while within Europe, there are also strong differences with respect to this dimension. U.S. researchers seem reluctant to use the masculinity dimension, possibly because of the label. Masculine/feminine can be misinterpreted as politically incorrect wording. At the time Hofstede labeled this dimension, there was no such thing as a political correctness movement. Yet for advertising and branding, this dimension can be used to distinguish important cultural differences with respect to values and motivations like achievement, accomplishment, and success.

An interesting observation on the cultural homogeneity of the Scandinavian countries is that they are not only a cluster of feminine cultures but also similar with respect to the other dimensions. This cultural homogeneity may have been the cause of Erik Elinder's statement in 1961, that cultural differences were decreasing. Elinder was a Swedish marketing executive who discovered that a campaign for a savings bank had identical results in all Scandinavian countries, and concluded that the same campaign could easily be extended to Europe.[48] At the time he may not have realized the scale and scope of his remark, which has been quoted ever since though it was based on an assumption valid only for Scandinavia, not for the rest of Europe. The Scandinavians are culturally very much alike, and very different from the rest of Europe. Erik Elinder fell into the trap of extending the findings of one cluster of similar cultures to an entire region, assuming all would be similar.

A marketing example of the difference between the feminine and masculine value systems was the "soap fight" between Procter & Gamble and Unilever in 1994. In April of that year, Unilever introduced its new stain-removing "power" formula detergents, under such brand names as Persil Power and OMO Power. Procter & Gamble charged that lab tests demonstrated the Unilever formula was causing clothes to rot. It was a very aggressive PR and advertising campaign. Unilever denied the charges, but reduced the amount of stain-reducing ingredient. P&G expected that their tough campaign, showing clothes torn to pieces after being washed in OMO Power, would make Dutch consumers reluctant to buy Unilever soap and cause distributors to pull the new product from their shelves. They didn't, or at least it took a long time before they did. Dutch distributors and consumers were so disgusted by the type of attack, which was so non-Dutch, that they supported the Unilever brand much longer than was expected.

Uncertainty Avoidance (UAI)

Uncertainty avoidance (UAI) can be defined as *"the extent to which people feel threatened by uncertainty and ambiguity and try to avoid these situations."* Life is unpredictable, and some people do not mind unpredictability or uncertainty while others hate uncertainty or ambiguity and try to cope with it by making rules and prescribing behavior. In cultures of strong uncertainty avoidance, there is a need for rules and formality to structure life. This translates into the search for truth and a belief in experts. Communication is more formal. Conflict and competition are threatening. People in strong uncertainty avoidance cultures have a higher level of anxiety

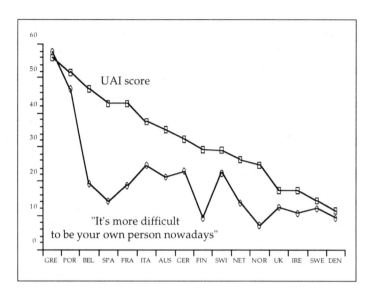

Figure 4.5 Correlation Between UAI and Strongly Agreeing With "It's More Difficult to Be Your Own Person Nowadays"
SOURCE: Data EMS (1995). Copyright © Inter/View.

and the show of emotions is accepted. People in strong uncertainty avoidance cultures build up tension, stress that must be released. This is done in many different ways. Members of strong uncertainty avoidance cultures are recognized as talking louder, using their hands while talking, driving their cars more aggressively, and embracing more emotionally. Members of weak uncertainty avoidance cultures tend not to show their emotions (e.g., the British "stiff upper lip") and are more tolerant drivers.

The tension caused by modern society appears to be experienced more strongly depending on the degree of uncertainty avoidance, as found in the answers to the following EMS 95 question: "It's more difficult to be your own person nowadays." The percentage of "strongly agree" answers appeared to correlate with the score on the uncertainty avoidance dimension, as illustrated in Figure 4.5.

Weak uncertainty avoidance cultures feel that there should be as few rules as possible. They believe more in generalists and common sense and there is less ritual behavior. Conflict and competition are not threatening.

Examples of countries that score high on Uncertainty Avoidance are Germany, Austria, and Japan. Examples of countries scoring low are Great Britain, Sweden, Denmark, and Hong Kong.

Differences between levels of uncertainty avoidance explain the difference in education systems between the Anglo-Saxon world and continental European countries. Germany—high on the uncertainty avoidance index—cherishes its specialized education with its apprenticeship system, while the British and the Americans are known for their liberal arts inclination and general business studies. The expert in strong uncertainty avoidance cultures must be a real expert, with degrees in specialized areas, in order to allow him- or herself to be called an expert. This is different in the United States, where anyone can become an expert because no one says what an expert is or must know. Americans can get themselves listed in *The Yearbook of Experts Etc.* for US$ 375.[49] This wish to be an expert is related to the masculinity dimension—status, wanting to stand out from the crowd—not to uncertainty avoidance.

The combination of masculinity and weak uncertainty avoidance, in particular, which combines the wish to be a winner with relative freedom from anxiety, appears to be indicative of creativity and innovation. It may explain why a relatively large number of creative advertising awards are won by the British and Americans. It also confirms Hofstede's findings that "the need for achievement," as measured by McClelland, is strongly correlated with the combination of weak uncertainty avoidance and strong masculinity.[50] Figure 4.6 shows the correlation between uncertainty avoidance and the EMS 95 response "strongly agree to the statement 'I like to stand out in a crowd' ": refer back to Figure 4.4 for the correlation of masculinity with this response. While the independent correlations between "I like to stand out in a crowd" and masculinity and uncertainty avoidance are 0.49^* and 0.51^*, respectively, the multiple correlation increases to $R = 0.63^{***}$.

Cultures of strong uncertainty avoidance feel the need to structure reality, but they may do this in different ways. Configuration with other dimensions will show differences in how reality is structured. If combined with individualism, the rules are explicit and written. Combined with collectivism, the rules are implicit and rooted in tradition. Differences in power distance have other implications. Combined with small power distance, the rules are internalized; one accepts the rules and that one has to abide by them. Combined with large power distance, one need not abide by the rules because they are externalized. Germans and French, both strong uncertainty avoidance cultures, like rules, but the Germans use them to structure themselves, the French to structure others. In French culture, reality is structured through conceptualization. This difference explains the propensity for the conceptual or the "grand idea" of the French, which is so

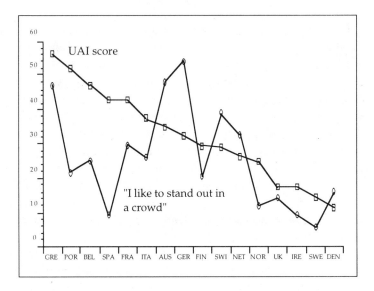

Figure 4.6 Correlation Between UAI and Strongly Agreeing With "I Like to Stand Out in a Crowd"
SOURCE: Data EMS (1995). Copyright © Inter/View.
NOTE: rho = 0.51*

different from the German thinking model. When the artist Christo suggested wrapping the Pont Neuf in Paris, it did not take the French long to agree. When he suggested wrapping the Reichstag in Berlin, it took the Germans years to say yes.

In academia, the combination of strong uncertainty avoidance and large power distance means that first there is a philosophy, a concept, then you get down to reality by finding the facts (Cartesian thinking). This is deductive thinking, as opposed to inductive thinking. The difference between deductive and inductive thinking runs parallel with the degree of uncertainty avoidance: Inductive thinking goes with weak uncertainty avoidance, deductive thinking with strong uncertainty avoidance. People of cultures in between tend to use both methods.

Long-Term Orientation (LTO)

Because of the Western bias of researchers, no dimension was originally found that explained the economic success of a number of Asian countries. Michael Bond, together with a number of Chinese social scientists, developed a Chinese Value Survey, resulting in a fifth dimension. Because this dimension includes the values of Confucian philosophy, it was originally labeled Confucian Dynamism. The Institute for Training in Intercultural Management (ITIM) also adopted this term. Hofstede, however, labeled it Long-Term Orientation, and that term is used in this book.

Long-term orientation is *"the extent to which a society exhibits a pragmatic future-oriented perspective rather than a conventional historic or short-term point of view."* Consequences of a high score on the long-term orientation index are: persistence (perseverance), ordering relationships by status and observing this order, thrift, and having a sense of shame. The opposite is short-term orientation, which includes personal steadiness and stability, protecting your "face," respect for tradition and reciprocation of greetings, and favors and gifts.[51] Focus is on pursuit of happiness rather than on pursuit of peace of mind. Most east Asian countries, particularly the ones with large Chinese populations, score high on the LTO index. Anglo-Saxon societies score low. Some non-Asian countries score medium or relatively high, such as Brazil and the Netherlands.

The combination of long-term orientation and collectivism results in family ties, long-term thinking, and other elements of Confucian philosophy such as filial piety and paternalism. This is reflected in the successful family entrepreneurship that makes east Asian development so different from Western development. Pragmatism is an important aspect of most east Asian cultures. They adapt to other cultures in such a way that Westerners are often fooled and think they are Westernizing.

The concept of truth, as it is experienced in the West, does not exist in east Asian cultures. The Western concept is supported by an axiom in Western logic that a statement excludes its opposite: If A is true, B, which is the opposite of A, must be false. Eastern logic does not have such an axiom. If A is true, its opposite B may also be true, and together they produce a wisdom that is superior to either A or B.[52] Pragmatism makes people prefer what works over what is "true" or what is "right."

Something that is often perceived as paradoxical in the measurements on this index is the combination of strong respect for tradition and short-term orientation in a large part of the Western world, while respect for old age and ancestor worship are such strong elements of Asian value systems. This is because the index measures the relative value given to one side over the other. If Asians value tradition, they value thrift even more. At the short-term orientation pole, personal steadiness and stability, if overly stressed, discourages initiative and entrepreneurship. On the long-term orientation pole, too much respect for tradition impedes innovation, so it is de-emphasized.[53] This reflects the desirable versus the desired: Tradition is important, but it is innovativeness that is desired. When studying how this is reflected in advertising, this gap between the desirable and the desired appears to be much stronger in Asia than in Europe and the United States, where tradition appears to be a common appeal in advertising. Particularly in China, pragmatism tends to overrule respect for tradition. An example is the 10-year Cultural Revolution that destroyed a priceless cultural heritage. It is not the first time such a frenzy has happened. Mao Zedong, the instigator of the Cultural Revolution, was inspired by the first emperor, Shi Huangdi, who unified China in 220 B.C.[54] He had all books destroyed and 463 philosophers buried alive in an attempt to remove the traditional Confucian thought from the collective Chinese memory. It was in vain: The emperor died after 11 years and the scriptures of Confucius and other philosophers, which had been memorized, were re-issued.[55] Yet pragmatism in accepting foreign habits in China has a limitation; they must fit *guo qing,* or "the Chinese national context." Good ideas applicable to China must be promoted; corrupted and inapplicable ideas must be discarded. Particularly for methods and ideas proposed to the Chinese by foreign governments, the expression "does not meet China's *guo qing*" is used. Confucian philosophy is a central part of that.[56]

The Japanese example of pragmatism is how, in the modernization process, the Western form was incorporated while ensuring full continuity of Japanese social patterns and cultural codes. The Japanese traditional patterns of familial hierarchical relationships, including values of emotional interdependence, reciprocal loyalties and obligations, and high levels of performance, shifted from rural family life to urban corporate life.[57]

A strong value in long-term orientation cultures is reverence for nature. This is also related to collectivism, so it is particularly in the configuration of long-term orientation and collectivism that harmony with nature plays such a strong role in people's lives. Nature and symbols of nature are an important part of advertising in Japan, China, and Chinese-related cultures.

Configurations of Dimensions

To illustrate the previous sections, the configurations of dimensions applicable to three cultures are described below.

The United States

The cultural dimensions of the United States are: an M-time culture, linear time-pattern, low-context, below average on power distance, high on individualism, high on masculinity, relatively weak in uncertainty avoidance, and with a short-term orientation.

The United States shows the following cultural characteristics:

- Short-term thinking, which influences all aspects of American life: the bottom line, success now rather than in the future, extremely short-range schedules
- Obsession with change, "new" and "better"
- More a credit card than a debit card culture
- Linear thinking; time is compartmentalized
- Hype, persuasive communication, and rhetoric
- Education valued only if it allows the individual to compete more effectively
- Expression of private opinions
- Equal opportunity
- Independence
- Need for privacy, universalistic thinking, ethnocentrism
- Winning, power, success, and status are important
- Strong role differentiation
- Humor, innovativeness, creativity
- Man must conquer nature
- Education teaches students to be "critical, makes them think." Students ask "why," not "how."

The Netherlands

The cultural dimensions of the Netherlands (and the Scandinavian countries) are: M-time culture, linear time-concept, low-context, small power distance, high on individualism, low on masculinity, of relatively weak uncertainty avoidance, relatively long-term orientation.

The Netherlands shows the following cultural characteristics:

- Longer-term thinking
- More a debit card than a credit card culture
- Traditional; reverence for the past
- Linear thinking, rhetoric

- Time is compartmentalized
- Need for privacy
- Equality, not so much in opportunity as in freedom and care
- Independence
- Universalistic thinking, preachers
- Winning is OK, but not its display, status not important
- Small role differentiation
- Consensus seeking, jealousy
- Thrift, perseverance
- Caring rather than winning is the ideal
- Education beyond the basic ability to get a job

Japan

The cultural dimensions of Japan are: a P-time culture, circular time concept, high-context, above average power distance, collectivistic, masculine, strong uncertainty avoidance, long-term orientation.

Japan shows the following cultural characteristics:

- The pressure on every Japanese person to know his or her place, to behave like his or her neighbors, not to shame his or her family, and to avoid jolting social harmony
- Dependence
- Private opinions not expressed
- Status is important to show power and success, but avoid standing out in a crowd: "the nail that sticks out will be hammered down"
- Long-term thinking
- A cash culture, not a credit card culture
- Thrift, perseverance
- Strong role differentiation
- Education is not based on teaching students to be critical: The very meaning of "to think" is differently understood. In Japanese culture it means something like "to find an answer which can be shared by others."[58] Students ask "how" instead of "why"
- Education has an intrinsic value, which cannot be measured purely in terms of the labor market
- "New" is accepted as a collective necessity, but basically the Japanese do not like change

- Obsession with cleanliness, purity
- Harmony with nature rather than conquest over nature

Conclusion

For people concerned with global marketing and communication, the most important aspect of culture is that it influences our perception—our own culture drives how we communicate and what we communicate. When developing messages, our automatic pilot takes over: We produce, create, and send what fits our own patterns of learning and our own pictorial conventions, our own language, our own vocabulary. This is often done irrespective of the vocabulary of the receivers of our messages, who do not belong to our own culture.

The way we perceive other cultures is from our own cultural mind-set, and it is very difficult not to take the ethnocentric point of view when classifying other cultures. Classification of cultures is necessary to develop marketing and advertising strategies in the global marketplace. Classifying cultures on dimensions has proved to be the most constructive method. It helps in vocalizing and labeling cultural differences and similarities.

A broad classification is the degree to which cultures contextualize, which is reflected in the type of communication cultures use. The difference between high- and low-context communication cultures helps us understand why, for example, Japanese and American advertising styles are so different, why the Japanese prefer indirect verbal communication and symbolism over the direct assertive communication approaches used by Americans. Other dimensions, such as different concepts of time, can explain major differences between East and West.

In order to construct a more refined classification system, Geert Hofstede developed a model of five dimensions for comparing work-related values, based on data collected in an extensive study. This model also proves to be useful for comparing cultures with respect to consumption-related values. As a result, it can explain the variety of values and motivations used in marketing and advertising across cultures.

The five dimensions can be used to explain differences in behavior influenced by culture that can be recognized in advertising. In Chapter 3 it was assumed that advertising, to be effective, must include values that match the values of the consumers being addressed. The 5-D model can be used to recognize these values and thus help develop more appropriate advertising. It can also explain differences in actual consumption behavior and product use and thus can assist in predicting consumer behavior or effectiveness of marketing strategies for cultures other than one's own. This will be particularly useful for companies that want to develop global marketing and advertising strategies.

Further understanding our own values and the receiver's values and how they may or may not match will be the topic of Chapter 5.

Notes

1. Hofstede, G. H. (1984). *Culture's consequences: International differences in work-related values.* Beverly Hills, CA: Sage, pp. 32-33.

2. Miracle, G. E. (1982). "Applying cross-cultural research findings to advertising practice and research." In A. D. Fletcher (Ed.), *Proceedings of the 1982 Conference of the American Academy of Advertising.* (Contact Robert King, AAA Executive Secretary, School of Business, University of Richmond, Richmond, VA 23173)

3. Hofstede (1984), *Culture's consequences,* pp. 32-33.

4. Gannon, M. J. (1994). *Understanding global cultures.* Thousand Oaks, CA: Sage.

5. Hall, E. T. (1984). *The dance of life.* Garden City, NY: Doubleday/Anchor, pp. 85-128.

6. De Mooij, M. (1994). *Advertising worldwide* (2nd ed.). Hemel Hempstead, Hertfordshire, UK: Prentice Hall International, pp. 131-132.

7. Ferraro, G. P. (1994). *The cultural dimension of international business.* Englewood Cliffs, NJ: Prentice Hall, pp. 50-51.

8. Doi, T. (1985). *The anatomy of self.* Tokyo: Kodansha International.

9. Hall, E. T. (1976). *Beyond culture.* Garden City, NY: Doubleday.

10. According to an unpublished survey done for the Fourth IAA Education Conference, Amsterdam, 1988.

11. Althen, G. (1988). *American ways.* Yarmouth, ME: Intercultural Press, p. 31.

12. Hall (1984), *The dance of life,* p. 62.

13. Hall (1984), *The dance of life,* pp. 16-27.

14. Hall (1984), *The dance of life,* pp. 32-33.

15. Hall (1984), *The dance of life,* pp. 33-34.

16. Adler, N. J. (1991). *International dimensions of organizational behavior.* Belmont, CA: Wadsworth, pp. 30-31.

17. Hall (1984), *The dance of life,* p. 86.

18. Ferraro (1994), *The cultural dimension of international business,* p. 94.

19. Roland, A. (1988). *In search of self in India and Japan.* Princeton, NJ: Princeton University Press, p. 302.

20. Hall, E. T. (1976). *Beyond culture.* Garden City, NY: Doubleday, pp. 17-24.

21. De Mooij (1994), *Advertising worldwide,* pp. 135-136.

22. This is demonstrated by the cause-and-effect approach in the Ishikawa or fishbone diagram, in Oakland, J. S. (1989). *Total quality management* (2nd ed.). Oxford, UK: Butterworth Heinemann.

23. Gudykunst, W. B., & Ting-Toomey, S. (1988). *Culture and interpersonal communication*. Newbury Park, CA: Sage, p. 52.

24. Kluckhohn, C. (1952). Values and value orientations in the theory of action. In T. Parsons & E. A. Shils (Eds.), *Toward a general theory of action*. Cambridge, MA: Harvard University Press; and Kluckhohn, R., & Strodtbeck, F. L. (1961). *Variations in value orientation*. Evanston, IL: Row, Peterson.

25. Ferraro (1991), *The cultural dimension of international business*, pp. 97-99.

26. Gudykunst & Ting-Toomey (1988), *Culture and interpersonal communication*, p. 52.

27. Doi (1985), *The anatomy of self*, pp. 147-148.

28. This section draws on Hofstede, G. (1991). *Cultures and organizations: Software of the mind*. New York: McGraw-Hill. Used with permission.

29. The European Media & Marketing Survey is executed by InterView International, address: Overtoom 519-521, 1054 LH Amsterdam, the Netherlands. Tel. +31-20-6070707; Fax. +31-20-6851621. The address for InterView North American Division is 103 Carnegie Center, Ste. 303, Princeton, NJ 08540, USA. Tel. +1-609-497-0613; Fax. +1-609-497-0665.

30. Reader's Digest Eurodata—A Consumer Survey of 17 European Countries, sponsored by The Reader's Digest Association, Inc. Published by The Reader's Digest Association, Limited, Berkeley Square, London W1X 6AB, United Kingdom.

31. Significance was established with the Spearman rank correlation coefficient, rho. Significance levels are indicated by * $p < .05$; ** $p < .01$; and *** $p < .005$.

32. The data for Luxembourg, the 17th country, are included in the EMS data for Belgium, while in the Eurodata report the data for Luxembourg are separate. The data of the Eurodata report are for the whole population; EMS data focus more on the level of managers.

33. Benedict, R. (1974). *The chrysanthemum and the sword*. Rutland, VT: Charles E. Tuttle, p. 47. (Original work published 1946)

34. Roland (1988), *In search of self in India and Japan*, p. 101.

35. "Perspectives." (1996, April 22). *Newsweek*, p. 7.

36. Roland (1988), *In search of self in India and Japan*, p. 280.

37. Gudykunst & Ting-Toomey (1988), *Culture and interpersonal communication*, pp. 42-43.

38. Roland (1988), *In search of self in India and Japan*, pp. 134 & 149.

39. Gudykunst & Ting Toomey (1988), *Culture and interpersonal communication*, pp. 42-43.

40. "America's strange clubs: Brotherhoods of oddballs." (1995, December 23). *The Economist*, p. 63.

41. Michael Hoppe, a German American management educator, replicated the IBM study on a population of political and institutional elites and found that Italy is much more collectivistic than the IBM scores lead one to believe. Hoppe's study also found differences with respect to Finland, which may be more individualistic than

the IBM scores indicate. Contradictory information about the level of individualism or collectivism in Italy is probably due to the fact that Italy is bi-cultural: The north is individualistic but the rest of the country is collectivistic. Hofstede's IBM data were mainly collected in the north, and he found strong individualism. Consumption and media behavior data are based on a country average; where these relate to individualism or collectivism, Italy tends to score similar to Spain, which is much more collectivistic.

42. Adler (1991), *International dimensions of organizational behavior,* p. 47.

43. Hall (1984), *The dance of life,* p. 86.

44. Malkin, E. (1994, October 17). "X-ers." *Advertising Age International,* pp. 1-15.

45. Private conversation with Donald Nekman, Denmark, May 1, 1995.

46. Information report "Bundesministerium für Familie, Frauen, Senioren und Jugend, 1991/1992," in *NRC Handelsblad,* December 8, 1994.

47. "Perspectives." (1996, April 22). *Newsweek,* p. 7.

48. Burghoorn, A. (1992). *Postmodernisme, globalisering en international advertising.* Unpublished master's thesis, University of Utrecht, the Netherlands.

49. Samuelson, R. J. (1995, June 5). "A nation of experts: If you think you're one, well, maybe you are." *Newsweek,* p. 33.

50. Hofstede (1991), *Cultures and organizations,* p. 124.

51. Hofstede (1991), *Cultures and organizations,* pp. 159-166.

52. Hofstede (1991), *Cultures and organizations,* p. 171.

53. Hofstede (1991), *Cultures and organizations,* pp. 168-169.

54. Han Suyin. (1994). *Eldest son.* London: Jonathan Cape, p. 392.

55. Ross, J. (1990). *The origin of Chinese people.* Petaling Jaya, Malaysia: Pelanduk Publications (M) Sdn Bhd. (Original work published 1916)

56. Yan, R. (1994, September/October). "To reach China's consumers, adapt to guo qing." *Harvard Business Review,* p. 229.

57. Roland (1988), *In search of self in India and Japan,* p. 129.

58. Joseph, J. (1994). *The Japanese.* New York: Penguin.

Values and Marketing

Values are said to be the basis for segmentation and positioning decisions. Ness and Stith[1] state that "successful marketing programs can only occur when the marketing mix of the product is matched with the values of the consumer." Vinson, Scott, and Lamont[2] mention that value acquisition is a sociocultural process and that different value orientations will lead to variations in preferences for products and brands. Values of both consumers and marketers are defined by their culture, hence the importance of understanding the value concept.

The Value Concept

A value is defined by Rokeach[3] as "an enduring belief that one mode of conduct or end-state of existence is preferable to an opposing mode of conduct or end-state of existence." A value system is "a learned organization of principles and rules to help one choose between alternatives, resolve conflicts, and make decisions."[4]

Values have cognitive, affective, and behavioral components. A value is a preference for one mode of behavior over another mode of behavior. One knows that one prefers order over chaos or chaos over order; most people know they prefer and should prefer love over hate, yet it may happen that one person hates another person. One can feel emotional over such preferences. Preferences can lead to action: changing chaos into order, if one prefers order over chaos. A value is a conception of the "desirable": the—generally—desirable is love, not hate; peace, not war. These are definable preferences.

Values are taught at an early age and in an absolute manner. They describe what people in general think the world ought to be in an absolute way. Freedom, peace—not a little bit of peace or a little bit of freedom. This is the desirable as opposed to the desired: The desired is what you want for yourself. The desired is not necessarily the same as what one "ought" to do. This distinction between the desirable and the desired is particularly meaningful for advertising. It will be further discussed in Chapter 8.

Rokeach states that "a person prefers a particular mode or end-state not only when he compares it with its opposite but also when he compares it with other values within his value system. He prefers a particular mode or end-state to other modes or end-states that are lower down his value hierarchy."[5] Thus, values include opposites, and there are different types of values in a value system which may have a different order of importance. Values are integrated in an organized system in which they are ordered in priority with respect to other values. Values can serve as standards that guide our choices, beliefs, attitudes, and actions.

Like other authors, Rokeach assumes (a) that the total number of values a person possesses is relatively small, (b) that all people everywhere possess the same values to different degrees, and (c) that the antecedents of human values can be traced to culture, society, and its institutions.

Terminal Values and Instrumental Values

Rokeach distinguishes two levels of values: terminal values and instrumental values. Terminal values refer to desirable end-states of existence. Instrumental values refer to desirable modes of conduct. Instrumental values are motivators to reach end-states of existence. Table 5.1 shows Rokeach's instrumental and terminal values, alphabetically arranged.[6] This list is based on a complete inventory of American values from the 1960s.

What people refer to as central or core values are usually terminal values. Moral values, including the norms of people or society, refer to modes of behavior. Social norms, or what one "ought" to do, how one "ought" to behave, are requirements for behavior in a specific society and more related to the instrumental values than the terminal values of that society.

Value System and Value Orientation

The notion of a value system implies a rank-ordering of terminal or instrumental values along a single continuum. A value orientation uses a multiple continuum and can be used to compare people along different dimensions or measurement systems. An example is the value orientation of Kluckhohn and Strodtbeck,[7] which includes both values and existential elements. The five dimensions of Kluckhohn and Strodtbeck are: (a) human nature is good or evil; (b) subjugation to, harmony with, or mastery over nature; (c) past, present, or future time perspective; (d) being, being-in-becoming, or doing; and (e) linearity, collaterality, or individualism. Within each dimension, a rank-order of values may exist.

TABLE 5.1 *Rokeach's Terminal Values and Instrumental Values*

Terminal Values	Instrumental Values
a comfortable life	ambitious
an exciting life	broad-minded
a sense of accomplishment	capable
a world at peace	cheerful
a world of beauty	clean
equality	courageous
family security	forgiving
freedom	helpful
happiness	honest
inner harmony	imaginative
mature love	independent
national security	intellectual
pleasure	logical
salvation	loving
self-respect	obedient
social recognition	polite
true friendship	responsible
wisdom	self-controlled

SOURCE: Reprinted with the permission of The Free Press, a division of Simon & Schuster, from *The Nature of Human Values* by Milton Rokeach. Copyright © 1973 by The Free Press.

Values, Attitudes, and Needs

Values guide and determine social attitudes and behavior. A value is a specific, single belief; it guides and determines actions, attitudes, and judgments. An attitude is an organization of several beliefs focused on a specific object or situation. A value is an enduring standard; an attitude is not a standard, but is object- or situation oriented. Values are more stable than attitudes and occupy a more central position in a person's cognitive system.[8] Needs can be innate and learned. Values are only learned. Animals can have needs, but they don't have values.

Classifications of Values and Lists of Values

The Rokeach Value Survey was one of the first to be used in marketing and has served as an example for many other value studies. A simpler approach to values, called List Of Values (LOV), was developed by Kahle and Goff Timmer.[9] LOV consists of nine values: a sense of belonging, excitement, fun and enjoyment in life, warm relationship with others, self-fulfillment, being well respected, a sense of accomplishment, security, self-respect. The nine items of LOV became the basis for the development of a new measurement scheme of the U.S.-Marketing Science Institute, called MILOV (Multi-Item List Of Values). The nine values resulting from MILOV are: Security, Self-Respect, Being Well Respected, Self-Fulfillment, Sense of Belonging, Excitement, Fun and Enjoyment, Warm Relationships, Sense of Accomplishment.

Values Are Enduring

Values are among the first things children learn, not consciously, but implicitly. Developmental psychologists believe that by the age of 10, most children have their basic value systems firmly in place.[10]

The search for changing lifestyles and trends is an integral part of the advertising world, and researchers regularly try to demonstrate that values change. What they usually find are changes in how people express their values, changes in the symbols and rituals of culture. Or, one can be misled by the behavior of members of a subculture, such as youth or businesspeople. Roland[11] gives the example of how an Indian man at work may dress in Western clothes and disregard intercaste rules in eating and other rituals, while strictly observing all of these codes and dressing traditionally at home. The core values of national culture appear to be very stable.

How enduring values are, is demonstrated by Yankelovich,[12] who states that despite increased affluence effect and other changes, many of America's most important traditional values have remained firm and constant. Despite the transformations in America's lifestyles, a number of core values, shared by virtually all Americans, have endured.

The unchanged values are:

- Freedom (valuing political liberty, free speech)
- Equality before the law
- Equality of opportunity (the practical expression of freedom and individualism in the marketplace)
- Fairness (placing a high value on people getting what they deserve as a consequence of their own individual actions)
- Achievement (a belief in the efficacy of individual effort: the view that education and hard work pay off)
- Patriotism (loyalty to the United States)
- Democracy (the belief that the judgment of the majority should form the basis of governance)
- American exceptionalism (a belief in the special moral status and mission of America)

- Caring beyond the self (concern for others, such as family or ethnic group)
- Religion (a reverence for some transcendental meaning)
- Luck (good fortune can happen to anyone at any time)

Yankelovich adds that this tiny cluster of values holds Americans together as a single people and nation; it is the unity amid the variety of American life.

Inglehart[13] offers relevant evidence on levels of satisfaction with one's life as a whole that appear to be stable over time. Data from Euro-Barometer surveys between 1973 and 1988 show that the levels of satisfaction as expressed in the surveys have remained more or less the same. There are remarkable cross-cultural differences: Consistently, the Danish, Dutch, and British publics show a higher level of satisfaction than the Italian, French, and German. These differences have remained stable over time. An explanation of these differences is not provided by Inglehart, but can be given by Hofstede's cultural dimensions. Uncertainty avoidance correlates negatively with feelings of well-being, and this remains stable over time. In the 1991 Reader's Digest Eurodata survey, the responses to the statement, "I am happy with the kind of life I lead" correlate negatively with the uncertainty avoidance dimension (rho = $-0.47*$).[14] *The Economist* publishes data annually on official aid expenditures by OECD countries and, each year, the most feminine cultures—Norway, Denmark, Sweden, and the Netherlands—are at the top of the list, while the masculine cultures are at the bottom: the United States is consistently at the bottom, as are, in varying order, Italy, Ireland, and New Zealand.[15]

Value Shift

Although values are enduring, some values may change over the long term. Wealth leads to individualism and poverty leads to collectivism. With better education, the level of power distance goes down. Yet relative differences remain, and some differences may even become stronger. At face value, people tend to become more individualistic, but individuation follows different patterns. Modernization, including industrialization and urbanization, is assumed to turn collectivistic societies into individualistic societies. Although urbanization tends to break up the joint household of the extended family in favor of more nuclear households, this does not imply decreasing extended family values. Roland[16] states that the Indian family always remains an extended one. The extended family maintains strong family ties, gets together on holidays, makes mutual decisions on important matters, and sometimes maintains joint ownership. Indian society and culture modernize by traditionalizing various foreign innovations. A class society has formed, but classes do not predominate over caste. Instead, caste associations have been formed to provide assistance for jobs, marriages, or loans, and castes have participated in the political process. The Japanese remain enmeshed within traditional family and group hierarchical structures although new skills and greater education have led to increased individuation. Modernization for the Japanese has reinforced the traditional Japanese ego-ideal into a total dedication to the task, which contributes to the good of the group.[17] The system of structural hierarchy of unquestioned subordination in large power distance cultures may change, but related dependency values included in a hierarchy by quality, deep respect for superiors, and reciprocal relationships remain.[18]

Age and point in time of people's lives can cause value differences. Hofstede mentions four different causes of differences in values among people of different ages and points in time. These are maturation effects, generation effects, Zeitgeist effects, and seniority effects.[19] Maturation effects mean that people's values shift as they grow older. Stress, for example is highest at middle age. Masculinity decreases with increasing age. Young people who want to make it in life generally adhere more to masculine values than those who have already made it. Youngest and oldest age categories are less individualistic. Generation effects occur when values are fixed in the young from a certain period and then stay with that age cohort over its lifetime. Drastic changes in the conditions of life during youth may lead to generations having different fixed values. The value shift of the generation of the 1960s is an example of a generation effect. Zeitgeist effects occur when drastic system-wide changes in conditions cause everyone's values to shift, regardless of age. In times of recession the degree of power distance may increase because equality is less functional, or it may lead to increased bureaucracy and shift to a stronger level of uncertainty avoidance. In Germany, between 1973 and 1977 (after the oil crisis), uncertainty avoidance increased. Also, both men and women shifted toward more masculine values. Seniority effects occur when the values of people who are more senior in an organization are measured. Seniority and age effects cannot be separated easily.

Cross-Cultural Value Research

Cross-cultural value studies are comparative studies between selected cultures. The limitations of these studies are that findings always relate only to the areas or countries studied and relate also to the value-perspective of the culture of the researcher. Surveys developed in one environment and used to measure values of another environment may lead to irrelevant results. Rokeach's list of (American) values has been used for value studies worldwide and applied to many other cultures for marketing and advertising purposes. At the time Rokeach developed his value survey, he already realized that values will vary by culture. There are three main consequences of using value studies developed in one culture for other cultures.

The first consequence of culture is a difference in rankings of priorities of values. In an exercise to find cross-cultural differences among American, Australian, Israeli, and Canadian students, Rokeach found differences in the ranking of the importance of the values in his list.[20] The Israeli students, in particular, deviated. For example, they cared more about being capable than being ambitious and they were less individualistic and more group oriented than the other students, all of whom were from Anglo-Saxon cultures (American, Australian, and Canadian). This supports Hofstede's findings on the Israeli culture—which is more collectivistic and of high uncertainty avoidance behavior, resulting in a higher regard for competence than is found in U.S. culture. Also, the lower priority given to being ambitious may be explained by the relatively low score of the Israelis on the masculinity index. Later studies by other scholars confirmed that surveys in other, non-American cultures will find different rankings of the same values.

A second consequence of culture is that the terminal values of one culture may be the instrumental values of another culture. Rokeach listed obedience, getting along well with others, and self-control as instrumental values.[21] In large power distance as well as in collectivistic cultures, however, obedience may well be a terminal value. Respect for elders, parents, or any higher placed person is ingrained in these cultures. Similarly, if the division between terminal and instrumental values were used in Asian cultures, getting along with others, or harmony, might be a terminal value rather than an instrumental one. A Belgian value, listed as the first terminal value by the Belgian Patrick Vyncke,[22] is having one's own house, one's own place under the sun. The Dutch consider this to be an instrumental value. The house is the instrument of security or care. And, indeed, the Dutch are very different from the Belgians, not only with respect to this value. Specific to the Belgians is their strong linkage to the soil of their birthplace, which is expressed by the saying, "a stone in your belly."

The third culture-specific aspect of values is that certain relevant values of one culture may not exist in another culture or the other way around. For example, in Rokeach's list of values, two important Asian values are missing:

perseverance and thrift. Relevant, culture-specific values can be found by looking at the important cultural concepts, which appear to be untranslatable into any other language or only into the languages of similar cultures. Due to the fact that some values cannot be translated, using a single value list for cross-cultural research will result in mistakes. Values will not be translated correctly or, in the translation process, will become different values. As a result, the data cannot be compared or the outcome is useless. In *The European* of November 8, 1995, the results of a world survey[23] were summarized. The survey was based on questions related to such values as responsibility and respect for others. What caused great doubt about the reliability and meaning of the whole survey was the remark that "the organizers had been confronted with translation difficulties." The example given was that the English word *imagination* translates as *verbeelding* in Dutch, which means conceitedness. Indeed, this is one of the two words provided in the dictionary, meaning "you think you are more than you are." It illustrates a relevant value of Dutch feminine culture, that one should not show off. The word that should have been used is *fantasie,* another translation possibility, which does not reflect negatively on the value found and better compares with the English concept imagination. The right choice can only be made by those who know the culture. Some values are so ingrained in culture that they are taken for granted, while others are given great emphasis because they are felt to be lacking in the society.[24] This represents the difference between the desirable and the desired. The desirable values are often the ones that are implicit, the desired the ones that are lacking. If the ingrained, implicit values of one culture are selected for a survey of other cultures, the results will be biased due to differences in relevance of the values and any related translation problems.

Priorities of Values Vary Across Cultures

Grunert, Grunert, and Beatty[25] compared values for two age groups in three countries (the United States, Germany, and Denmark), based on Kahle's LOV instrument, and found that ratings varied, particularly with respect to the values fun and enjoyment and self-fulfillment. Danish respondents, independent of their age, rated fun and enjoyment much higher than both German (from former West Germany) and U.S. respondents. The latter, on the other hand, rated self-fulfillment higher. The differences between the students and their parents must be due to the

TABLE 5.2 *Value Chosen as Most Important for Two Age Groups in Three Countries*

	Students			Parents		
Values	**USA %**	**Germany %**	**Denmark %**	**USA %**	**Germany %**	**Denmark %**
Sense of belonging	2.1	20.6	6.1	7.0	38.2	24.2
Fun and enjoyment	14.9	6.9	23.0	2.3	0	3.3
Warm relationships	8.5	14.5	12.2	11.6	3.6	9.9
Self-fulfillment	27.7	13.7	10.1	9.3	8.2	2.2
Being well-respected	7.1	3.1	4.7	2.3	4.5	5.5
Excitement	1.4	4.6	2.0	0	0	0
Sense of accomplishment	11.3	5.3	8.1	9.3	8.2	15.4
Security	10.6	5.3	4.1	11.6	18.2	9.9
Self-respect	16.3	26.0	29.7	46.5	19.1	29.7
Total	100	100	100	100	100	100
n of respondents	141	131	148	43	110	91

SOURCE: Grunert, Grunert, & Beatty (1989).

maturation effect. Table 5.2 shows the rankings of values chosen as most important for two age groups in three countries.

Kamakura and Mazzon[26] found substantial differences between the United States and Brazil for the Rokeach terminal values. Although family security, world peace, and freedom have consistently been important values in the United States, true friendship, mature love, and happiness appear to be the most important values in Brazil. Kamakura and Mazzon, comparing rankings of 1971 and 1981, also found that the ranking of values in the United States had been quite stable over time. Table 5.3 shows a comparison of value priorities between Brazil (1988) and the United States (1971 and 1981).

Culture-Specific Values

Knowing that the Rokeach values are typical American values, one would expect that countries with different cultures would develop their own lists of values. This is only a very recent development. Scholars and researchers

TABLE 5.3 *Comparison of Value Priorities in the United States and Brazil (overall ranks)*

Terminal value	Brazil 1988	USA 1981	USA 1971
True friendship (close companionship)	1	10	10
Mature love (sexual and spiritual intimacy)	2	14	14
Happiness (contentment)	3	5	6
Inner harmony (freedom from inner conflict)	4	13	12
A world at peace (free from war and conflict)	5	2	1
Freedom (independence, free choice)	6	3	3
Family security (taking care of loved ones)	7	1	2
Equality (brotherhood, equal opportunity for all)	8	12	4
Self-respect (self-esteem)	9	4	5
Wisdom (a mature understanding of life)	10	6	7
A comfortable life (a prosperous life)	11	8	13
A sense of accomplishment (lasting contribution)	12	7	11
A world of beauty (beauty of nature and the arts)	13	16	15
Pleasure (an enjoyable, leisurely life)	14	17	16
Social recognition (respect, admiration)	15	18	17
Salvation (being saved, eternal life)	16	9	9
National security (protection from attack)	17	11	8
An exciting life (a stimulating, active life)	18	15	18

SOURCE: From "Value segmentation: A model for the measurement of values and value systems," by W. A. Kamakura & J. A. Mazzon (1991), in *Journal of Consumer Research, 18,* 208-218.

in some countries are developing lists of values for their own countries— the culture-specific values of their countries. An example is a list of Belgian values presented in this section. Another way of observing culture-specific values is by analyzing questions used for local psychographic or lifestyle research. The questions or statements used reflect culture-specific values, and cultural dimensions can be recognized in the questions. To demonstrate this, a few questions from an Indian survey are included. The same is done with respect to a Japanese survey. A third way to find culture-specific values is to observe the characteristics of cultures on the Hofstede dimensions and link them with other relevant research, as Hofstede did with respect to the masculinity/femininity index.

Masculine and Feminine Values

Hofstede[27] correlated gender stereotypes found by the Japanese market research unit Wacoal in a study in eight Asian countries with the masculinity index scores. The findings of this secondary research confirmed a strong role differentiation in masculine cultures and a weak role differentiation in feminine cultures. This was expressed by the degree to which "typical" masculine and feminine values were shared by males and females. In the Wacoal study on average responsibility, decisiveness and ambitiousness were values seen as predominantly masculine and gentleness as predominantly feminine. In Japan, the most masculine culture in the study, 76% of respondents saw responsibility as masculine and 8% as feminine. In the most feminine culture, Thailand, 92% saw responsibility as masculine and 66% as feminine. In feminine cultures, men and women are seen as more responsible than in masculine cultures. In masculine cultures decisiveness, liveliness, and ambition are considered primarily masculine, whereas caring, gentleness, and humility are considered primarily feminine. In feminine cultures, these traits are considered to apply more equally to men and women alike. Masculine countries differentiate more in the characteristics associated with the two sexes. Love and family life are more often seen as separated, whereas in the feminine countries they are expected to coincide. Common gender stereotypes appear to be more pronounced in countries that score high on the masculinity index and less pronounced in countries labeled as feminine.

Belgian Values

A list of values developed by a Belgian scholar, Patrick Vyncke,[28] shows values not found in Rokeach's list (see Table 5.4). This list includes individualistic values such as self-esteem, self-interest, and "doing your own thing." It reflects the masculine values of success, status, and prestige. Most interesting is the fact that the first eight values are all related to strong uncertainty avoidance, which is a characteristic of Belgian culture. Owning your own house is a form of security; so are thrift, progeny, health, safety, being able to count on people, and being without pain. In particular, the statement "keep everything, all you have, as it is," reflects the reluctance to change that is characteristic of a strong uncertainty avoidance culture. The value progeny is reflected in the importance of children in Belgian society. According to the Reader's Digest Eurodata Survey, Belgians, of all Europeans, own the most insurance saving plans for their children's education.

TABLE 5.4 *List of Belgian Values*

1. Having your own house, a place "under the sun"

2. Thrift, frugality

3. Progeny, having descendants

4. Health, a healthy life

5. Safety, living in a safe world

6. Security, being able to count on people

7. Being without pain, fear, or misfortune

8. Keeping everything, all one had, as it is

9. Paying attention to oneself, self-interest

10. Romanticism, being in love, romantic love

11. Erotic love, sex, sensuality, seduction

12. A strong, intimate, and mature partner relationship

13. Love for children

14. Strong friendship, comradeship, "mateship"

15. Strong family ties, good family relationships

16. A better world for one's fellow man

17. A better environment, love of nature

18. Self-esteem, self-respect

19. Being respected by others

20. Being admired, having prestige, status, success

21. Leadership, power

22. Ability to be oneself as one is

23. Freedom, independence, doing one's own thing

24. Development of one's own abilities, creativity

25. Having one's own lifestyle

26. Being without stress, having peace, inner harmony

27. Having an active, exciting, adventurous life

28. Enjoying the simple things in life

29. Leading a prosperous, comfortable, luxurious life

SOURCE: Vyncke (1992), *Imago-Management.* Used with permission of Mys & Breesch, Ghent, Belgium.

TABLE 5.5 *Ten of 74 Questions Reflecting Indian Values*

1. "I do not wear clothes that are considered disrespectful in our society even though I would like to" (1).

2. "I am uncomfortable chatting with men other than my immediate relatives" (8).

3. "In today's world, it is important for a man and woman to get to know each other well before they get married" (9).

4. "It is important that we obey our elders" (20).

5. "I generally have my meals along with the rest of the family" (40).

6. "I don't feel confident shopping alone except for groceries" (41).

7. "I like the idea of staying in a joint family" (42).

8. "Our lives are determined by what is written in our stars—we can do very little to change it" (54).

9. "When we have visitors at home, I serve a variety of foods, even if it means a drain on my budget" (68).

10. "I do not complain about products which do not meet my expectations" (74).

SOURCE: Shunglu & Sarkar (1995).

Indian Values

The values of the extended family are predominant in Indian culture, although individuality is richly developed in Indians, including a large degree of freedom in feeling, thinking, and cultivation of one's inner life. Competitive individualism, however, is severely frowned upon in Indian society because it can disrupt relationships by hurting others' feelings.[29]

Statements used in psychographic research tend to reflect culture. Examples of such statements are presented in Table 5.5, showing a list of 10 questions, out of a total number of 74, used in an Indian survey.[30] The questions in the table were selected from the full list because they reflect culture so evidently. To show how they rank in the total list, the table also provides (in parentheses) the original numbers of the questions in the survey.

India is a large power distance and medium collectivistic culture, masculine, and of relatively weak uncertainty avoidance. Large power distance is recognized in Questions 1 and 4, expressing respect for elders and in Question 10, expressing dependence. Collectivism is recognized in Questions 5, 6, 7, and 9, reflecting the extended family, a preference for not being alone, and catering to visitors, even beyond one's financial means. Also, typically Indian historical values and practices are reflected, such as a segregated society and the arranged marriage.

East Asian Values

East Asian values, reflected in psychographic research and in communication, are: long-term orientation, pragmatism, perseverance, thrift, preference for utility rather than innovation per se, having a sense of shame,
willingness to subordinate oneself to a purpose, and living in harmony with
nature and one's fellows. Two east Asian values are frequently found in
marketing and advertising: harmony and nature. They are characteristic of
the combination of long-term orientation and collectivism and, although
here explained for Japanese culture, are applicable to a number of east Asian
cultures.

Harmony. One of the most important basic Japanese values is harmony
(*wa*): walk together, think together, dine together. Related is empathy
(understand and anticipate the feelings of others), respect for age, and
honesty. Honesty cannot be related to the Western concept of truth. The
Japanese concept of honesty is linked to respect. For example, government
should not treat us as children, but as grown-ups.

Nature. East Asian cultures are not normative cultures. When the
Japanese speak of the providence of nature, they refer to a natural order that
they believe to be the fountainhead of all existence. In the Christian world,
God is the fountainhead of all existence and humans seek comfort from God.
In Japan, human beings seek comfort by attempting to immerse themselves
in nature. Christianity is normative; it poses a strong division between good
and evil. East Asian culture is not normative. Nature is not normative.
Another explanation of the reverence for nature is that the Japanese turn to
nature because there is something unsatisfying in the way they deal with
human relations, where the surface is always glossed over and conflict is kept
in the shadows. Living with the strong distinction between dealing with
people in one's inner circle and one's outer circle can be very complicated
and stressful. Nature does not have this distinction and can therefore be
trusted completely.[31] Relating to nature is not as confusing as relating to
human beings. Thus, nature has a relaxing function. The Japanese turn to
nature for healing when their hearts are split.

Japanese Values

Japanese values reflect a medium to large power distance, collectivistic,
very masculine, strong uncertainty avoidance culture with a high score on

the LTO index. Japanese culture is extremely competitive. A central dimension is an internalized high level of skill and craftsmanship, an aesthetic ideal of perfectionism, and a strong drive for task accomplishment. The high score on the LTO dimension explains the cultivation of will and persistence for overcoming obstacles and accomplishing difficult work.[32]

The late Kazuaki Ushikubo[33] studied people's wants in Japan and developed a model for structuring wants. This structure is based on 12 Japanese core values. From 1982 onward he carried out an annual survey among 3,000 respondents, presenting them with 12 statements. Respondents received a number of stickers to distribute over the value statements to show their preference. This technique circumvents the problem of Asians not being able to think in opposites. Ushikubo found four clusters of basic values, which he named Change, Participation, Freedom, and Stability.

Statements are:

1. "To keep friends is very important." This relates to the element "family and friends" in the participation cluster. "Friends" in this statement applies to the members of the in-group. It does not relate to the Western concept of friendship, but to "correct behavior vs. the others in your group."

2. "Want to refresh from a tired brain or body." This statement is related to relaxation and is part of the stability cluster.

3. "Want to learn knowledge faster than other people." Values related to this statement are part of the change cluster.

4. "Identity of myself is important." This question relates to freedom, and fits with the "individuality" trend. It is an example of a value that is emphasized because it is lacking in society.

5. "Have a happy time with friends and family." The Japanese word is *danran*, which has no equivalent in English, according to Ushikubo. It means having a happy time, enjoying open-hearted conversation with your family and good friends. It is part of the participation cluster.

6. "To live without fear—safety." This is included in the stability cluster.

7. "To create something and upgrade my ability." This is included in the change cluster.

8. "Live easy, I do not care about my surroundings." This me-ism, wanting to be yourself, outside the group, is included in the freedom cluster.

9. "Do well with all people around me." This relates to social life, included in the participation cluster.

10. "Want to be healthy." This is included in the stability cluster.

11. "To live in loneliness, have a lonely time." This means voluntary solitude, included in the freedom cluster.

12. "Want to have stimulation, change in my life, diversion, new things." This is included in the change cluster.

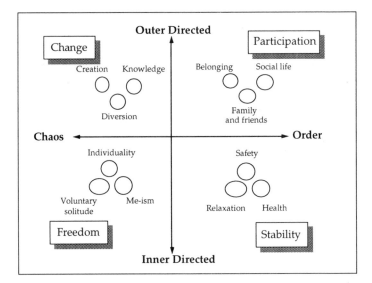

Figure 5.1 Japan: "Freedom and Order"
SOURCE: Kazuaki Ushikubo (1986).

Although the freedom cluster, defining individuality (individuality, me-ism, and voluntary solitude), has increased during the past 14 years, in 1995 it was still indicated by only 10% of the respondents. It illustrates the different meaning of freedom in Japan: individuality, me-ism, thus escaping the (sometimes) stifling conformity of the group.

Ushikubo presents the most important values in Japanese society on three axes. One of these is additional to the two axes of the model presented in Figure 5.1. The third axis is optimism-pessimism.

The three axes are described as follows:

1. Modern-traditional. There is a trend toward tradition. This is not the same as "back to tradition," which implies linear thinking and which is not Japanese. Instead, it is a spiral movement. The Japanese feel they have gone through a number of phases. In circular thinking, they now reenter a phase in which they have been at some time in the past. There is no forward-backward thinking in this, but a continuous movement in which traditional values now fit, which is part of the upward spiral.

2. Social, society versus me. This represents Japanese thinking about the relationship between society and the self. This is a relatively new trend in Japanese values; complex and confusing. It is collective thinking about individualism. This kind of reflection does not fit in the hectic life of the Japanese.

3. The brightness or darkness of the mind to the future (optimism/pessimism with respect to the future). Because of the poor economy in 1995, the Japanese scored pessimistic.

Cross-Cultural Use of Value Studies

Value studies are used to position brands by using bi-polar systems. When using a semantic differential or any other type of bi-polar axis system to measure values or image, success depends on the dimensions selected and the relevance of the dimensions. If poles from one culture are used for research in another culture, values become irrelevant, and other culturally significant values may be omitted or the results may be useless because of interpretation problems. Smaller markets often have no funds available to develop local value studies. For those markets, studies developed for other cultures are sometimes translated. Some international advertising agencies use one list, based on American values but presented as universal, to position brands worldwide. As we have seen, there are values that just do not exist in American lists of central values, such as thrift and perseverance, yet they are very important for a large part of the world population.

Similar things happen within Europe. A French study structures meanings in a framework made up of two axes with the opposite poles harmony/conflict and order/freedom. This way of structuring meaning represents French culture: order/freedom reflects large power distance and harmony/conflict reflects strong uncertainty avoidance. A model like this will not fit in neighboring cultures such as the United Kingdom and the Netherlands, to which it was exported. These countries are of small power distance and weak uncertainty avoidance, in contrast to France where the model was developed.

Values Don't Translate

Values are the core of culture, which explains why culturally meaningful values do not easily translate. Values have to be labeled, and if the labels are translated but the values are not comparable, the result is nonsensical. Because the value system is different, the translated label may even reflect another value. A single label may then reflect a positive value in one culture and a negative value in another culture. Thus, translation of some of the values on American value lists into other languages will result in meaningless concepts or may turn positive concepts into negative ones. For example, some values that are positive in the United States are negative values in Scandinavia, the Netherlands, and, to a lesser degree, in France and Spain. A number of values of individualistic cultures are nonexistent in collectivistic cultures, or the English words used for them mean something else. Benedict[34] states, "Both the Chinese and the Japanese have many words meaning 'obligations.' The words are not synonyms and their specific meanings have no literal translation into English because the ideas they express are alien to us [i.e., Americans]." The translation of Rokeach values has resulted in new concepts that cannot be compared with the original meanings.

Examples of untranslatable words and concepts were given in Chapter 3. Such words and concepts are very important for advertising, because they are meaningful concepts that communicate a message instantly. During the past century, the Dutch coffee producer Douwe Egberts (Sara Lee/DE) has built a high market share in the Netherlands by consistently connecting coffee with the typically Dutch togetherness concept, which cannot be implanted in other parts of Europe except in the similar cultures of Scandinavia.

Certain often-encountered values have a significantly different loading in one country than in another. Values like patriotism and nationalism are more meaningful to some countries than to others, often depending on their histories. For countries that have always had open borders, such as the Netherlands, these values are neither meaningful nor important. Nationalism is a concept that is discussed in many ways, in the social sciences, political science, in literature. Harry Mulisch, a well-known Dutch writer,[35] says it is all a matter of language:

> if people start shouting "Deutschland, Deutschland," it may sound frightening [i.e., to the Dutch], on the other hand one cannot think of a couple of Germans starting to shout: "Die Bundesrepublik, Die Bundesrepublik." The Dutch cannot imagine themselves shouting "Holland, Holland." If someone in the Netherlands were to declare himself ready to die for his country, people would start laughing.

With respect to national feeling, expressing very well how ingrained and enduring national values are, more or less shaping a cultural identity, Mulisch says: "One *is,* one cannot *become* a Dutchman, a Frenchman, an American, any more than a Terrier can become a Greyhound." Feelings of nationality may vary between individualistic and collectivistic cultures. For the former, a "nation" is the abstract ultimate unit to which one chooses to belong, and it is abstract. For Americans, it is loyalty to the

Stars and Stripes, not to the current president. For members of collectivistic cultures, one is more implicitly part of a "grand family" in which a ruler has the role of the benevolent father, and loyalty is more automatic. This explains how in Japan, a culture based on personal ties, the Emperor was and still is a symbol of loyalty far surpassing a flag.[36] For the Japanese of the 1990s, national security means security from crime, fire, hospitalization. Patriotism does not exist: "we are no nation, we have no nation, we have only government." The Japanese don't think of nationality. A nation does not exist in their mind.[37] Globalization may increase peoples' feelings of nationalism, which express feelings of cultural identity. The nation one belongs to may be the most appropriate label for expressing one's cultural identity.

Happiness is one of the most important American values. Yet the idea that the pursuit of happiness is a serious life goal by which the State and family are judged is unthinkable to the Japanese. To the Japanese, the supreme task in life is fulfilling one's obligations. Pleasure or happiness is a relaxation that can easily be given up in order to fulfil one's obligations.[38] This may explain why "happy endings," including solutions to problems, are rare in Japanese novels and plays as opposed to American novels and plays where people are supposed to live happily ever after.

Another Western value, romantic love, is underplayed by the Chinese but is cultivated by the Japanese. Erotic pleasure, on the other hand, is a moral issue or even a taboo to the Americans, whereas the Japanese see no need to be moralistic about sex pleasures. In Indian culture, too, the erotic is more accepted and expressed.[39]

Salvation, an American value, when translated into Dutch seems to be irrelevant. All concepts related to religion or to belief in higher beings are culture-bound. The Japanese cannot cope with concepts relating to God at all. For them, the concept of salvation is nonexistent. When they seek comfort, they seek it in nature, which is not related to the concepts of Christianity.

Belonging is an important end-goal for individualistic cultures: Being "by yourself" is not always desirable, so one has to make an effort to be with others. For collectivistic cultures, belonging is part of existence: The individual exists only as part of the group. Individuals are part of, belong to, an inner circle consisting of a number of people who can be well defined. For the individual, the group is a basic, vital spiritual property; being isolated from it would, more than anything else, be to lose the self completely in a way that would be intolerable.[40]

Achievement is a word that is difficult to translate into the Dutch language. According to McClelland,[41] an American researcher, it is one of the three important motives that drive workers. The three are: the needs for achievement, for power, and for affiliation. Achievement is a typically Anglo value complex. It is valid for cultures that score high on the Hofstede dimension masculinity (importance of visible results) and low on uncertainty avoidance (willingness to run risks). This combination is the recipe for the economic success of Anglo-Saxon culture, as it is a component of entrepreneurial activity. Other cultures show other components of success. Yet achievement has been declared a universal motive. The French, Swedes, Dutch, and Japanese will either not use the word or will change its meaning into something with greater culture-fit. Thus in Japanese it has become "inner harmony, personal attainment."

Just as many Asian concepts are not understandable to Westerners, a number of Western concepts are beyond understanding to the Japanese and other Asian cultures. Particularly the abstract, remote from daily life, such as a world at peace or striving for quality of life are concepts they have difficulty coping with. The Japanese can better handle pragmatic, down-to-earth thinking. This implies that the notion of a "concept" is not familiar to their way of thinking, either. Peace, not the large concept of peace, but peace nearby, means health, safety, and having good people around you.

The word *freedom* has different connotations for different cultures. Its interpretation depends on the cultural and environmental context of a people. The concept of freedom as described by U.S. students studying in the Netherlands, meant "free enterprise." Dutch students at the same time described freedom as "freedom to express your feelings, to be yourself." In 1996, Russian students from Western Siberia associated the word *freedom* primarily with "not being in prison" and secondarily with freedom from pollution and freedom of speech.[42] To the Japanese, freedom means "to behave as you please, to transcend the group."[43] Freedom is experienced by the Japanese as "having individual ideas, escape from spiritual bondage." The Western-style idea of freedom serves as a basis for asserting the precedence of the individual over the group, which is not seen as desirable in Japanese society. The Japanese word used to translate the English word *freedom* (*jiyu*) is of Chinese origin. It means to behave as one pleases, without considering others, which for a collectivistic society basically means disharmony and thus is negative and the opposite of freedom. As liberty and freedom in the West signify respect for the human being, the concept has become ambiguous, to say the least to the Japanese.[44]

The Rokeach value a comfortable life is linked with material prosperity. To the Japanese it means to be rich, not in money, but spiritually, to be without fear, have stability, no change, good relations, a good house. The desirable appears to be a life without change. Japanese society obviously is not a jealous society. If you are rich, well off, you are supposed to show it. This explains the desire for original brands, fakes are not tolerated in this concept.

The Rokeach value self-respect or self-esteem is related to the concept of "self" of an individualistic society. This is of lesser importance to Asian cultures than it is to the Western world. Self-respect (*jicho*) in Japan means restraint, which is the opposite of the American value, which includes values like character, reputation, and prestige. A major dimension of Japanese self-esteem relates to reflecting well on the family and work group through high performance, thus gaining their respect. Indians' inner feelings of esteem are deeply tied up with family reputation.[45]

Asking people of different cultures to define a word like *pleasure* leads to long sentences and explanations, suggesting that it has different connotations in different cultures. Because it is frequently used in advertising, understanding its meaning and connotations in other cultures is important. In Japan, pleasure is a personal feeling of pleasure, related only to the inner circle. It seems to be more like the Spanish concept of *placer,* which reflects a wide variety of feelings of social and inner enjoyment.

The concept of friendship used as a value in global marketing is ambiguous. It does not exist in Japanese society. It is known and used because it is an often-encountered American word, but those whom you call your friends are basically members of the inner circle. True friendship is made to mean "understanding how to communicate." This is very different from the Western concept of friendship, where you can make friends and lose friends (see also Chapter 4, under "Individualism/Collectivism"). Americans call people friends who are merely acquaintances in the European concept of the word *friend.* In the Japanese outer circle you have no friends. Rarely might you find a new friend in your work. As a result, asking Japanese respondents to choose the degree of importance of true friendship is a nonsense question. Japanese cannot express the importance of true friendship. This also holds true in China and in other collectivistic cultures, though more strongly in some than in others.

In most collectivistic cultures, showing people alone in an advertisement would mean they have no identity, they do not belong, or to use a Western saying: They have no friends. The concept of friendship is an ambiguous one for many cultures. This is caused by the way the word *friend* is used in different cultures and the different ways one distinguishes a friend. In continental Europe, only close friends are on a first-name basis. Dealing with everybody on a first name basis, as the Americans do, confuses the friendship concept. It is particularly confusing to Germans, for whom the wider usage of the word *friendship* is too ambiguous, as is illustrated by the reaction to a *Newsweek* article about service:[46]

> Germans, like most Europeans, are more distant with customers than Americans are used to, but can hardly be summed up as unfriendly. The artificial friendliness commonly practiced by shop assistants and restaurant staff in America would be off-putting to Germans. Who wants to be on a first-name basis with a waiter who'll be forgotten promptly after the meal?

The Value Concept in Marketing and Advertising

The value concept is used in two different ways. It refers to people and to objects. People are said to have values and objects are said to have values. Applied to branding, a brand will be a strong brand if people's values match the values of the brand. *Branding* means adding values to products, and advertising is an important instrument for achieving this.

Values play an important role in consumer behavior because they influence choice. They can be arranged in the order of their relative importance to individuals, groups, and societies. Values provide consumers with standards for making comparisons among alternatives. Consumers' value systems can be divided into three groups:[47]

1. Central values: the core values of the individual's value system
2. Domain-specific values: values acquired in specific situations or domains of activities
3. Product-specific values: evaluations of product attributes

Examples of different domains include economy, religion, politics, work, and consumption. In using values to evaluate products and brands, the values of interest are product-specific values applied to product categories or specific brands. Examples are values related to purity, cleanliness with respect to detergents, pleasure or security for automobiles, and self-respect (in the Western sense) or beauty/aesthetics for cosmetics.

Instrumental and central values are a key aspect of advertising strategy. Modern advertising strategy development includes (a) selecting values or end-states to emphasize in advertising, (b) determining how advertising will connect the product to key end-states, and (c) developing advertisements connecting the product to the end value. Values offer an opportunity to differentiate brands by going beyond a focus on attributes and benefits, or the deliverance of higher-level consequences to consumers. Adding values creates association networks that distinguish the brand vis-à-vis the competitive brands in the category and thus can help build strong positions for brands.

Value Structure Maps

A tool for strategy is the Value Structure Map (VSM), which describes how a particular group of subjects tends to perceive or think about a specific product or brand.[48] A value structure map links the product's attributes and benefits to values.

Attributes can be concrete or abstract; benefits can be functional or psychosocial consequences of the product's attributes. Value structure maps provide a structure of people's associations with a brand at the three levels: attributes, benefits, and values. They show how the types of associations that people make between a specific attribute of a product and its subsequent benefits and values are connected. This connection, developed by Gutman, was presented as the means-end chain model.[49] Gutman formulates the essence as follows: Means are objects (products) or activities in which people engage; ends are valued states of being such as happiness, security, accomplishment. A means-end chain is a model that seeks to explain how the choice of a product or service facilitates the achievement of desired end-states. Such a model consists of elements that represent the major consumer processes that link values to behavior.[50] Rokeach's distinction of instrumental and terminal values compares with the means and ends. The technique used to develop means-end chains is laddering, an in-depth, one-on-one interviewing technique used to develop an understanding of how consumers translate the attributes of products into meaningful associations with respect to the self.[51] By using this laddering technique, sets of linkages can be determined between perceptual elements, which are then represented at different levels of abstraction. Figure 5.2 shows three levels of associations for toothpaste, and Figure 5.3 shows six levels of (hypothetical) associations for Coca-Cola. An example of a Value Structure Map is the hypothetical VSM for BMW of Figure 5.4, including a number of Rokeach's terminal and instrumental values as well as one Asian value, harmony with nature.

Advertisers who want to differentiate a brand can follow different routes via attributes and benefits to reach end values. In this system the product attributes may be the same worldwide, yet different end values may be connected to the attributes (to be found through research), reflecting different cultures. An example of a route in the VSM for BMW is selecting, for

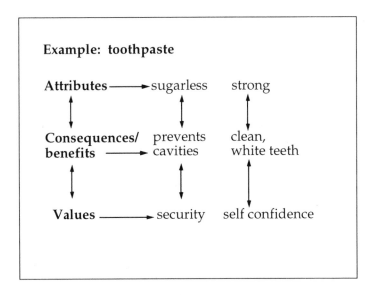

Figure 5.2 Three Levels of Association: Toothpaste

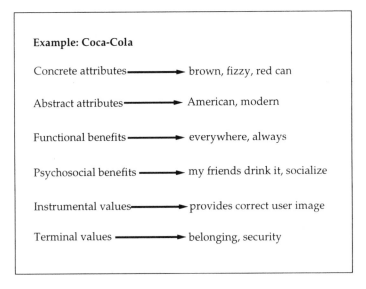

Figure 5.3 Six Levels of Association: Example: Coca-Cola and Young People

example, one attribute, a Strong Motor, and one end value, an Exciting Life, and following the route Fast Acceleration → Imaginative, Daring → Personal Enjoyment → Independence to Exciting Life. Another route takes the same attribute as a starting point but continues via Safe to Protects the Family, to

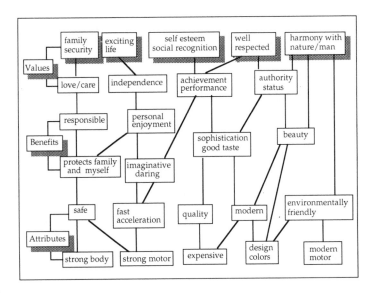

Figure 5.4 Value Structure Map for BMW—Hypothetical

Responsible, to Love/Care, to Family Security. This could be an example of a route for a feminine culture. Focus on individualism could lead to another route: from Strong Motor to Safe, to Protects Myself, to Personal Enjoyment, Independence, and an Exciting Life. Different routes can be followed, depending on the target group, the culture, and the competition. In a multinational campaign targeted at countries that are similar with respect to one or more dimensions, it may be possible to select one route with values the different countries have in common. Two other VSMs presented in Figures 5.5 and 5.6 offer examples.

These VSMs were developed by a group of Spanish and German students who, in casework, had to develop a common strategy for Spain and Germany for the beer brand Corona Extra. First they selected the attributes and then tried to find common terminal values. What they found the cultures to have in common were Friendship, Distinguished, and Acceptance. The Spanish found Belonging and Stability to be important terminal values with Self-esteem and Being With Others as instrumental to the terminal values. The Germans found that Self-esteem was a terminal value for them and that Stability and Being With Others were instrumental to the terminal value Self-esteem. They concluded that only the two routes leading toward Belonging and Stability for Spain and to Self-esteem for Germany could not be used for a common strategy, while Friendship, Distinguished, and Acceptance, which they formulated as terminal values, could be shared and used for one common strategy.

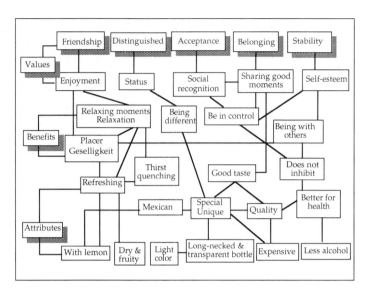

Figure 5.5 Value Structure Map for Corona Extra—Spain

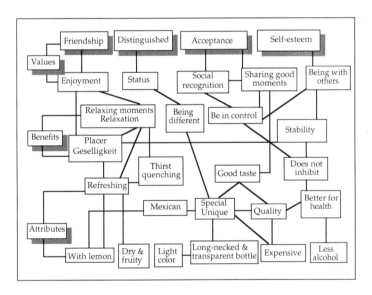

Figure 5.6 Value Structure Map for Corona Extra—Germany

Lifestyle Research

Lifestyle research for marketing aims to group people according to their value systems as expressed by their lifestyle. Lifestyle research usually is of the typology type. A typology describes more or less easy to imagine, ideal types.[52] Lifestyle studies originated in the United States, which was natural because it is a huge, relatively homogeneous market. The oldest value research used for marketing is the VALS segmentation system, developed by SRI International in Menlo Park, California. It uses a questionnaire asking motivations and demographic characteristics that are seen as strong predictors of a variety of consumer preferences in products, services, and media. The VALS segmentation system sorts respondents into an eight-part typology. The types are: Actualizers, Fulfilleds, Achievers, Experiencers, Believers, Strivers, Makers, and Strugglers.[53]

Sometimes studies of different countries use similar English-language labels for different typologies or classification cues. One example is the difference between the group Achievers in VALS and the Japanese Lifestyle study by Dentsu. The description of this type in VALS is as follows: "Achievers tend to be successful career and work-oriented people who like to be in control of their lives. They value stability over risk and are committed to work and family. They like to live conventional lives. Image, prestige products are important as they demonstrate success." Hiroe Suzuki of Dentsu's Information Technology Center distinguishes four life models in Dentsu's Lifestyle Study:[54] Achiever, Intelligent, Group Merit, and Membership Dependent. Key words in the description of the achiever in this study are: "Enterprising; attaches importance to individuality; attaches importance to human relationships. The achiever practices innovative consumption, which is a reflection of an enterprising personality whose aim is a Japanese style society of successful people." Another example is the use of the labels inner-directed and outer-directed. This distinction in the VALS study refers to people who make their own rules as opposed to those take their cues from the world around them. In Ushikubo's model, discussed under "Japanese Values" earlier in this chapter, the words refer to the inner and outer circles.

VALS is used worldwide, although the values included in this study are typical for the United States. A number of lifestyle studies are conducted for use by international marketing. Most describe typologies and focus on changes in people's lifestyles for use in new product development, new product introduction, and the positioning of brands. They do not describe cultural dimensions for developing effective advertising.

Conclusion

In modern marketing and advertising, values are used to differentiate and position brands vis-à-vis competitive brands. Previous chapters have described how values vary by culture. As a result, value studies developed in one culture cannot be used in other cultures. Yet value and lifestyle studies based on the Rokeach Value Survey are used worldwide, although the values in this survey are typical for the American culture. When translated into other languages, they may become meaningless, or positive values may turn into negative values.

Values are also stable, which means that the core values of a culture either do not change or change only over longer periods of time—not within the lifetime of current marketing and advertising people. This seems to be paradoxical, as the marketing and advertising world shows a preoccupation with change and is in continuous pursuit of new trends and changing lifestyles. Those who are involved in value and lifestyle research have to be aware of the fact that new lifestyles generally concern the expressions of culture. The core values, so useful for differentiating brands at a higher level, are stable. Understanding that the values of one culture cannot be used indiscriminately in another culture should lead toward more refined value studies for developing effective global marketing and advertising strategies. Value Structure Maps are valuable tools that enable companies to develop standardized products and differentiate them by adding value, using the core values of national culture. It will become increasingly important to be able to recognize the values of national culture as, with increased globalization, cultural identity will be of growing importance to consumers in the global marketplace.

Transplanting surveys developed in one environment to another that differs significantly cannot lead to an effective strategy. People's values vary by culture and researchers' values differ as well. If there is no match between the culture reflected in a research model and the culture of the country in which it is applied, the outcome will not be meaningful for the latter country. Using axes of one culture to position brands in another culture is an interesting but not very efficient exercise.

Notes

1. Ness, T. E., & Stith, M. T. (1984). "Middle-class values in blacks and whites." In R. E. Pitts & A. G. Woodside (Eds.), *Personal values and consumer psychology*. Lexington, MA: Lexington Books, p. 232.

2. Vinson, D. E., Scott, J. E., & Lamont, L. M. (1977). "The role of personal values in marketing and consumer behavior." *Journal of Marketing.*

3. Rokeach, M. (1973). *The nature of human values.* New York: Free Press, p. 5.

4. Rokeach (1973), *The nature of human values,* p. 5.

5. Rokeach (1973), *The nature of human values,* p. 10.

6. Rokeach (1973), *The nature of human values,* p. 28.

7. R. Kluckhohn & F. L. Strodtbeck's *Variations in value orientation,* cited on p. 22 of M. Rokeach (1973), *The nature of human values.*

8. Herche, J. (1994). *Measuring social values: A multi-item adaptation to the list of values. MSI Report Summary* (Report No. 94-101). Marketing Science Institute, 1000 Massachusetts Ave., Cambridge, MA 02138; tel. (617) 491-2060.

9. Kahle, L. R., & Goff Timmer, S. (1983). *A theory and method for studying values and social change: Adaptation to life in America.* New York: Praeger.

10. Hofstede, G. (1991). *Cultures and organizations: Software of the mind.* New York: McGraw-Hill, p. 8.

11. Roland, A. (1988). *In search of self in India and Japan.* Princeton, NJ: Princeton University Press, p. 94.

12. Yankelovich, D. (1994). "How changes in the economy are reshaping American values." In H. J. Aaron, T. E. Mann, & T. Taylor, (Eds.), *Values and public policy.* Washington, DC: Brookings Institution, pp. 23-24.

13. Inglehart, R. (1990). *Culture shift in advanced industrial society.* Princeton, NJ: Princeton University Press.

14. Reproduced from Reader's Digest Eurodata—A Consumer Survey of 17 Countries, sponsored by The Reader's Digest Association, Inc.

15. "Emerging market indicators: Official aid by OECD countries for the years 1994 [1995, 1996]." (1994, July 9 [1995, July 8; 1996, June 29]). *The Economist.*

16. Roland (1988), *In search of self in India and Japan,* pp. 90-93.

17. Roland (1988), *In search of self in India and Japan,* p. 131.

18. Roland (1988), *In search of self in India and Japan,* pp. 102-103.

19. Hofstede, G. H. (1984). *Culture's consequences: International differences in work-related values.* Beverly Hills, CA: Sage, pp. 232-251.

20. Rokeach (1973), *The nature of human values,* p. 90.

21. Rokeach (1973), *The nature of human values,* p. 15.

22. Vyncke, P. (1992). *Imago-Management: Handboek voor Reclamestrategen.* Ghent, Belgium: Mys & Breesch, Uitgevers & College Uitgevers, p. 134.

23. Helgadottir, B. (1995, November 2-8). "The qualities we prize in children: Description of findings of a world survey by International Research Associates INRA (Europe)." *The European,* p. 4.

24. Helgadottir (1995), "The qualities we prize in children."

25. Grunert, K. G., Grunert, S. C., & Beatty, S. E. (1989, February). "Cross-cultural research on consumer values." *Marketing and Research Today,* pp. 30-39.

26. Kamakura, W. A., & Mazzon, J. A. (1991). "Value segmentation: A model for the measurement of values and value systems." *Journal of Consumer Research, 18,* 208-218.

27. Hofstede, G. H. (1996, July). "Gender stereotypes and partner preferences of Asian women in masculine and feminine cultures." *Journal of Cross-Cultural Psychology, 37*(4), 524-537.

28. Vyncke (1992), *Imago-Management,* pp. 133-135.

29. Roland (1988), *In search of self in India and Japan,* p. 240.

30. Shunglu, S., & Sarkar, M. (1995, May). "Researching the consumer." *Marketing and Research Today,* p. 124.

31. Doi, T. (1985). *The anatomy of self.* Tokyo: Kodansha International, pp. 147-156.

32. Roland (1988), *In search of self in India and Japan,* p. 131.

33. Kazuaki Ushikubo, who passed away in February 1996, was president of Research and Development, Japan. He developed a model describing Japanese values that is described in Kazuaki Ushikubo (1986). A method of structure analysis for developing product concepts and its applications. *European Research.* Quotes in this chapter are from a conversation I had with Mr. Ushikubo in November 1995. Research & Development gave permission to use Mr. Ushikubo's statements and model with the note that the text only partially represents the total concept of CORE, R&D's proprietary lifestyle analysis.

34. Benedict, R. (1974). *The chrysanthemum and the sword.* Rutland, VT: Charles E. Tuttle, p. 99. (Original work published 1946)

35. Mulisch, H. (1995). *Bij gelegenheid.* Amsterdam: Uitgeverij de Bezige Bij.

36. Benedict (1974), *The chrysanthemum and the sword,* p. 129.

37. Descriptions and quotes are from a private conversation with Kazuaki Ushikubo, President, Research and Development, Tokyo, Japan, November 1995.

38. Benedict (1974), *The chrysanthemum and the sword,* p. 192.

39. Benedict (1974), *The chrysanthemum and the sword,* p. 183; and Roland (1988), *In search of self in India and Japan,* pp. 109-110, 262.

40. Doi, T. (1973). *The anatomy of dependence.* Tokyo: Kodansha International, p. 135

41. Hofstede (1991), *Cultures and organization,* p. 124.

42. Students' answers during a seminar on Marketing and Culture for Russian students from Western Siberia, organized by the Finnish Marketing Institute, Brussels, October 2, 1996.

43. Doi (1973), *The anatomy of self,* p. 85.

44. Doi (1973), *The anatomy of self,* pp. 84-86.

45. Roland (1988), *In search of self in India and Japan,* pp. 131, 203; Benedict (1974), *The chrysanthemum and the sword,* p. 290.

46. "Letters: A failing role model? [Letter from Mike Dunn of Bamberg, Germany]" (1996, April 16). *Newsweek.*

47. Vinson et al. (1977), *The role of personal values.*

48. Olson, J. C., & Reynolds, T. J. (1983). "Understanding consumers' cognitive structures: Implications for advertising strategy." In *Advertising and consumer psychology.* Lexington, MA: Lexington Books.

49. Gutman, J. A. (1982). "Means-end chain model based on consumer categorization processes." *Journal of Marketing, 46*(2), 60-72.

50. Gutman (1982), "Means-end chain model," p. 60.

51. Reynolds, T. J., & Gutman, J. (1988, February-March). "Laddering theory, method, analysis, and interpretation." *Journal of Advertising Research.*

52. De Mooij, M. (1994). *Advertising worldwide* (2nd ed.). Hemel Hempstead, Hertforshire, UK: Prentice Hall International, pp. 156-162.

53. Information from the Internet, June 1995.

54. Received from Hiroe Suzuki, November 1995. Earlier description in: Suzuki, H. (1990, June 18-20). "Japanese Lifestyle, Life Models and Applications to Creative Concepts." *ESOMAR Conference on America, Japan and EC '92: The Prospects for Marketing, Advertising and Research,* Venice.

Culture and Consumer Behavior

How people behave and what motivates them is largely a matter of culture. How they relate to each other in the buying process, whether their decisions are individual decisions or group decisions, all is influenced by the culture to which they belong. Consequently, theories of consumer behavior are not culture-free. U.S. concepts of marketing and consumer behavior, when used in other cultures, should be adapted. This chapter provides an overview of culture-bound topics of consumer behavior theory and will point out the influences of culture.

Classification of Consumption Values

To structure the discussion of theories related to consumption behavior, a classification of consumption values developed by Sheth, Newman, and Gross[1] is used. The theory is based on the fundamental premise that market choice is a multidimensional phenomenon involving multiple values. Five values are identified as impacting market choice behavior. These are functional value, social value, emotional value, epistemic value, and conditional value. These values are related to concepts of consumer behavior.

Functional values[2] relate to the satisfaction derived from the utilitarian and physical attributes of an alternative, and to needs. Various authors have classified needs. An example is Maslow's hierarchy of needs. Needs influence decision making, and need arousal is perceived as an integral part of the motivation process in buying behavior. Needs are culture-bound.

Social value[3] relates to the perceived utility of an alternative as a result of its association with one or more social groups. Concepts connected with this value are social class, reference group, opinion leadership, diffusion of innovations, and symbolic value. Symbolic value refers to the symbolic meaning of products and brands; it says something about the social world of those who consume them. This symbolic content of products has led authors to relate product choice to personality and to state that people see products as extensions of themselves. The role of reference groups, opinion leadership, innovativeness, and the concept of personality are culture-bound.

Emotional value[4] relates to the product's ability to arouse specific emotions. Emotions driving market choice can be positive or negative. Important research areas are motivation research, research on personality, and nonverbal processing. Sheth et al.[5] state that "because emotional value is non-cognitive by nature, research pertaining to non-verbal or visual information processing is also relevant."

Epistemic value[6] is related to novelty seeking, curiosity arousal, knowledge seeking, and the willingness to innovate. Core elements are curiosity and the desire for novelty and complexity. Stimuli are the unfamiliar, ambiguous, or complex. Curiosity is assumed to underlie many consumer decisions. The desire for novelty, variety, and exploration is assumed to be universal for humankind. Nevertheless, the degree of innovativeness varies by culture.

Conditional value[7] relates to the capacity to provide temporary functional or social value in the context of specific circumstances. A simple example is birthday cards, which only have value related to birthdays.

The following sections will describe the concepts of consumer behavior that are influenced by culture.

Group and Reference Group

It is generally accepted that consumption and decision making behavior is influenced by group membership. Groups and their influence on consumer behavior form an important subject of consumer behavior theory. Examples of frequently mentioned reasons why people are part of or join a group are[8]

- to achieve a task that cannot be completed alone
- to obtain friendship, companionship, and support
- to obtain status or to exercise power
- to get a source of warmth and psychological security
- to get power, as in joining a trade union
- because we have no choice, we are born male or female and we are born into a particular family

This is a Western-centric list of reasons. The basic assumption is that people can choose group membership. In Western literature, reference groups are distinguished as membership groups or nonmembership groups influencing behavior. The role of the group, its reference function, and the individual's place and role in the group vary by culture. In individualistic cultures, one is born into a nuclear family that may influence one's social class. But people can change social class, as upward or downward mobility is relatively easy. This is not so easily done in collectivistic cultures. In individualistic cultures, children are stimulated within the family to develop their own, distinct identity. In collectivistic cultures, one is born as part of a group and that group is one's identity. In individualistic cultures, the individual is given precedence over the group. Belonging to any group represents a free and voluntary association that can be broken whenever the individual so desires. Typical symbols of individualism are the various types of social clubs. Motives for joining clubs vary by culture. In large power distance cultures and masculine cultures, the need for status to be derived from group membership will be important. Feminine cultures tend to see status as negative, and their reason for joining a club will be driven more by affiliation needs.

The degree of uncertainty avoidance will play a role in the type of reference group: professional or formal rather than informal. The influence of the members of the group on buying behavior will vary. Power distance and related dependency needs will cause a more dominant role of elders and superiors in decision making. In collectivistic cultures, if an individual makes the decision, that decision will be made in consensus with the group, so it is not an individual decision. Group conformance is strong. Consensus seeking will also play a role in feminine cultures. In feminine cultures, the marriage partner plays a strong role in decision making. This is demonstrated by the negative correlation between masculinity and involvement of the partner in the choice of make and model of the main car in the household, as EMS 95 data show (see Figure 6.1).

The chart in Figure 6.1 shows how countries that are geographically close may need radically different approaches. Denmark and Germany, although sharing a geographical border, are far apart in this chart. So are Belgium and the Netherlands. An example of how strongly this difference can affect advertising is a 1996 television commercial for the Renault Mégane (automobile). It depicts a man who wants to surprise his wife with the new Renault Mégane, at the same time demonstrating the short brake path. He stops in front of what he thinks is his house, shouting "Darling, I have bought the Renault Mégane," and it appears he has entered his neighbor's—similar—house because he is not used to the short brake path. The text of this Belgian commercial was changed radically for the Netherlands, although it was in the same language, as part of Belgium and the Netherlands share the same language. In Belgium, apparently, the husband

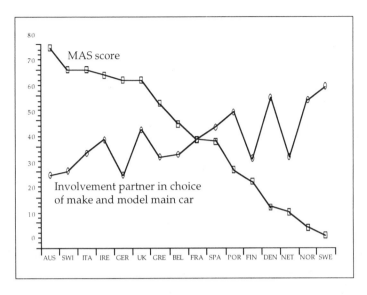

Figure 6.1 Correlation of MAS and Involvement Partner in Choice of Make and Model of Main Car (EMS 95)
SOURCE: Data EMS (1995).Copyright © Inter/View.
NOTE: rho = –0.63***

can buy a car without consulting his wife, but this is not done in the Netherlands. (Note: In this chart the Netherlands score relatively low on involvement of partners as the EMS respondents show a relatively high ownership of company cars.)

In collectivistic cultures, members of the inner and outer circles play different roles. While in individualistic cultures few other people will influence decision making, which is an individual activity, Japanese housewives refer to an average group of eight other housewives who influence their decision making.[9] This explains the success of network marketing in collectivistic cultures. The success of Yakult (a milk-based morning drink) in Japan was the result of door-to-door sales and network marketing, while in Europe the mass media had to be used.

Family type will influence buying behavior. Elders such as grandparents play a more important role in large power distance and collectivistic cultures than they do in small power distance and individualistic cultures. In masculine cultures, which have strong role differentiation, housewives will not share their chores with their husbands to the degree that they do in feminine cultures. Whether the women or the men do the food shopping in Europe correlates with the MAS dimension: In masculine cultures, men are less involved in the shopping chores than in feminine cultures.[10] In segregated societies the actual purchasing behavior is different, as women will not always be able to do their own shopping.

Decision Making

The fundamental assumption in decision-making theory is that decisions do not "happen," someone "makes them." This is a Western view. The Japanese are more likely to prefer events to shape whatever actions are required, to stand back from an event rather than attempt to control it by decision making.[11] A fundamental difference between individualistic and collectivistic cultures is between decision making by the individual or by the group.

Another important difference is between internal and external locus of control. The belief in the West that the locus of control resides in the individual and that behavior is a function of the individual's own action, is deeply implanted in decision theory. External locus of control is part of collectivistic cultures, where people are used to the fact that other people may make decisions about them and for them. This is reinforced by large power distance, where the power holders will ultimately make the decisions. Particularly the combination of large power distance, collectivism, and strong uncertainty avoidance appears to be linked with external locus of control. When collectivistic cultures are low in uncertainty avoidance, external locus of control does not operate. When an individualistic culture is feminine, people take other people's opinions into consideration and, therefore, are controlled externally more than people in masculine, individualistic cultures.[12] Feminine cultures are also more intuitive.

The need for information and the type of information desired will vary for low-context and high-context cultures. The degree of importance of the source of information and the credibility of the source will vary according to the degree of power distance, individualism, and uncertainty avoidance. Buyers in high-context, collectivistic cultures will seek more social information than those in low-context, individualistic cultures. Strong uncertainty avoidance will lead to the need for more, structured, and detailed information. Club Méditerranée "learned that Japanese tourists crave infinite detail in their travel plans. So, along with brochures and activity schedules for the villages they'll visit, Club Med sends them maps of airports at both ends of the trip, showing toilets, customs booths, and other facilities."[13]

The relationship orientation of collectivistic cultures as opposed to the task orientation of individualistic cultures will be reflected in the decision-making behavior of sellers and buyers. Members of collectivistic cultures invest time in building relationships with their business partners. As a result, the negotiating and buying process takes much longer than in individualistic cultures with their focus on efficient use of time and the accomplishment of the task. Expectations buyers have of sellers, the degree of trust needed, will vary by culture. Trust is an important choice criterion in collectivistic cultures. Trust in the company more than brand personality will drive sales.

Time Orientation and Decision Making

The time orientation of participants in the decision-making process is an important cultural dimension. Little research has been done on the influence that variations in time orientation have on decision making by consumers and industrial buyers. Bergadaà[14] defines consumer behavior as a process of activities in a certain time span, a process leading from initial motivation to decision, to the act of buying and its consequences. The subjective vision of past and future are part of this. This process description represents the linear, monochronic time concept, which is different from the circular and polychronic time concept. In a polychronic culture, future plans are changed if more important situations arise, and appointments may be easily changed. This is opposed to behavior in monochronic cultures, where people are so attuned to time that it determines and coordinates relations with others. A change of appointment is perceived as unpleasant.

A sharp difference between Americans and Japanese is the difference between control of time (management of deadlines) and control of human relationships. To a lesser degree, this is similar to the differences among countries in Europe, for example between the Germans and the Spanish. What colloquially is called the "mañana syndrome" (postponing decisions) may affect decision making. The mañana syndrome can be explained by strong uncertainty avoidance combined with large power distance and collectivism. Strong uncertainty avoidance causes people to postpone decisions, large power distance implies that power holders may overrule. In collectivistic societies, also, fate is assumed to play a role.

Cultures with a linear time concept, where time is dealt with as something tangible, will be motivated by time-saving appeals. Efficiency and time-saving appeals are very much part of the individualistic, Western world and not of collectivistic cultures. Another difference related to time orientation is the thought that a decision or expressed buying intent will lead to action. People with an action attitude actively seek progress, alternatives, self-improvement. People with a reaction attitude will wait with action until confronted with a new situation. This behavior is not necessarily related to expressed intentions.

Another difference is between people who make definite, concrete plans with well-described actions and people who leave their plans more abstract, more philosophical, without a specific sequence of actions. Differences can lead to wrong expectations with respect to buying intentions. If 55% of the people who try a new product in Italy say they will definitely buy it, the product will probably fail. But in Japan, if 5% say they will definitely buy it, the product is likely to succeed.[15] It is tempting to use the Hofstede dimensions and differences in time orientation to try to explain the fact that members of Catholic and Latin-language cultures tend to overclaim their purchase intentions, while the Protestant cultures do this to a lesser extent. Cultures with a Confucian influence tend to follow the middle way and avoid extreme responses like "I definitely will buy." This phenomenon is related to differences in responding to bi-polar scales and to the degree of external or internal locus of control. If one is used to fate or power holders interfering at any time in the realization of an expressed intention, and if cancelled appointments are acceptable, this is part of daily life, thus part of people's values. This is reflected in the way buying intention is expressed. Extreme Response Style (ERS), or the tendency to score in the extremes of a bi-polar scale, may have the same origin. In collectivistic cultures, people do not like to say no and in large power distance cultures there is a need to please, resulting in "yesmanship."

The Decision-Making Unit

The number of members in the decision-making unit (DMU) varies; so does the importance of the individual members. The average size of the decision-making team within the EU varies from 10 in France, to 8 in Germany, 6 in Italy, 10 in Sweden, and 9 in Britain.[16] Also, the members of the DMU behave differently, related to the country's management style and culture. In Britain, specialist expertise is not highly regarded. Decisions tend to come about by informal consensus developed in meetings, discussions, and out-of-office contacts among middle managers. Top management normally refuses any routine contacts with suppliers. This relates to the high level of delegation, a characteristic of small power distance cultures. In France, although middle or specialist managers may be consulted, in the end the President Directeur Général must give permission (large power distance behavior). In the Netherlands, business relationships seem more relaxed and informal (influenced by affiliation needs of the feminine culture). In Italy, businesses have to take relatively large amounts of time and resources to deal with industrial relations problems. Successful managers have to be flexible improvisers. Authority may be delegated to trusted individuals rather than to holders of particular job-titles, so that finding the right decision maker is an art. Interpersonal contact is of great importance. Business relationships are based on mutual dependence and a sense of mutual obligation. A distinctively Spanish (large power distance and collectivistic) company is likely to have a strong leader, an entrepreneurial autocrat with boldness and personal charisma. Good personal relations are necessary to prevent middle management blocking approaches, and anything important may have to be sent "up the line" for final approval.

In large power distance cultures, the boss will make the decision and the roles of influentials below his or her level will be much less important than in small power distance cultures. In the latter cultures, secretaries have an important influence on decisions related to their work, such as for office equipment. Truck drivers may be consulted in decision making on investments in the company's fleet. The decision-making process will also vary according to the degree of masculinity. In feminine cultures, where reaching consensus is important, all people concerned must be allowed to give their opinion, while in masculine cultures decisiveness is seen as a virtue that will make the decision-making process more expedient.

Opinion Leaders

Opinion leaders are strong, informal sources of product information. Opinion leaders achieve their status through technical competence, social accessibility, and conformance to system norms. They serve as role models and play an important role in the process of diffusion of innovations.

People with technical competence, or competent people in general, are favored in strong uncertainty avoidance cultures. Masculine cultures have high regard for the successful. Conformance to group behavior and group norms will be important in collectivistic cultures and the opinions of elders are more relevant than in individualistic cultures. In large power distance cultures, the power holders in particular may have an important role as opinion leader.

Diffusion of Innovations

Consumers' degree of innovativeness influences their propensity to try new products. Various researchers have found differences among individuals with respect to innovativeness. It was found to be positively related to the ability to deal with abstractions, the ability to cope with uncertainty, with openness to change, education, and science.[17] As innovativeness is related to tolerance for ambiguity and deviant ideas, culture will play a role, too, and members of weak uncertainty avoidance cultures may be more innovative than members of strong uncertainty avoidance cultures. How innovativeness operates in cultures depends on its configuration with other dimensions. The configuration of four of Hofstede's dimensions can explain why Anglo-Saxon countries tend to include more innovative people than do other cultures. Their configuration of dimensions is rather unique. They show small power distance behavior, thus favoring independent minds. They are very individualistic, wanting to do things their own way. They are masculine, characterized by a winning mentality, and, due to their weak uncertainty avoidance, are not hindered by fear of what is new or strange. Members of such cultures are relatively more inventive and innovative. Power distance and individualism influence innovativeness in cultures in another way. While it is internalized in the person in small power distance and individualistic cultures, in large power distance and collectivistic cultures, it is externalized. In the latter, the degree of innovation depends on the power holders and group process. This may explain the fact that the United Kingdom has produced more Nobel Prize winners than China, although the Chinese are a relatively weak uncertainty avoidance culture and in the far past have proved to be extremely innovative. The Chinese invented a number of processes or instruments that were not discovered or acknowledged in the West until more than a thousand years later. Examples of inventions are the process of making steel from crude iron (2,000 years), deep drilling for natural gas (1,900 years), the circulation of blood (1,800 years), and the wheelbarrow (1,300 years).[18] In China, the incentive for inventions was service to the overlord or emperor, not personal ambition.

Rogers[19] identified five categories of (American) consumers according to their degree of acceptance of new products. These five categories of adopters are often illustrated in a normal distribution curve. They are called Innovators, Early Adopters, Early Majority, Late Majority, and Laggards. Innovators represent 2.5% of (American) society; they are described as venturesome individuals who are willing to take risks. Early Adopters (13.5%) are the ones who take up new ideas, which are taken up by the Innovators who serve as role models. The Early Majority (34%) are risk avoiders, but are relatively deliberate in their purchasing behavior. The Late Majority (34%) are skeptical and cautious of new ideas. Laggards (16%) are very traditional. The percentages as well as the time span of the adoption process may vary by culture. More innovative cultures are expected to have a larger percentage of Early Adopters than less innovative cultures. Collectivism plays another role. Particularly in Japan, after acceptance, the spreading of new products is rapid. On the one hand, change is not appreciated so adoption of new ideas and products takes longer. Yet the need for conformance leads to faster adoption as soon as an opinion leader has taken the lead. In individualistic and strong uncertainty avoidance cultures the adoption process takes longer because what is new is dangerous, and that relates to each person individually.

Brand Loyalty

Members of cultures with a large power distance and collectivism configuration are found to show a higher degree of brand loyalty. Conformance to the group plays a role: Choosing another brand than the group-members or changing brands distinguishes a person from the group. It is preferable to choose the popular or perceived popular brands.

Large power distance implies respect for the status quo, the "proper place" of the power brand, the brand with the highest market share. In Asia, big market-share brands are the kings of their "brand world" and consumers in Asia believe in them implicitly.[20] This is the reason brands like Coca-Cola, Nescafé, and San Miguel have such high and sustained market shares in a number of Asian countries. Being big automatically provides trust. This trust, combined with the conformance need of collectivistic societies, leads to high brand loyalty. This will be reinforced by uncertainty avoidance in cultures scoring high on that dimension. Consequently, it will be very difficult for new entrants in these markets to gain market share.

Needs

Consumption decisions can be driven by functional or social needs. What to some appear to be functional needs, to others are social needs. What in one culture may be a functional need can be a social need in others. The bicycle is a functional need to many Chinese, who need it for transportation, while it is a social need to many Americans, who use it for socializing or fitness. Clothes are functional, fashion is not, and the degree to which people pay attention to their appearance varies by culture. Members of small power distance and weak uncertainty avoidance cultures are generally not well groomed as compared with members of large power distance and strong uncertainty avoidance cultures. Particularly in strong uncertainty avoidance cultures, people are well groomed. It is one way of facing a threatening world. Observant travelers

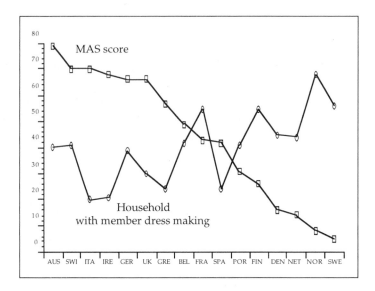

Figure 6.2 Correlation of MAS and Household With Member Dressmaking (Eurodata 91)
SOURCE: Data reproduced from Reader's Digest Eurodata—A Consumer Survey of 17 European Countries, sponsored by The Reader's Digest Association, Inc.
NOTE: rho = −0.73***

in Europe may have noticed the difference between the careful manner of dressing by the Belgians, French, and Italians as opposed to the carefree (sometimes sloppy) way of dressing by the Dutch, Danes, and British. In large power distance cultures, people dress according to occasion. The need for dressing up in collectivistic cultures is to reflect well on the family. Roland[21] notes that urban Indian women spend much more time and effort on personal grooming and dress when they go out in public in India than they do when going out in public in New York. In feminine cultures, people like making their own clothes more than in masculine cultures, according to the negative correlation between masculinity and the number of households with a member who does dressmaking, as illustrated in Figure 6.2.

Use and ownership of one product or product category may satisfy a variety of different needs across cultures. When buying automobiles, the main influence on the choice between a new or a second-hand car may be income. The choice also appears to be influenced by culture. The respondents to the EMS 95 survey, who are of a relatively high income class, report culture-bound behavior with respect to buying new or second-hand automobiles. This influence of culture is confirmed by the Reader's Digest

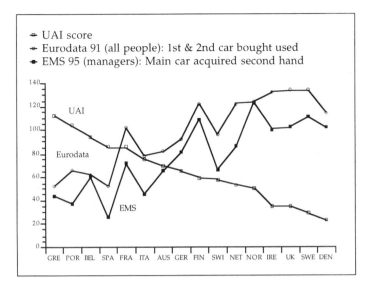

Figure 6.3 Correlation of UAI and Second-Hand Cars (Eurodata 91 & EMS 95)
SOURCE: Data reproduced from Reader's Digest Eurodata—A Consumer Survey of 17 European Countries, sponsored by The Reader's Digest Association, Inc., and EMS (1995). Copyright © Inter/View.
NOTE: Eurodata: rho = −0.87***; EMS 95: rho = −0.84***

Eurodata Survey. There appears to be a strong correlation between buying new cars and strong uncertainty avoidance, as presented in the chart in Figure 6.3.

The need for wristwatches varies by culture. To some, a watch is a high-priced status object, to others it has functional value. The type of watch, the value, and the number of watches people wear are culture-bound. Responses to an EMS 95 question asking the value of watches owned shows a correlation between femininity and low-cost watches (under £100), which implies that people in masculine cultures have more high-cost watches (see Figure 6.4). Expensive watches are status articles, a lesser need in feminine cultures. There also appears to be a correlation between uncertainty avoidance and the number of watches people own (see Figure 6.5).

In both Figure 6.4 and Figure 6.5, the Swiss respondents show deviant behavior, which may have two reasons. First, the Swiss respondents in the survey were of relatively high income levels and second, Switzerland is known for its watch industry.

Long-term orientation appears to influence the use of credit cards. Although the LTO dimension has not yet been measured robustly, and thus a significant correlation could not be demonstrated, there is a strong

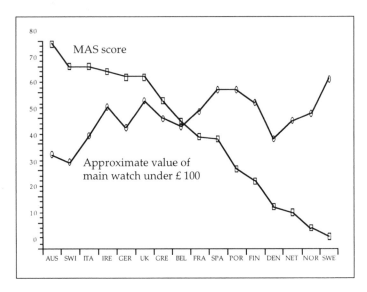

Figure 6.4 Correlation of MAS and Watches Under £100 (EMS 95)
SOURCE: Data from EMS (1995). Copyright © Inter/View.
NOTE: rho = 0.51*

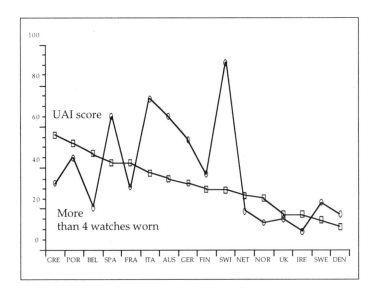

Figure 6.5 Correlation of UAI and 4+ Watches Worn (EMS 95)
SOURCE: Data from EMS (1995). Copyright © Inter/View.
NOTE: rho = 0.56*

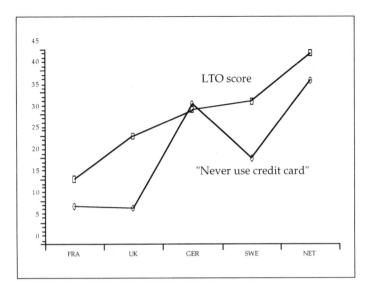

Figure 6.6 Correlation of LTO and No Credit Card (EMS 95)
SOURCE: Data EMS (1995). Copyright © Inter/View.
NOTE: rho = 0.80

indication of an influence on credit card behavior, as illustrated in Figure 6.6. Long-term orientation cultures use fewer credit cards than short-term orientation cultures.

The need for insurance products is influenced in various ways—in general, by the degree of individualism. In collectivistic cultures, the extended family or other in-groups function as a safety net. Figures 6.7 and 6.8 illustrate the correlation between individualism and ownership of life insurance and home insurance in Europe. In these charts, Italy behaves more like Spain, which reinforces my assumption that Italy is more collectivistic than Hofstede's data indicate, as pointed out under "Individualism/Collectivism (IDV)" in Chapter 4.

At face value, one would expect members of strong uncertainty avoidance cultures to own more insurance products than members of weak uncertainty avoidance cultures, yet the opposite appears to be the case: Personal ownership of insurance and pension-related investments as reported in EMS 95, and ownership of private pension savings plans in Reader's Digest Eurodata, appear to correlate negatively with uncertainty avoidance (see Figure 6.9). This implies that individuals of strong uncertainty avoidance cultures tend to buy fewer insurance and pension-related investments personally. This confirms that uncertainty avoidance is not the same

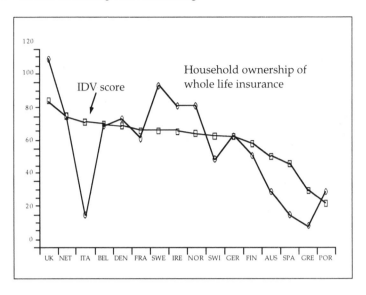

Figure 6.7 Correlation IDV and Household Ownership of Whole Life Insurance (Eurodata 91)
SOURCE: Data reproduced from Reader's Digest Eurodata—A Consumer Survey of 17 European Countries, sponsored by The Reader's Digest Association, Inc.
NOTE: rho = 0.63***

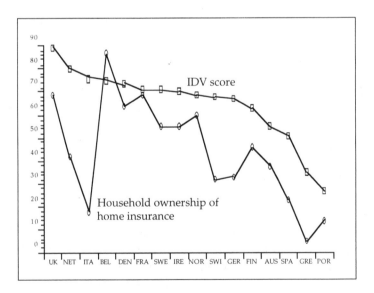

Figure 6.8 Correlation of IDV and Household Ownership of Home Insurance
SOURCE: Data reproduced from Reader's Digest Eurodata—A Consumer Survey of 17 European Countries, sponsored by The Reader's Digest Association, Inc.
NOTE: rho = 0.64***

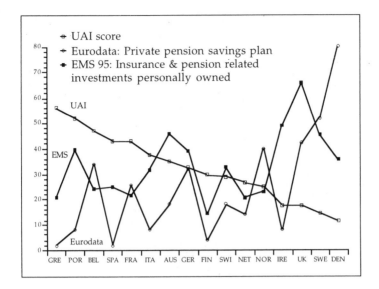

Figure 6.9 Correlation of UAI and Personal Pension Insurance Products
(Eurodata 91 & EMS 95)

SOURCE: Data reproduced from Reader's Digest Eurodata—A Consumer Survey of 17 European
Countries, sponsored by The Reader's Digest Association, Inc., and EMS (1995). Copyright © Inter/View.
NOTE: Eurodata 91: rho = −0.59**; EMS 95: rho = −0.64***

as risk avoidance. Insurance products eliminate risk. Members of weak
uncertainty avoidance cultures may make a cool calculation of risk and insure
themselves; for members of strong uncertainty avoidance cultures, it is a
more emotional reaction. This paradoxical behavior can be compared with
fast driving by members of strong uncertainty avoidance cultures, whereas
members of weak uncertainty avoidance cultures generally are slower and
more tolerant drivers.

In strong uncertainty avoidance cultures, the company's or government's role may be stronger with respect to pension-related insurance.
Generally, authorities in strong uncertainty avoidance cultures have a
stronger influence on people's lives than in weak uncertainty avoidance
cultures with stronger "citizen competence."[22]

Competence is a desirable value in strong uncertainty avoidance cultures. This value is expressed by the high regard for the professional, the
expert, and the need for technology and detail. Thus, in strong uncertainty
avoidance cultures, do-it-yourself products will either be less popular or have
to be accompanied by detailed instructions. Figure 6.10 shows that in strong
uncertainty avoidance cultures in Europe there are fewer households with

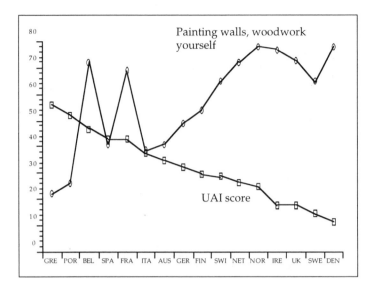

Figure 6.10 Correlation of UAI and Household Member Does Painting of Walls, Woodwork (Eurodata 91)

SOURCE: Data reproduced from Reader's Digest Eurodata—A Consumer Survey of 17 European Countries, sponsored by The Reader's Digest Association, Inc.

NOTE: rho = –0.67***

members who paint walls or woodwork than in weak uncertainty avoidance cultures. Machines or electronic products that can be manipulated—compared with those that are automatic—will be more popular in strong uncertainty avoidance cultures. Products with which people can show their professionalism will be more popular than products obviously designed for the amateur, such as autofocus cameras. There is, indeed, a significant correlation between uncertainty avoidance and camera buyers who buy autofocus cameras, as illustrated in Figure 6.11.

Maslow's Hierarchy of Needs

Maslow's[23] hierarchy of needs is based on the assumption that a person's behavior is directed at satisfying needs and that some needs will take precedence over others when the individual is faced with choices as to which needs to satisfy. Maslow's hypothesis is that a satisfied need is no longer a motivator and that a person will try to satisfy the lowest unsatisfied need in a hierarchy before trying to satisfy needs higher in the hierarchy. Physiological needs will take precedence over security or safety,

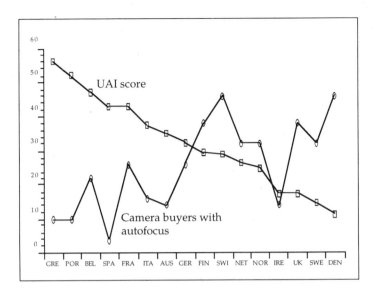

Figure 6.11 Correlation of UAI and Camera Buyers With Autofocus (Eurodata 91)
SOURCE: Data reproduced from Reader's Digest Eurodata—A Consumer Survey of 17 European
Countries, sponsored by The Reader's Digest Association, Inc.
NOTE: rho = −0.72***

the need for group membership, or esteem needs. The ultimate need, then, is self-actualization. Figure 6.12 depicts Maslow's hierarchy.

In textbooks, Maslow's hierarchy of needs is generally presented as a universal model. Authors are increasingly questioning Maslow's theory. Rice[24] presents a few problems with respect to the theory, one of which is that self-actualization and -esteem needs are likely to be a function of each individual's self-perception, which is socially conditioned. The question then is whether we are describing an innate need or something that may be defined by family, gender, culture, and class. Inglehart[25] states that there is little evidence to support Maslow's hypothesis that there is a universal order among the nonphysiological goals. A universal human pattern may be that physiological needs take precedence over higher-order needs, but the ranking of the nonphysiological needs varies across cultures. Adler[26] reports a number of studies that demonstrate how culturally defined needs are. The individual's frame of reference is in part determined by culture and will determine the needs and their order of importance.

Self-actualization is a highly individualistic U.S. motive. In collectivistic cultures, what will be actualized is not the self but the interest and honor of the in-group—not its individual members. The Japanese do use the concept

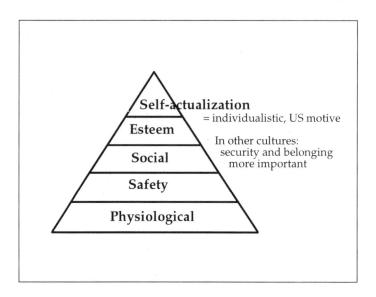

Figure 6.12 Maslow: Hierarchy of Needs

self-actualization, but in another context and related to what was earlier described as individuality (see Chapter 4, under "Individualism/Collectivism (IDV)"). It represents something that is different from the U.S. concept. In collectivistic cultures, belonging and safety will converge: It is very risky to distinguish oneself from the group. Security or safety is likely to prevail over other needs where uncertainty avoidance is strong. Belonging will prevail over esteem in feminine cultures, but esteem over belonging in masculine cultures.[27] The security-esteem combination will be important for masculine cultures of strong uncertainty avoidance, and security-belonging for feminine cultures of strong uncertainty avoidance. In feminine cultures, self-actualization presupposes consensus, which carries elements of both esteem and belonging.

Attitude

Attitude is a much used concept in consumer behavior theory. The definition given by Engel, Blackwell, and Miniard[28] is, "an overall evaluation that enables one to respond in a consistently favorable or unfavorable manner with respect to a given object or alternative." People's attitudes are guided by their values; values are the standards according to which people form their attitudes. Generally, people behave in a manner consistent with their attitudes. On the other hand, behavior drives attitudes and attitudes drive behavior. We have developed our attitudes as a result of prior experience, and many attitudes can be traced back to our childhood. As a result, attitudes have a cultural component.

Motivation

The study of motivation, the mixture of wants, needs, and drives within the individual, is seen as of prime importance to understanding behavior. Motivation research seeks to find the underlying "why" of our behavior; it seeks to identify the attitudes, beliefs, motives, and other pressures that influence our purchase decisions. In the 1950s, researchers such as Ernest Dichter used Freudian psychoanalytical ideas to explain behavior on the basis of unconscious motivation. Motivation theories are particularly based on Freud's idea of anxiety, which is related to his own culture.

There is a strong relationship among values, attitudes, needs, and motivations. Rokeach states that values have a strong motivational component, as well as cognitive, affective, and behavioral components. Instrumental values are motivating because their components are instrumental to the attainment of desired end-goals.[29] Vyncke[30] relates motivations to values: "motivations are a limited set of fundamental, motivating factors, which are the primary determinants of the human value system." Thus, Vyncke situates the value concept between the motivation and attitude concepts, quoting Dhalla and Mahatto:[31] "An individual's value system canalizes motivations, and tells him what attitudes he should hold." Because of their link with values, motivations are not universal, although many authors, following Maslow's assumption about universality of needs and motivations, state that they are universal.

Understanding the variations in what motivates people is important for positioning brands in different markets. It explains differences in brand loyalty, brand preference, brand image, and the like. Differences in sensitivity to certain product attributes and advertising appeals can be explained by culturally defined motives. An example is how motives for buying automobiles vary by culture. Although safety, when mentioned, will be a top-priority motive, it is also an implicit part of modern automobiles. Safety is, however, an important motive for feminine cultures, as it is a means of protecting loved ones and thus satisfies a need for caring and quality of life. Feminine cultures have no interest in powerful motors, they don't even know the power of their car engines, as compared with masculine cultures. This was demonstrated by the correlation of the masculinity dimension and answers

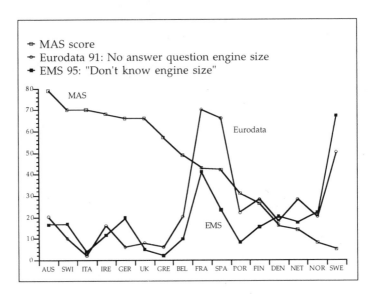

Figure 6.13 Correlation of MAS and Knowledge of Engine Size of Car
(Eurodata 91 & EMS 95)
SOURCE: Data reproduced from Reader's Digest Eurodata—A Consumer Survey of 17 European
Countries, sponsored by The Reader's Digest Association, Inc., and EMS (1995). Copyright © Inter/View.
NOTE: Eurodata 91: rho = −0.62***; EMS 95: rho = −0.52*

to questions about the engine size of the main car in the Eurodata Survey of
1991, as well as in EMS 1995. The more masculine the culture, the more
knowledge about the engine size, as illustrated in Figure 6.13. For cultures
of different configurations, other motives appear to be overriding. Figure
6.15 shows motives for buying automobiles in cultures clustered according
to two of Hofstede's dimensions: masculinity and uncertainty avoidance.
These motives, found by analyzing advertising, are the appeals used by
advertisers of successful car brands. Two culture clusters in the diagram are
also clusters of large power distance cultures in which style and design of
automobiles was found to be a frequently used appeal. The need for
distinctive style fits with the need for status in large power distance cultures.
This was confirmed by EMS 95 data, which showed a correlation between
power distance and the response "strongly agree" with the statement "I like
cars with individualistic styling." This is illustrated in Figure 6.14.

The upper left-hand quadrant of Figure 6.14 shows the configuration
of femininity and weak uncertainty avoidance. In this culture cluster, people
have a preference for safety to protect their family and for saving money.
Saving money is a frequent claim in advertising in these cultures. The upper
right-hand quadrant shows a cluster of cultures with the configuration
masculinity and weak uncertainty avoidance. People in these cultures tend

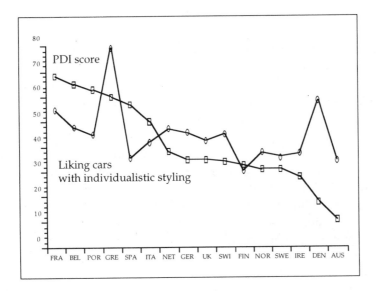

Figure 6.14 Correlation of PDI and Strongly Agree With "I Like Cars With Individualistic Styling" (EMS 95)
SOURCE: Data EMS (1995). Copyright © Inter/View.
NOTE: rho = 0.47*

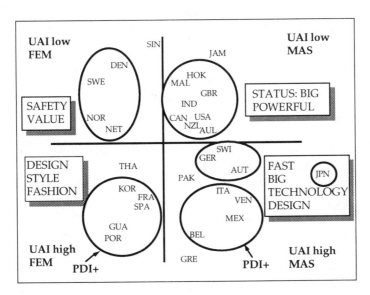

Figure 6.15 Buying Motives for Automobiles
NOTE: AUL = Australia, AUT = Austria, BEL = Belgium, CAN = Canada, DEN = Denmark, FRA = France, GER = Germany, GBR = Great Britain, GRE = Greece, GUA = Guatemala, HOK = Hong Kong, IND = India, ITA = Italy, JAM = Jamaica, JPN = Japan, KOR = Korea, MAL = Malaysia, MEX = Mexico, NET = the Netherlands, NOR = Norway, NZL = New Zealand, PAK = Pakistan, POR = Portugal, SIN = Singapore, SPA = Spain, SWE = Sweden, SWI = Switzerland, THA = Thailand, USA = the United States, VEN = Venezuela.

to have a need for status. They have a preference for cars with big, powerful motors. The lower right-hand quadrant shows the cluster of cultures with the configuration of masculinity and strong uncertainty avoidance. People in strong uncertainty avoidance cultures are aggressive drivers, and they prefer cars with rapid acceleration. This seems paradoxical, as one would expect to see risk aversion translated into a safety motive. Not so: The explanation is that people of strong uncertainty avoidance cultures build up stress, which they also want to release. Fast and aggressive driving is a sort of safety valve. But cars must also be technologically advanced, well designed, and well tested. In the lower left-hand quadrant, in the combination of feminine and strong uncertainty avoidance, one sees the need for "sporty" driving, fast acceleration but not so aggressive. This is combined with a preference for design, but more in the art/fashion sphere, pleasure and enjoyment.

An example of the contrast between masculinity and femininity is provided by the anecdote about an American car company selling their cars in the Netherlands. One model was offered for a very favorable price, including a powerful motor, to which the Dutch were not accustomed. The distributor insisted that another version with a smaller motor be developed. The counterargument was that this version would not be cheaper, as it would have to be developed specially so the car with the large motor would cost the same as a car with a smaller motor. This was not an argument for the Dutch: A small motor was enough, there was no need for a bigger motor; worse, the strong motor suggested they would be paying too much. Only the car with the smaller motor would sell, even if it cost more.

Emotion

Emotion tends to be described as a process that involves an interaction between cognition and physiology. The complete emotional experience includes cognitive components involving beliefs, values, and evaluation, as well as physiological changes producing feelings and desires leading to expressive behavior. Another typology is that of emotional content. An approach to emotional content is to make lists of emotions, differentiating between positive and negative emotions like pleasantness/unpleasantness, favorability/unfavorability.[32] From time immemorial, thinkers about emotion have shown a tendency to list what they regard as basic emotional types, like love, hatred, desire, joy, sadness, admiration, and sorrow.

The use of "emotions" in advertising originated in the United States and is a reaction to the strong historical focus on argumentation, persuasion, and information. Early in the 1980s, the American advertising industry realized that using advertising mainly at the attribute and benefit levels had resulted in parity advertising. Any manufacturer claiming superiority on the basis of attributes finds competitors responding with identical or even better claims in a short span of time. In the 1980s, the use of emotions in advertising was a response to that problem and the need to stand out from an increasingly cluttered advertising environment.[33] Yet, in the United States, where along with a trust in facts goes a distrust of emotions, advertisers tend to be afraid of emotional advertising, and they think the rational appeals for their products and services are much more important than the consumer thinks they are. The discussion of this aspect of "emotion" is related to the assumptions of how advertising works (see Chapter 7 under "Informational Versus Emotional").

Another aspect of emotion is the way it is vocalized and visualized. Cultures vary, particularly with respect to whether people show emotions at all or how they show them. In collectivistic cultures, only positive emotions can be shown because a display of negative emotions will decrease harmony in the group. Cultures of weak uncertainty avoidance tend not to show emotions. The British "stiff upper lip" can serve as an example. Cultures of strong uncertainty avoidance show their emotions but in many different ways, such as talking loudly, using their hands when talking, crying, laughing, and so on. In some countries, the word *emotional* in itself is popular in advertising—for example, the word *emozione* in Italian advertising. Across cultures, the ways people show such emotions as love, joy, sadness, and embarrassment are very different. Those who rely on so-called mood boards to visualize different brand positions cannot use the same visuals to express moods across cultures.

The Concepts of Self, Personality, and Identity

One aspect of Western marketing is the focus on product attributes that are to distinguish the user's self from others. The self is said to have an "I" component (the personal, private, individual "I") and a "ME" component (the socially acceptable "ME"), with internalized, learned, and accepted norms and values. In Western theories, another distinction is between the actual self and the ideal self. People will buy products that are compatible with their self-concept, or rather that enhance their "ideal-self"-image. Frequently mentioned drives related to the ideal-self are self-esteem, self-actualization, and the need for achievement.

Our self-concept also is the image we carry in our mind of the type of person we are and whom we desire to be.[34] Our self-image reflects how we see our own personality. A personality is a collection of traits that makes a person distinctive.[35] Implicit in the concept of personality is the individual-istic notion that people should distinguish themselves from others, as opposed to conformance to the group in collectivistic cultures.

The concept of self, as used in consumer psychology, is based on the Western-centric psychoanalytic theory of the self and personality. Central to the psychoanalytic value system as it originated in the United States, is the focus on a mental health model of individual autonomy in which the individual sharply differentiates between inner images of self and other; of norms of self-reliance, self-assertion, self-actualization; and a high degree of relatively open verbal self-expression. A youth has to develop an identity that enables him or her to function independently in a variety of social groups, apart from the family. Failing to do so can cause an identity crisis. The mental health models of collectivistic cultures are different. Whereas Ameri-can personality development is based on striving for autonomy and initiative in young children, Indian and Japanese development, for example, is based on encouragement of dependency needs in the earlier phases of childhood and negotiating in the complex familial hierarchical relationships.[36] Conse-quently, Indian psychiatric leaders view the Western mental health norms as inappropriate to Indian psychological development and functioning in the extended family and culture, and thus not at all universal.[37]

Viewing the self in individualistic terms implies that the self is an entity unto itself and exists apart from the groups to which the individual belongs.[38] Members of collectivistic cultures conceive of the self as part of the group to which they belong. The self is based on the individual's transactions with his or her fellow human beings. As a result, for members of collectivistic cultures, self-esteem—if used as a concept—is not linked to the individual but to relationships with others. The self is defined through a web of social and personal relationships. In Japan, "respecting yourself" means always showing yourself to be the careful player; it does not mean, as in English usage, consciously conforming to a worthy standard of conduct.[39] In India, "we"-self-regard means that feelings of inner regard or esteem are experi-enced not only around oneself or one's own body image, but equally around the "we" of the extended family, particular community (*jati*), and other groups one belongs to.[40] In collectivistic cultures there is no such thing as self-promotion as in individualistic cultures. The self is never free, but is bound by moral obligations. In Japan, the absence of self can be explained in terms of the individual's submersion in or submission to the group. Loss of the world to which one belongs is normally experienced as a loss of the self.[41] In Japan, people do not ascribe integrated personalities to fellow human beings. Behavior is relative to the circle within which it appears; it is related to context, thus personality is contextual. Western personality means consistency, acting in character. Men and women picture themselves as acting as particular kinds of persons, not as different persons in different situations or contexts.[42] If used in Japan, the notions of personality or identity relate to freedom. Doi[43] states that the Japanese experience long ago taught the psychological impossibility of freedom. For the Japanese, freedom in practice existed only in death.

So, when referring to the self across cultures, there are different concepts. Roland,[44] for the purpose of cross-cultural psychology, distinguishes between a familial self and an individualized self. For members of individualistic cultures, the individualized self is dominant and for members of collectivistic cultures, the familial self is dominant. Roland found the familial self in the psychological makeup of Indians and Japanese and of persons coming to psychoanalysis in America from various Mediterranean cultures—such as Hispanics, Italians, and Greeks. The familial self can be explained as a basic inner psychological organization that enables people to function well within the hierarchical intimacy relationships of a collectivistic culture. The familial self is a "we" self, relational in different contexts. It includes a private self and a public self. The private self operates in interdependence with others of a person's in-group. There is emotional connectedness, empathy, and receptivity to others. Reciprocal responsibilities and obligations are traditionally defined. This private self is kept quite secret and is communicated mainly indirectly and by subtle nonverbal gestures.[45] It is through the public self that the social etiquette of relationships with the outer group are maintained in varying interpersonal contexts. The inner psychological organization of members of individualistic cultures such as the United States, or the individualized self, enables them to function in highly mobile societies where autonomy is granted or even imposed. This individualized self is characterized by an individualistic "I"-ness.

Related to the familial self are personal emotional needs for sociability, dependence, security, and status, fulfilled through strongly affective intimacy relationships in the extended family and other in-groups. In contrast, in the West—and in America in particular—the individual tries to fulfil these needs through friends and other social groups in a mobile society where emotional ties tend to be temporary. Dependency needs are suppressed, particularly in masculine societies, because of competition.

Although most Western authors agree that the self-concept is influenced by social factors, such as the family, reference groups, social class, subculture, and culture, the distinction between the individualized self of individualistic cultures and the familial self of collectivistic cultures has consequences beyond social ones. One has therefore to be careful with extending concepts relating to the Western concept of self to other cultures, particularly collectivistic ones. Examples are personal drives such as self-esteem, self-confirmation, self-consistency, self-actualization, recognition, exhibition, dominance, independence, and the need for achievement.

Also within the Western, individualistic world, concepts related to the self are culturally defined. Freud's concepts related to the self, quoted in so many textbooks on consumer behavior, are culturally determined. In developing his concepts of the Id, Ego, and Superego, Freud was a true product of Austrian-Hungarian culture. Austria and Hungary score extremely low on power distance and high on uncertainty avoidance. Strong uncertainty avoidance implies that parents raise their children with the message that life is threatening, dangerous, so the children have to create structures to cope with threat. If combined with large power distance, this attitude does not pose a problem for children, as parents will create the structures for them. Parents guard and guide their children. Small power distance, however, implies that children become independent at an early age and have to structure reality for themselves. This leads to frustration. Freud's Superego is meant to control the Id, thus taking the role of the parent. It serves as an inner uncertainty-absorbing device.[46] One conclusion is that if Freud's theory is true or useful, it will be most useful for the Austrians and Hungarians and other cultures of a similar configuration of dimensions. It will be less useful for cultures of weak uncertainty avoidance, such as the United Kingdom and Scandinavia, or for cultures of large power distance, such as French and Asian cultures.

In modern Western marketing practice and theory, identity and personality are used as metaphors to define brand positions. Brand personality is the outside, what one sees of the brand, and brand identity includes the traits, the characteristics of the brand. Brand identity is the "soul" of the brand. Culture's consequence is that the concepts of brand personality and brand identity are metaphors that are less understandable and thus less useful to collectivistic cultures.

Words for the concepts identity and personality do not even exist in the Chinese and Japanese languages. There is a Japanese translation of the English word *identity*—"to be aware of one-self as oneself"—but its significance as a technical concept lies in the suggestion that this awareness of self is constituted on the basis of connections with others. The *katakana* (the Japanese language system that uses foreign words) word for *identity* is used.

But using the word does not necessarily imply that the same values are included. Efforts to compare American and Japanese brand personalities are therefore useless efforts.

Conclusion

Most concepts and theories of consumer behavior are Western-centric. Worldwide, students and practitioners have learned about consumer behavior with the help of theories developed for American culture. To use them properly, they must be adapted. What people buy and why they buy certain products is influenced by their cultural values. A number of examples were mentioned in this chapter, such as number and value of wristwatches bought, autofocus cameras, do-it-yourself products, and whether people buy new or second-hand cars. Finding such strong correlations between actual buying behavior and cultural dimensions is exciting and assuring. Most value research relies on what people say about their values, be it indirectly. Finding the relationship between value differences and actual consumption behavior provides stronger proof.

A number of theories of consumer behavior commonly found in textbooks were reviewed in this chapter. Group membership and roles of group members vary by culture and this influences decision-making and choice behavior. Motives for buying products vary among and within geographic areas. Countries may share a border but be far apart with respect to buying motives. With respect to saving money or getting value for money as a motive for buying automobiles, Singapore and the Netherlands are closer than the Netherlands and Belgium (see Figure 6.15).

The concepts of self, identity, and personality are integral parts of consumer psychology. They also are Western-centric concepts. They are used in theory, in practice, and in research. Using the concept and wording in cultures whose language has no words for them because the concept does not exist, is asking for trouble. Clients must distrust research agencies who do so.

For developing effective marketing strategies, it is important to distinguish between behavior that is strongly influenced by cultural values and behavior that is more influenced by economic variables. At face value, there must be an economic motive behind preferring second-hand cars over new cars. Yet this also is influenced by culture. Another example in this chapter is the market for insurance and pension-related products. Markets with low insurance buying behavior may be perceived as potential growth markets.

However, if buying behavior is influenced by collectivistic values, it will be more difficult to be successful in these markets than in the individualistic markets one is used to, and different approaches may be needed.

The evidence provided in this chapter may lead academics and researchers to develop theories for their own culture, resulting in a better understanding of how advertising works in their own country. Like the concepts discussed in this chapter, the assumptions of how advertising works are culture-bound. They will be discussed in Chapter 7.

Notes

1. Sheth, J. N., Newman, B. I., & Gross, B. L. (1991). *Consumption values and market choices.* Cincinnati, OH: South-Western, pp. 18-22.

2. Sheth et al. (1991), *Consumption values,* pp. 32-38.

3. Sheth et al. (1991), *Consumption values,* pp. 38-49.

4. Sheth et al. (1991), *Consumption values,* pp. 50-79.

5. Sheth et al. (1991), *Consumption values,* p. 58.

6. Sheth et al. (1991), *Consumption values,* p. 62.

7. Sheth et al. (1991), *Consumption values,* pp. 69-78.

8. Rice, C. (1993). *Consumer behaviour: Behavioural aspects of marketing.* Oxford, UK: Butterworth Heinemann, pp. 215-235.

9. Interview with Kazuaki Ushikubo, November 1995.

10. For the 16 European countries in the Reader's Digest Eurodata Survey 1991, the correlation between "women main food shoppers" and MAS is 0.53*. Omitting the more developing three European countries, Greece, Portugal, and Spain, which appeared to show very different behavior, the correlation became 0.68*** (13 countries).

11. Stewart, E. C. (1985). "Culture and decision making." In W. B. Gudykunst, L. P. Stewart, & S. T. Ting-Toomey (Eds.), *Communication, culture, and organizational processes.* Beverly Hills, CA: Sage, pp. 177-211.

12. Gudykunst, W. B., & Ting-Toomey, S. (1988). *Culture and interpersonal communication.* Newbury Park, CA: Sage, p. 147.

13. Toy, S. (1995, October 16). "Storm, terrorists, nuke tests—Why is Club Med smiling?" *Business Week,* p. 20.

14. Bergadaà, M. M. (1990, December). "The role of time in the action of the consumer." *Journal of Consumer Research, 17,* 289-302.

15. *Nielsen SRG News Asia Pacific,* No. 80. February 1996.

16. Wolfe, A. (1991, May). "Stalking Euro-buyers in their lairs." *Business Marketing Digest,* pp. 87-94.

17. Sheth et al. (1991), *Consumption values,* p. 69.

18. Temple, R. (1986). *China.* London: Multimedia Publications.

19. Rogers, E. M. (1962). *Diffusion of innovations.* New York: Free Press.

20. Robinson, C. (1996). "Asian culture: The marketing consequences." *Journal of the Market Research Society, 38*(1), 55-66.

21. Roland, A. (1988). *In search of self in India and Japan.* Princeton, NJ: Princeton University Press.

22. Hofstede, G. (1991). *Cultures and organizations: Software of the mind.* New York: McGraw-Hill, p. 126.

23. Maslow, A. H. (1954). *Motivation and personality.* New York: Harper & Row.

24. Rice (1993), *Consumer behaviour.*

25. Inglehart, R. (1990). *Culture shift in advanced industrial society.* Princeton, NJ: Princeton University Press, chap. 4.

26. Adler, N. J. (1991). *International dimensions of organizational behavior.* Belmont, CA: Wadsworth, pp. 152-154.

27. Hofstede (1991), *Cultures and organizations,* p. 126.

28. Engel, J. F., Blackwell, R. D., & Miniard, P. W. (1990). *Consumer behavior* (6th ed.). Chicago: Dryden.

29. Rokeach, M. (1973). *The nature of human values.* New York: Free Press, p. 14.

30. Vyncke, P. (1992). *Imago-Management: Handboek voor Reclamestrategen.* Ghent, Belgium: Mys & Breesch, Uitgevers & College Uitgevers, p. 87.

31. Dhalla, N. K., & Mahatto, W. H. (1976). "Expanding the scope of segmentation research." *Journal of Marketing, 40,* 37.

32. Holbrook, M., & O'Shaughnessy, J. (1984). "The role of emotions in advertising." *Psychology & Marketing, 1*(2), 45-60.

33. Holman, R. H. (1986). "Advertising and emotionality." In R. A. Peterson, W. D. Hoyer, & W. R. Wilson (Eds.), *The role of affect in consumer behavior: Emerging theories and applications.* Lexington, MA: D. C. Heath.

34. Bovée, C. L., & Arens, W. F. (1992). *Contemporary advertising.* Homewood, IL: Irwin.

35. Wells, W., Burnett, J., & Moriarty, S. (1992). *Advertising: Principles and practice* (2nd ed.). Englewood Cliffs, NJ: Prentice Hall, p. 162.

36. Roland (1988), *In search of self in India and Japan,* p. 314.

37. Roland (1988), *In search of self in India and Japan,* p. 60.

38. Gudykunst & Ting-Toomey (1988), *Culture and interpersonal communication,* p. 82.

39. Benedict, R. (1974). *The chrysanthemum and the sword.* Rutland, VT: Charles E. Tuttle, p. 219. (Original work published 1946)

40. Roland (1988), *In search of self in India and Japan,* p. 242.

41. Doi, T. (1973). *The anatomy of dependence.* Tokyo: Kodansha International, pp. 135-139.

42. Benedict (1974), *The chrysanthemum and the sword,* p. 195.

43. Doi (1973), *The anatomy of dependence,* pp. 94-95.

44. Roland (1988), *In search of self in India and Japan,* pp. 3-13.

45. Roland (1988), *In search of self in India and Japan,* p. 83.

46. Hofstede, G. (1984). *Culture's consequences: International differences in work-related values.* Beverly Hills, CA: Sage.

Culture and How
Advertising Works

Because the United States is the birthplace of modern advertising techniques, it is not surprising that American cultural assumptions have become the standard by which the working of advertising is measured and the basis for philosophies of how advertising works, including related theories of how people process information. If we want to understand how advertising works across cultures, we'll first have to learn how communication works. Styles of communication vary by culture. One of the clearest distinctions is between high-context and low-context communication. Related to this distinction is the way people process communication and their expectations of the role, purpose, and effect of communication.

Is advertising persuasive by nature or can it have another role in the sales process? Philosophies of how advertising works will be related to the prevailing communication styles and intellectual style of the culture of the philosopher. The hierarchy of effect model of how advertising works is a true product of sequential, cause-effect thinking. Research styles and advertising measurement criteria are the consequence of the assumption of how advertising works, which in turn will influence the way advertising is developed.

Communication Styles

An understanding of general communication styles of cultures, and styles of mass communication in particular, should be helpful in understanding different advertising styles. Studies of related areas, such as content analysis of television programs or literature, may help determine basic differences between communication styles. American television, for example, is more action oriented than Finnish television. Domestically produced Finnish video dramas are much more static. They sacrifice action and setting for dialogue and extreme close-ups. But between the

Scandinavian countries and Finland, differences in style also exist. Finnish directors of TV dramas are more interested in the relationship between people whereas Scandinavian directors emphasize movement and space.[1] Both the Russians and the Japanese depict boredom in their novels, while American novels do not do much with the theme. "Fun is not a Russian concept," says Moscow sociologist Maria Zolotukhina on the difficulties faced by the creators of a Russian version of the popular American's children's television program *Sesame Street*.[2] The "happy ending" is rare in Japanese novels and plays, while American popular audiences crave solutions.[3] This is reflected in American TV dramas and commercials. Also, Gerbner's[4] work can be used to understand more generally how communication works, particularly his cultivation theory, which is that the media cultivate attitudes and values in a culture. The media do not create them, they must already be there. Content analysis reveals the values embedded in the total message system of a culture.[5]

I'll discuss two ways to analyze communication styles across cultures. First there is the distinction between high-context and low-context communication. Second, studies of interpersonal communication across cultures will be adapted. Styles of interpersonal communication are: direct versus indirect, verbal versus nonverbal, and variations in verbal and nonverbal styles. They relate to high- and low-context communication.

High-Context and Low-Context Communication

Context, or the information surrounding an event, is inextricably bound up with meaning. If people have extensive information networks among family, friends, colleagues, and clients and are involved in close relationships with each other, communication generally is high-context. In high-context cultures, people implicitly and imperceptibly collect information from their networks. People who do not have many information networks require a great deal of detailed information from other sources. Their approach to life is highly segmented, and they focus on bits of information. Their communication is low-context.

High-context people tend to become impatient or irritated when low-context people give them information they don't need because they already know it through their network. People from low-context cultures are at a loss when high-context culture people do not provide enough information.

In order to communicate effectively across cultures, the correct level of contexting must be found. Too much information may make people feel as if they are being talked down to; too little may mystify them. Hall[6] places

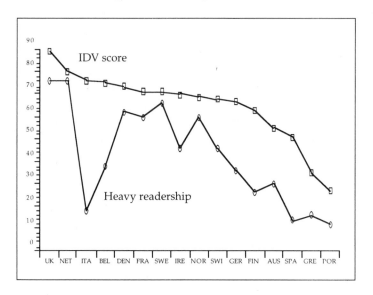

Figure 7.1 Correlation Between IDV and Heavy Readership = 12 + Books in Past Year
SOURCE: Data reproduced from Reader's Digest Eurodata—a Consumer Survey of 17 European Countries, sponsored by The Reader's Digest Association, Inc.
NOTE: rho = 0.76***

people on a sliding scale from low-context to high-context. The Germans and Americans are on the low-context side of his sliding scale and the French, Spanish, Italians, peoples of the Middle East, and the Japanese on the high side. With respect to advertising, high-context can be recognized by the use of indirect communication using less copy and more symbols. Low-context communication cultures tend to use more copy, argumentation, facts, and data than high-context cultures.

Hofstede[7] found a correlation between high- versus low-context and the collectivism/individualism dimension. Individualistic cultures are generally low-context and collectivistic cultures are generally high-context. Indicators for low- versus high-context are verbal versus visual communication, reading versus watching TV, or perception of newspapers versus television as useful sources of information. Figure 7.1 shows the correlation between individualism and heavy readership for 16 countries; the data are from the Reader's Digest Eurodata Survey. Data from the Eurobarometer for 12 countries show a correlation between individualism and people's choice of medium as their main source of information about new developments that affect people's lives. This is shown in Figure 7.2.

What is relevant for the media in general is also relevant for advertising: There is a significant correlation between individualism and finding adver-

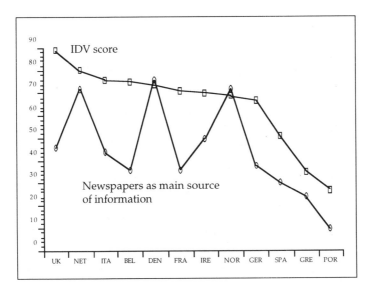

Figure 7.2 Correlation Between IDV and Newspapers as Main Source of Information About New Developments That Affect People's Lives
SOURCE: Data Eurobarometer (1993)
NOTE: rho = 0.59*

tising on television a useful source of new product information, as illustrated in Figure 7.3. In this chart, the United Kingdom, Ireland, Denmark, and Italy are seemingly high-context, although they score high on the IDV dimension. For each country there are different explanations. Italy may be more collectivistic than the Hofstede-IBM data show, as discussed in Chapter 6 under "Needs." Denmark's history of television advertising is short, which may cause a bias in how people relate to television advertising. The United Kingdom and Ireland show high-context communication advertising, although they are individualistic cultures. Generally, homogeneous cultures show more high-context communication than heterogeneous cultures. This phenomenon was also mentioned in Chapter 4 under "High-Context and Low-Context Cultures."

Direct Versus Indirect Modes of Communication

Individualistic cultures generally use a direct mode of communication. In collectivistic cultures, people prefer indirect communication. In collectivistic cultures "face saving" in particular plays a role, and a direct mode of communication is perceived as highly threatening and unsettling to one's own face.[9] Individualistic, low-context cultures (the Anglo-Saxon world and

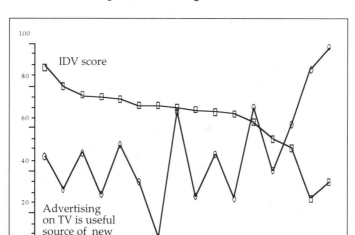

Figure 7.3 Correlation Between IDV and Regarding TV Advertising as a Useful Source of New Product Information
SOURCE: Data EMS (1995). Copyright © Inter/View.
NOTE: rho = 0.47*

northern Europe) emphasize individual value orientations, linear logic, and direct verbal interactions. Collectivistic, high-context cultures (most of Asia, the Arab world, and Latin America) emphasize group value orientations, circular logic, and indirect verbal interactions.

The individualistic verbal and nonverbal communication style suggests that intentions and meanings are displayed clearly and expressed explicitly through direct communication. A contextual verbal and nonverbal style implies that intentions and meanings are situated within the larger shared knowledge of the cultural context and are implicit.[10] Styles of individualistic cultures include control, confrontation, problem solving, and direct address of the public. Styles of collectivistic cultures show a dependency and trust-generating orientation, indirect speech acts, and contextual (role-oriented) nonverbal acts.[11]

Verbal Communication Styles

For the purpose of understanding intercultural interpersonal communication, Gudykunst and Ting-Toomey[12] distinguish four verbal communication styles: direct versus indirect, elaborate versus succinct, personal versus contextual, and instrumental versus affective. In their description, they use Hofstede's dimensions and Hall's high- and low-context distinction.

The direct versus indirect style refers to the extent speakers reveal their intentions through explicit verbal communication. In the direct style, wants, needs, and desires are expressed explicitly. The indirect verbal style refers to verbal messages that conceal the speaker's true intentions. Wordings such as "absolutely" and "definitely" to express buying intentions are an example of the direct style, while "probably" or "somewhat" are examples of the indirect style. The direct verbal style is part of individualistic cultures, the indirect style is part of collectivistic cultures.

The elaborate versus succinct verbal style encompasses three verbal styles: elaborate, exacting, and succinct. Elaborate verbal style refers to the use of rich, expressive language. The exacting style is a style in which neither more nor less information than is required is given. The succinct style includes the use of understatements, pauses, and silences. Silences between words carry meaning. High-context cultures of moderate to strong uncertainty avoidance tend to use the elaborate style. Arab cultures show this elaborate style of verbal communication, using metaphors, long arrays of adjectives, flowery expressions, and proverbs. Low-context cultures of weak uncertainty avoidance (the United States, the United Kingdom) tend to use the exacting style. The succinct style is found in high-context cultures of high uncertainty avoidance (Japan).

Verbal personal style is individual-centered language, whereas verbal contextual style is role-centered language. Verbal personal style enhances the "I" identity, and is person oriented (English), while verbal contextual style emphasizes the sense of a context-related role identity (Japanese, Chinese). The two styles focus on "personhood" versus "situation" or "status." Verbal personal style is linked with small power distance (equal status) and low-context, while verbal contextual style is linked with large power distance (hierarchical human relationships) and high-context. Verbal contextual style includes different ways of addressing different persons, depending on their status. For example, the Japanese language adapts to situations in which higher- or lower-placed people are addressed.

The instrumental verbal style is sender-oriented language usage while the affective verbal style is receiver oriented. The instrumental style is goal oriented, the affective or intuitive style is process oriented. The speaker using the instrumental style consciously constructs the message for the purpose of persuading and producing attitude change. The affective style is based on the assumption that human beings will adapt to their environment rather than exploit it. The instrumental style is part of individualistic, low-context cultures, while the affective style is part of collectivistic, high-context cultures.

Nonverbal Communication Styles

The degree to which people prefer nonverbal communication, such as using symbols, is defined by culture and related to high- and low-context. Gudykunst and Ting-Toomey refined this distinction to explain differences in interpersonal communication.[13] They developed a two-dimensional grid of interpersonal nonverbal styles, using the high- and low-context dimension and Hofstede's dimensions of individualism/collectivism, power distance, and uncertainty avoidance. Their grid includes four nonverbal style possibilities: unique-explicit nonverbal style, unique-implicit nonverbal style, group-explicit nonverbal style, and group-implicit nonverbal style. The two basic dimensions used are identity-communality, which echoes the self-orientation of individualism versus the group orientation of collectivism, and accessibility-inaccessibility, which reflects the power distance and uncertainty avoidance dimensions. Accessibility-inaccessibility refers to the degree to which the home environment emphasizes the openness or closedness of occupants to outsiders. Strong uncertainty avoidance people perceive outsiders as more threatening than weak uncertainty avoidance cultures do, and power distance reinforces that.

The grid, although theoretical and applied to interpersonal communication, may well be used for mass communication. Advertising styles of different countries can be recognized and placed in the quadrants. The grid in Figure 7.4 is an adapted version. The unique-explicit nonverbal style in the upper left-hand quadrant of Figure 7.4 fits individualistic cultures of small power distance and weak to medium uncertainty avoidance. The uniqueness of the person or the brand, the importance of identity and personality, are reflected in this style. The advertising styles of the United Kingdom, the United States, and Germany can be recognized. All three countries show high use of the "personalized lecture" style in advertising. This is the type of advertising in which an identified or well-known presenter or celebrity endorses the product. Many Procter & Gamble television commercials using the testimonial format look like they are carefully directed to focus on the personality of the endorser and not to include any implicit nonverbal behavior. In cultures of stronger uncertainty avoidance, the execution of the visuals will be more detailed or demonstration will be added. That is the style in Germany, where visuals are more exact than in weak uncertainty avoidance cultures.

The upper right-hand quadrant of Figure 7.4 shows the unique-implicit nonverbal style, which expresses both uniqueness and inaccessibility. In interpersonal communication, this style fits individualistic cultures of large

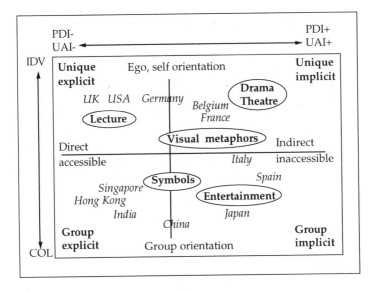

Figure 7.4 Nonverbal Communication Styles and Advertising
SOURCE: Gudykunst & Ting-Toomey (1988). Adapted by De Mooij, 1997.

power distance combined with moderate to strong uncertainty avoidance. The configuration fits France and Belgium, where implicit nonverbal communication styles are used more than in the northern European countries. Theater-style advertising, visual metaphors, and symbols are used to create both a suggestion of uniqueness and positioning of the product or brand in its "proper place," as fits large power distance cultures. Although in the United States the "drama" style is also used, it is more popular in France and other countries fitting in the upper right-hand quadrant. "Drama" is an advertising form in which actors play real-life or imaginary situations involving a product. The interaction provides the message. It is a more indirect style, used more in France, Belgium, and Italy, where the drama tends to be more theatrical and indirect than in the Anglo-German cultures.

The group-implicit nonverbal style fits cultures with the configuration of collectivism, strong uncertainty avoidance, and large power distance. In the lower right-hand quadrant of Figure 7.4 are the countries in which nonverbal communication is more indirect, is less likely to offend, and thus upholds public face. It is subdued and works on likability. The use of symbols is characteristic of this style. The preference for entertainment as a basic advertising form in Japan is an example of this nonverbal communication style. If celebrities are involved, they rarely address the audience explicitly, they play a more symbolic role, and they associate more with the product rather than endorse it.

According to the grid in Figure 7.4, the group-explicit nonverbal style is the style of collectivistic cultures of small or medium power distance and weak or moderate uncertainty avoidance. Nonverbal communication style must ensure group norms and help maintain face. Symbols are important in advertising in these cultures, but the audience is more directly addressed. Ting-Toomey puts Hong Kong and Singapore in the lower left-hand quadrant. Singaporeans are indeed direct in their communication and Hong Kong, too, fits in this quadrant. So does India, which is confirmed by Roland,[14] who states that "Indian modes of communication operate more overtly on more levels simultaneously than do the Japanese."

France: High-Context or Low-Context?

Hall and Hofstede contradict each other with respect to one country: France. France is an individualistic culture, yet according to Hall it is high-context. Indeed, a relatively high use of symbols can be seen in French advertising. Gudykunst and Ting-Toomey[15] confirm the correlation between context and individualism/collectivism. An explanation for the high use of symbolism in French communication is that French communication shows the unique implicit nonverbal style, including the use of symbolism, which may easily be confused with high-context. Maleville[16] also noted the inconsistency with respect to France. In French business-to-business advertising she found many devices for making information explicit, which did not fit with Hall's categorization of France as a high-context culture. She compared this inconsistency with another of Hall's concepts, that of polychrony versus monochrony. Hall[17] states that the French picture themselves as monochronic, consistent with systematized linear culture in the Cartesian sense. Intellectually and philosophically, the French can be monochronic but still be polychronic in the context of daily life, particularly in interpersonal relationships. Hall states that there is nothing unusual about people actually being one way but having a different image of themselves. Maleville extends this thinking to contextualization: Although the French may prefer implicit communication, explicitness is considered to sell better to business.

The Purpose of Communication

Communication styles, the supposed working of communication in general, and intellectual styles define how professionals think advertising works. Psychology and sociology are the disciplines on which advertising theory is primarily based. Western sociologists and psychologists concentrate on studies of peoples from Western societies and are more likely to construct theories that are based on Western constructs of reality.[18] For example, the theory of information processing is based on cognitive psychology with a bias toward the use of verbal material and linguistic performance, disregarding pictorial and other nonlanguage stimuli. It thus disregards an important data source for international advertising. Visuals are as convention-based as language, and all pictures must be interpreted according to learned patterns—just like reading words or recognizing numbers.[19]

A frequently used communication model in advertising theory is the Shannon-Weaver model,[20] in which the sender encodes and transmits a message and the receiver receives and decodes it. The Shannon-Weaver definition of communication, "all the procedures by which one mind may affect another," was operationalized in a mathematical model that provided a precise, quantified measure of information. Shannon originally used the expression "communication theory" to mean the study and statement of the principles and method by which information is conveyed.[21] This early focus on transmitting information has been the origin of current practice. The model has no provision for nonverbal content, which may make up a large part of cross-cultural exchange. It omits many aspects of communication.

Americans view communication as a process of transmitting messages for the purpose of control. They see it as a means to persuade others, to change attitudes, and to influence or condition behavior. Carey[22] states that European cultures view communication as a process through which a shared culture is created, modified, and transformed. Across cultures, people have different assumptions of the role of communication and advertising in business and society and there is no single philosophy of how advertising works. In the United States, advertising as a form of communication is seen as persuasive by nature. In Japan, the purpose of advertising is to create a good relationship between people and products.[23]

Information Processing

Information processing theory is a psychological approach to analyzing how people acquire, organize, and use information to assist choice behavior. The underlying assumption is that people want to solve problems and choose rationally. Under this assumption, symbolic, hedonistic, and aesthetic motives underlying people's choices are not taken into account. The assumption that choice behavior is rational is disputed in the Western world and can be even less generalized for consumers in non-Western cultures. Miracle[24] mentions the contrast between "Western" consumers and Japanese consumers with respect to information processing. Western consumers, generally speaking, tend to process information about a product or company and use the information to make up their minds whether or not, or what, to purchase. In contrast, Japanese in their decision making tend to depend at least in part on members of their in-group or on people who in other ways merit their trust.

How people acquire, organize, and utilize information is related to how they have learned to process information. It is related to the type of information they are used to. People of high-context cultures, used to symbols, signs, and indirect communication, will process information in a different way than people of low-context cultures who are used to explanations, persuasive copy, and rhetoric. In low-context communication, information is in the words; in high-context communication, information is in the visuals, the symbols, and the associations attached to them. Researchers of low-context cultures tend to define visual communication as noninformational, which can result in measurement bias if information cues are used to compare advertising between high- and low-context cultures.

There are significant cross-cultural differences in pictorial perception. Imagery is an important element of advertising, yet it is undervalued in research because of the historical focus on verbal communication. Scott[25] comments on this bias reflected in the use of the term "copy theory" instead of "advertising theory." The phrases "copy research" and "copy testing," used for testing effectiveness of advertising including visuals, demonstrate the bias toward thinking in verbal stimuli.

Distinctive thinking patterns playing a role in information processing are emphasized in associative versus abstractive thought and inductive versus deductive thinking. People with associative patterns tend to prefer oral, face-to-face communication, while people with an abstractive thought pattern tend to prefer written instructions. Inductive-thinking people start with facts, data, and draw conclusions from those. Deductive-thinking people start with a philosophy, a theory, and assemble facts and data to prove it. There is a relationship between the degree of uncertainty avoidance and thinking pattern. Strong uncertainty avoidance cultures tend to think deductively, whereas weak uncertainty avoidance cultures think inductively. This difference can be recognized in the academic style of the United States with its focus on empiricism, and the continental European style with more focus on theory. Associative thinking is found in high-context cultures and in cultures combining strong uncertainty avoidance with large power distance. France, Italy, and Spain are countries in which associative thinking is strong.

People of strong uncertainty avoidance cultures have a need to structure reality. When combined with small power distance (Germany, Austria) the structuring is internalized in the person. When combined with large power distance (France, Italy, Spain) the structuring is externalized, through conceptualization. The Germans and the French both like rules, but the Germans use them to structure themselves and the French to structure others.[26]

In advertising, differences in thinking patterns affect the balance between copy and visuals. The existence and appreciation of specific advertising styles and basic advertising forms is a reflection of culture. Of French magazine advertising, 90% is said to be visuals; of German magazine ads, 80% is copy, as was discovered by Euro Disney in Paris, where management originally thought they could use one standardized message for all countries in Europe.[27]

An example of the difference between visual and verbal orientation is the difference in timing and frequency of verbal or visual mention of the brand name in commercials.[28] In a typical Japanese television commercial, the first identification of a brand, company name, or product occurs later than in a typical U.S. television commercial. Japanese advertisers tend to take more of a commercial's time to develop trust, understanding, and dependency. In Japan, the brand name is shown for a longer time than in the United States, where it is more often verbally mentioned.

Informational Versus Emotional

The American assumption that advertising's main role is to provide information as part of the persuasive process has undervalued other elements of advertising. It was not so long ago that advertisers started to realize that the consumption experience also includes emotional components. Consumers' emotions were recognized as having a significant influence on purchase and consumption decisions. As a result, "emotional," "transformational," "evaluative," or "feeling" messages are often contrasted with "rational," "informational," "factual," or "thinking" appeals. This suggests that emotions do not carry information. "Logical, objectively verifiable descriptions of tangible product features" and "emotional, subjective impressions of intangible aspects of the product" are seen as contrasting.

Discussions of emotion have often been hampered by a lack of agreement on how emotion differs from rational concepts and from other, nonrational concepts, like drives, needs, and affect. In some studies it even seems to be related to "feeling," to "soft" sell as opposed to "hard" sell, to "indirect" as opposed to "direct" communication.

Rossiter and Percy[29] distinguish between emotional stimuli and emotional responses. Emotional stimulus-response connections are either (a) genetically programmed or (b) well established by previous learning. Examples of stimuli to elicit various emotions mentioned by Rossiter and Percy are: heard words and sound effects, music, seen words, pictures, color, and movement. Emotional responses are primarily bodily responses to which verbal labeling and visual imagery may be connected. Typical emotions may be connected to specific motivations. Examples given are problem removal portrayed by annoyance with the problem followed by relief, or social approval ending with brand usage that flatters the user. Emotional responses include physiological changes producing feelings and desires leading to expressive behavior.

Although a number of studies indicate that there are universal emotions, such as happiness and sadness, rules for emotional displays are culture specific. Expressive behavior varies by culture. This makes the emotional behavior of people of one culture often not understood by members of another culture. What Americans call "emotional" is often perceived as "sentimental" by members of other cultures. Typologies of emotional content can be useful to measure the effectiveness of emotional appeals for one culture, but not for others.

Because of the strong focus on verbal communication, particularly in low-context cultures, advertising people tend to think of the rational elements as the "content" and the emotional element as "execution" and to see them as separate entities. But execution is content. One cannot separate what is said from how it is said. This is the core of the problem of transferring advertising to other cultures—because how you say something is even more culturally defined than what you say.

The above may demonstrate that comparing advertising across cultures by using the distinction emotional/informational is an ethnocentric measurement method. It is related to the history of advertising and advertising styles in the United States. Cultures in which argumentation and persuasiveness based on facts and data are less effective advertising styles (collectivistic and feminine cultures) will have a different view of the concept of emotion in advertising. Reactions to emotional behavior in advertising will vary with the level of uncertainty avoidance.

Persuasive Communication

In his article on objectivity in marketing theory and research, Hunt[30] states: "Communication may either be successful (persuasive) or unsuccessful (unpersuasive)." The focus on persuasiveness and rhetoric, recognized in the "rhetorical turn" in social science, such as advocated in economics by McCloskey,[31] is of Anglo-Saxon origin and reflects the characteristics of a masculine culture. For Americans, advertising is synonymous with persuasive communication. Persuasiveness, repetition, and the hard sell arise from a model in which "advertising and consumer are on two sides of a counter, and that some kind of confrontation is taking place with one side trying to persuade the other to change attitude or behavior."[32] The frequently used persuasion test to measure advertising effectiveness is based on this pattern of thinking. The basic procedure is measurement of purchasing intentions before and after exposure, which reflects a digital, cause-effect way of thinking.

Persuasion means to "cause someone to do something, specially by reasoning, urging or inducing."[33] It is synonymous with "to win over." The persuasive communication function of advertising appears to be viewed with a bias toward rational claims, direct address of the public, or a hard sell. All elements of advertising, words and pictures, tend to be evaluated on their persuasive role in the sales process. Although in other cultures sales will also be the ultimate goal of advertising, advertising's role in the sales process is obviously different. In collectivistic cultures, the use of a hard sell, or directly addressing consumers, turns them off instead of persuading them. Although U.S. studies[34] have shown that persuasion tests (preference shifting) are also adequate for measuring the effectiveness of emotional or image/mood advertising in the United States, it seems inappropriate to use persuasion tests based on rational, linear processing to test advertisements meant for people who have a different information processing system. Zinkhan[35] confirms that American concepts do not necessarily explain advertising realities in Russia or in Latin America or in the Arab world. Neither do they in Europe. Yet, time and again, the effectiveness of advertising across cultures is measured by testing persuasiveness. Using U.S.-cultural concepts to find an explanation for how advertising works in other cultures may not be very effective. An example is the statement that "in exploring the causes of the soft sell in Japanese advertising, a natural question to ask is how the persuasive process is supposed to work at the individual level in Japan."[36] The answer is that there is neither a persuasive process nor is it useful to look at how advertising works at the individual level. In Japan, advertising cannot persuade the individual directly, it must adapt to the group influence, defining group membership rather than the "self." And the "group" includes Japanese in the same age, sex, and interest category. This explains the existence of so many niche, special-interest magazines in a highly segmented magazine market, with a special magazine for each segment.

Likability

In advertising effectiveness research in the Western world, it was recently recognized that persuasion measures do not capture a key element in the link between communication and the thoughts and behavior of consumers. That missing link is the degree to which an advertisement has personal significance for the consumer. When people experience advertising they do not behave as passive, objective receivers of messages about brands. They interpret the advertisement for themselves, using their own "world-view" as an interpretative filter. They associate it with other information.[37] Next to persuasion, therefore, likability has become a measure to predict sales. Aspects that contribute to the likability of advertising are:[38]

- "Meaningful" (worth remembering, effective, believable, true-to-life, not pointless)
- "(Does not) rub the wrong way" (not irritating, worn out, phoney)
- "Warmth" (gentle, warm, sensitive)

This view of how consumers relate to advertising may be a better approach to apply to advertising across borders than the persuasion model. It certainly will be a better effectiveness measurement for Japanese advertising where pleasing the consumer is one of the objectives of advertising.

How Advertising Works

Most models of how advertising works are based on an assumed hierarchy of effects and on sequential thinking. Although academics worldwide have modified this hierarchy of effects model, the sequential way of thinking remains the basis of much of the thinking about how advertising works.

The Hierarchy of Effects

The underlying assumption about how advertising works is that advertising takes people from one stage to another. These "linear or sequential" or "transportation" models are based on a logical and rational process.[39] The assumptions are that perception is a (Western) logical process and universal for humankind. But this is Western thinking, and there are more systems of logic in the world, not necessarily based on the sequential process. This hierarchy of effects model has strongly influenced American advertising style and the style used by U.S. advertisers elsewhere. Nevett[40] even states that it has constrained American managers. Later models, too, such as the FCB matrix,[41] which categorizes products according to the degree of involvement and cognitive-affective attitude components, are derived from the concept of multiple hierarchies. Some measurement systems are based on this hierarchy of effects thinking, for example the day-after recall (DAR) as a pretesting technique. DAR results are biased against commercials that depend on mood or feeling and in favor of advertisements explicitly stating selling points.

High and Low Involvement

One of the early sequences in how advertising works was that people would first learn something about a product or brand, then form an attitude or feeling, and consequently take action, which meant purchasing the product or at least going to the shop with the intention of buying. This sequence is called "learn-feel-do." It was later seen as mainly applicable to products of "high involvement," such as cars, for which the decision-making process was assumed to be highly rational. This so-called high-involvement model assumes that consumers are active participants in the process of gathering information and making a decision. In contrast, there are low-involvement products, such as detergents or other fast-moving consumer goods, with related low-involvement behavior when there is little interest in the product. The concept of low involvement is based on Herbert Krugman's[42] theory that television is a low-involvement medium that can generate brand awareness but has little impact on peoples' attitudes. The low-involvement sequence was assumed to be "learn-do-feel." Again, knowledge comes first, after that purchase, and only after having used the product would one form an attitude.

The FCB planning model[43] suggests four sequences in the process by which advertising influences consumers: (a) learn-feel-do, (b) feel-learn-do, (c) do-learn-feel, and (d) do-feel-learn. The first two sequences are related to high involvement: the first with respect to knowledge and the second with respect to feelings. The third and fourth sequences are low involvement, regarding thinking and feeling, respectively. Miracle[44] argues that for the Japanese consumer another sequence is valid: feel-do-learn. Japanese advertising is based on building trust, a relationship between the company (rarely are there brands) and the consumer. The purpose of Japanese advertising is to please the consumer and to build "dependency" (*amae*[45]), and this is done by the indirect approach. As a result, "feel" is the initial response of the Japanese consumer, after which action is taken: a visit to the shop to purchase the product. Only after this comes knowledge. Miracle suggests that this sequence also applies to Korean and Chinese consumer responses. It may well apply to all collectivistic cultures.

Argument From Consequence

Later models continue to follow the assumption that the advertising concept is what classical rhetoricians call an "argument from consequence," following the cause-effect way of thinking. Petty and Ciacoppo's[46] elaboration likelihood model (ELM) is one of the most advanced U.S. models of how advertising works. Taking into account the role of involvement, it states that persuasion follows a central route, peripheral route, or both. Within the central route, a person engages in thoughtful consideration of the issue-relevant information (i.e., the arguments) within a message. If the person lacks the motivation or ability to undertake issue-relevant thinking, persuasion follows a peripheral route.

Various studies have been conducted to find the influence of pictures, in both the central route and the peripheral route, reviewing affective responses as determinants of persuasion. Conclusions such as "the persuasion process may be more complex than is suggested by a 'picture evokes effect' sequence"[47] demonstrate the sequential thinking of how advertising works. They also reflect the assumption that this sequential process is based purely and solely on the persuasiveness of communication.

With respect to television commercials, it is important to understand that each image follows another because the commercial's creator designed that particular sequence of images to achieve a particular effect.[48] This, again, is linear thinking about how communication processing works.

Expectancy theory, which claims that people of Western cultures are driven by the expectation that their acts will produce results,[49] is also behind the Western philosophy of how advertising works. People vary across cultures in the amount of control they believe they have over their environment. Most Americans strongly believe that they control their environment; Moslems believe that things will happen only if God wills them to happen; and the Chinese believe in "joss" or luck, without there being any causal relation between one event and another. Differences between internal and external locus of control were discussed with respect to decision making in Chapter 6 under "Decision Making."

Styles of Research

Advertising research is dominated by the American information processing approach with its focus on verbal information. There is an implicit assumption that consumers see ads in terms of logical, rational "reason-why" arguments. This is in line with the assumptions discussed in the previous section. For researchers of one culture, operating on one set of assumptions, it is difficult to measure the effects of communication fabricated in another culture and based on an altogether different set of assumptions. Styles of research resulting from different intellectual styles will influence the way people of different cultures think about how advertising works. Also, within the "Western" world there appear to be fundamentally different approaches. The differences between East and West are even more difficult to understand. Differences in thinking patterns are greatest between the Western world and the cultures of Asia. Understanding how advertising works in Asian countries asks for understanding the culture. Japanese advertising relies heavily on the indirect, soft approach or entertainment, an advertising style that generally is not assumed to be effective in the United States and other Western cultures. The explanation given by the Japanese is that this style appeals to the inner circle, whereas the direct approach is for the outer circle and thus does not appeal to the emotions, does not reach the heart of the people. Generally, the indirect approach in advertising, as favored by the Japanese, can be explained by collectivism: Addressing the individual directly would alienate him or her from the group. Another explanation for the indirect or entertainment style, an important advertising form in Japan, is the duality of *honne* and *tatemae,* the heart, feelings, and drives and the conventions of behavior. The Japanese experience difficulty with the dual structure of *tatemae* and *honne,* and "when realizing that it is difficult to live in that world, poems are born."[50] This corresponds with the overriding need for advertising to be entertaining, not lecturing. The Japanese prefer reserve over eloquence, the indirect approach over rhetoric.

Models of How Advertising Works

Franzen,[51] in his inaugural lecture as Professor of Advertising at Amsterdam University, described seven different models of how advertising works: the sales-response model, the persuasion model, the involvement model, the awareness model, the emotions model, the likability model, and the symbolism model. These can be linked to different ways of thinking about how advertising works and may be well used to explain how advertising works for different cultures. I have added hypotheses about which model might fit which culture best.

1. The sales-response model is based on the simple stimulus-response model. The message is very direct, with the only objective being direct sales—the "buy now" strategy. This is the ultimate Anglo-Saxon model, based on short-term effect. It will fit cultures of the configuration of small power distance, individualistic, masculine, weak uncertainty avoidance, and short-term thinking.

2. The persuasion model can be compared with the "injection needle" theory of how communication works. The objective is short-term shift of attitude, buying intention, and brand preference through providing arguments. The "lecture" advertising form, which uses presenters, demonstrations, and testimonials, fits this model. All are based on direct communication. The model is based on the assumption that advertising should be persuasive and direct. It fits cultures with the configuration low power distance, individualistic, and masculine, thus the United States, England, Germany, Switzerland, and Austria.

3. The involvement model has as its objective the building of relationships between consumers and brands by creating emotional closeness. The philosophy behind this model is that the brand must become a "personality" to which human characteristics are attributed. Advertising must transfer associations from the brand to the consumer. This model is based on a more indirect advertising process. It will fit relatively well in feminine and individualistic cultures, thus the Netherlands, Scandinavia, and France.

4. The awareness model is primarily based on creating awareness in order to differentiate brands from similar brands. Association, metaphors, humor, and other forms of indirect advertising are based on this model. This is a model that, depending on the execution, may well cross borders. It may fit well in those cultures that need awareness as part of building trust, thus collectivistic cultures (e.g., Spain, Asia, Latin America). Because of its lack of persuasiveness, it may not work in cultures of the configuration masculine, individualistic (United States, England, Germany).

5. The objective of the emotions model is to create a positive attitude and brand loyalty. It builds a connection between brands and emotions. The type of emotion is often linked with the product category. This is the model

for collectivistic and feminine cultures, for building relationships and trust. The emotions as such and the intensity will vary across cultures according to the level of uncertainty avoidance.

6. The likability model is based on the assumption that liking the advertisement will lead to liking the brand. In countries used to the direct approach, thus conditioned to expect arguments and persuasion, this is not a good model. This is the model of how advertising works in collectivistic cultures. It may work best in weak uncertainty avoidance cultures, but that depends on the execution format. The type of presentation will decide the sort of entertainment. Likability is the most important criterion for Japanese advertising, where the objective of advertising is to make friends with consumers and get them to trust and depend on the seller. This goal is achieved by telling a story or by entertaining the audience; to put the consumer in a good mood, to induce him or her to go to the shop where real information about the product is available.

7. The objective of the symbolism model is to turn the brand into a symbol, a code, to help distinguish the consumer from other consumers. It gives cohesion to a subculture. This model is very culture specific. Symbols reflect culture: They can be symbols of status, success, self-expression, stability, or any other reflection of culture. Symbols are the communication mode of cultures of large power distance combined with strong uncertainty avoidance, but also of collectivistic cultures, thus all of Asia, France, and the south of Europe.

Conclusion

How communication works in general and, related to that, how advertising works, is culture-bound. In one culture, advertising is persuasive by nature, in another it is meant to build trust between companies and consumers. Thus, models of one culture cannot be projected to other cultures. The basic difference is between communication styles. The different verbal and nonverbal communication styles can be recognized in both interpersonal and mass communication, and culture clusters can be defined in which one or the other style prevails. The ability to distinguish among the different communication styles is the first step to understanding why an advertisement cannot be equally effective in all cultures. The next step is to understand that the way people process information is based on cultural learning. For some, pictures contain more information than words; for others, the only way to convey meaning is verbal. A large part of the advertising world still thinks about advertising as a stimulus-response model. Human perception is not a simple reception of stimuli, however. We try to match external stimuli with internal patterns of thought or concepts. These internal patterns are learned and thus influenced by culture. Advertising is effective when this match is achieved. If the advertising message is a stimulus that does not match internal patterns of the target group, the advertising effort is wasted. That is what is happening with a lot of global advertising, because one message, one stimulus for the whole world cannot match all of the internal patterns of all of the world's populations. Local people have implicit ideas about how advertising works in their own culture, which often do not go beyond gut feeling. Academics and researchers across cultures have disputes about the different theories of how advertising works. Maybe no one is right, or maybe all are right if each looks at how advertising works from the perspective of her or his own culture, which may indeed be very different from the perspective of their counterparts in other cultures. The consequence of the different roles of advertising across cultures for international advertisers is that they cannot use one standard for measuring effectiveness worldwide.

Notes

1. Levo-Henriksson, R. (1994). *Eyes upon wings: Culture in Finnish and US television news.* Doctoral dissertation. Research Report 1/1994. Oy. Yleisradio Ab. Helsinki, p. 84.

2. "Perspectives." (1996, September 9). *Newsweek,* p. 11.

3. Benedict, R. (1974). *The chrysanthemum and the sword.* Rutland, VT: Charles E. Tuttle, pp. 165, 192-193.

4. Relevant literature: (1) Gerbner, G., Gross, L., & Melody, T. (1973). *Communication technology and social policy.* New York: Wiley-Interscience. (2) Gerbner, G., Gross, L., Morgan, M., & Signorelli, N. (1980). "The mainstreaming of America: Violence profile no. 11." *Journal of Communication, 30*(3), pp. 10-29. (3) Signorelli, N., & Morgan, M. (Eds.). (1990). *Cultivation analysis: New directions in media effects research.* Newbury Park, CA: Sage.

5. Fiske, J. (1982). *Introduction to communication studies* (2nd ed.). New York: Routledge, p. 150.

6. Hall, E. T., & Reed Hall, M. (1983). *Hidden differences: How to communicate with the Germans.* Germany: Stern.

7. Hofstede, G. H. (1991). *Cultures and organizations: Software of the mind.* New York: McGraw-Hill, p. 60.

8. From: *Knowledge of and attitudes to biotechnology: The influence of national cultures* (Report for the European Commission, 30 June 1995 [Contract No. BIO2-CT-0608]).

9. Gudykunst, W. B., & Ting-Toomey, S. (1988). *Culture and interpersonal communication.* Newbury Park, CA: Sage, p. 87.

10. Gudykunst & Ting-Toomey (1988), *Culture and interpersonal communication*, p. 90.

11. Gudykunst & Ting-Toomey (1988), *Culture and interpersonal communication*, p. 93.

12. Gudykunst & Ting-Toomey (1988), *Culture and interpersonal communication*, pp. 99-115.

13. Gudykunst & Ting-Toomey (1988), *Culture and interpersonal communication*, pp. 43-50.

14. Roland, A. (1988). *In search of self in India and Japan*. Princeton, NJ: Princeton University Press, p. 284.

15. Gudykunst & Ting-Toomey (1988), *Culture and interpersonal communication*, pp. 40-43.

16. Maleville, M. (1993). "How boringly respectable can you get? A study of business slogans in three countries." *Toegepaste Taalwetenschap, 2*(3), p. 197.

17. Hall, E. T. (1983). *The dance of life*. Garden City, NY: Doubleday/Anchor, p. 113.

18. Ferraro, G. P. (1994). *The cultural dimension of international business*. Hemel Hempstead, Hertfordshire, UK: Prentice Hall International, p. 5.

19. Scott, L. M. (1994). "Images in advertising: The need for a theory of visual rhetoric." *Journal of Consumer Research, 21*(September), 269.

20. Shannon, C., & Weaver, W. (1949). *The mathematical theory of communication*. Urbana: University of Illinois Press.

21. Buttle, F. A. (1995). "Marketing communication theory: What do the texts teach our students?" *International Journal of Advertising, 14*, 297-313.

22. J. Carey, "Communication and culture," in *Communication Research,* April 1975, cited in Lannon, J. (1994). "Mosaics of meaning: Anthropology and marketing." *The Journal of Brand Management, 2*(3).

23. Dentsu Inc. (1994). *Japan 1995 marketing and advertising yearbook*. Tokyo: Dentsu Inc., p. 199.

24. Miracle, G. E. (1987). "Feel-do-learn: An alternative sequence underlying Japanese consumer response to television commercials." In F. G. Feasley (Ed.), *The proceedings of the 1987 Conference of the American Academy of Advertising*. (Contact Robert King, AAA Executive Secretary, School of Business, University of Richmond, Richmond, VA 23173)

25. Scott (1994), *Images in advertising*, pp. 261-263.

26. Thanks to Bob Waisfisz, of ITIM, who analyzed and explained this to me.

27. van Nieuwstadt, M. (1995, November 15). "Disney past zich aan Europa aan." *NRC Handelsblad.*

28. Miracle, G. E., Taylor, C. R., & Chang, K. Y. (1992). "Culture and advertising executions: A comparison of selected characteristics of Japanese and US television commercials." *Journal of International Consumer Marketing, 4*(4), 89-113.

29. Rossiter, J., & Percy, L. (1987). *Advertising and promotion management*. New York: McGraw-Hill, pp. 206-215.

30. Hunt, S. D. (1993). "Objectivity in marketing theory and research." *Journal of Marketing, 57*(April), pp. 76-91.

31. McCloskey, D. N. (1985). *The rhetoric of economics* (Series in the Rhetoric of the Human Sciences). Madison: University of Wisconsin Press.

32. Lannon, J. (1994). "Mosaics of meaning: Anthropology and marketing." *The Journal of Brand Management, 2*(3), 160.

33. *Webster's new twentieth century unabridged dictionary* (2nd ed.). (1979). Englewood Cliffs, NJ: Prentice Hall.

34. Rosenberg, K. E., & Blair, M. H. (1994, July/August). "Observations: The long and short of persuasive advertising." *Journal of Advertising Research,* pp. 63-69.

35. Zinkhan, G. M. (1994, March). "International advertising: A research agenda." *Journal of Advertising, 23*(1), 11-17.

36. Johansson, J. K. (1994, March). "The sense of 'Nonsense': Japanese TV advertising." *Journal of Advertising, 23*(1).

37. Blackston, M. (1996, February). "Can advertising pre-tests predict the longevity of advertising effects?" *Marketing and Research Today, 24*(1), 11-17.

38. Biel, A. L. (1990, September). "Love the Ad. Buy the product?" *Admap.*

39. Lannon, J. (1992, March). "Asking the right questions—What do people do with advertising?" *Admap,* pp. 11-16.

40. Nevett, T. (1992). "Differences between American and British television advertising: Explanations and implications." *Journal of Advertising, 21*(4), 61-71.

41. Vaughn, R. (1980, June 9). "The consumer mind: How to tailor ad strategies." *Advertising Age.*

42. Krugman, H. E. (1965). "The impact of television advertising: Learning without involvement." *Public Opinion Quarterly, 29*(Fall), 349-356.

43. Vaughn (1980), "The consumer mind."

44. Miracle (1987), "Feel-do-learn."

45. *Amae* (Takeo Doi [1973], *The anatomy of dependence,* Kodansha International) can be explained as follows: The Japanese divide their lives into inner and outer sectors, each with its own, different standards of behavior. In the inner circle, the individual is automatically accepted, there is interdependence and automatic warmth, love, or *amae,* of which the best translation is "passive love" or dependency. Members of the inner circle experience this *amae* between each other, but it does not exist in the outer circle. You lose *amae* when you enter the outer circle. You don't expect *amae* in the outer circle.

46. Petty, R. E., & Ciacoppo, J. T. (1986). "The elaboration likelihood model of persuasion." In L. Berkowitz (Ed.), *Advances in experimental social psychology* (Vol. 19). New York: Academic Press. Also in: *Communication and persuasion: Central and peripheral routes to attitude change* (1986), New York: Springer.

47. Miniard, P. W., Bhatla, S., Lord, K. L., Dickson, P. R., & Unnava, H. R. (1992). "Picture-based persuasion processes and the moderating role of involvement." *Journal of Consumer Research, 18*(June), 92-107.

48. Unnava, H. R., & Burnkrant, R. E. (1991, May). "An imagery-processing view of the role of pictures in print advertisements." *Journal of Marketing Research,* pp. 226-231.

49. Adler, N. J. (1991). *International dimensions of organizational behavior.* Belmont, CA: Wadsworth, p. 158.

50. Doi, T. (1985). *The anatomy of self.* New York: Kodansha America / Tokyo: Kodansha International, p. 62.

51. Franzen, G. (1994, September 16). *Reclame: Geloofshandeling of verkoopinstrument?* Unpublished Inaugural Lecture as Professor of Advertising, University of Amsterdam.

CHAPTER 8

Value Paradoxes in Advertising Appeals

Three aspects of advertising can be pointed out that are each prone to influence by culture: (a) the values and motives included in the appeal, the central message; (b) the basic advertising form, which is related to the advertising styles of cultures; and (c) the execution: the casting and activities of people, the setting, and the interrelationship. This chapter will focus on the appeals in advertising.

Appeals in Advertising

The appeal in advertising is a comprehensive concept. The appeal includes values and creative strategy. Wells, Burnett, and Moriarty[1] define an appeal as "something that makes the product particularly attractive or interesting to the consumer." Examples of appeals provided by Wells and colleagues are security, esteem, fear, sex, and sensory pleasure. The appeal is also used to describe a general creative strategy. Emphasis on the price is an economy appeal. A status appeal is used for presenting quality, expensive products.

The combination of the appeal (including motives), advertising form, and execution will reflect cultural values. In this chapter I will focus on how appeals reflect the core values of culture and link them with the five Hofstede dimensions. Advertising appeals do not necessarily follow the norms of a culture, they may even go against them. To understand this, we first have to return to the value paradox.

The Value Paradox: The Desirable and the Desired

Some values can easily be recognized as a reflection of culture. Self-actualization, self-interest, and self-esteem are examples of such values. They fit individualistic cultures. Achievement reflects masculinity. Doing it your own way, going it alone are expressions of values of an individualistic culture. But belonging is also a strong value of individualistic cultures. This seems paradoxical. That is because there are often opposing elements in one value. Thus, advertising appeals or claims may represent two opposing statements about values. This is related to the desirable and the desired, the distinction between what people think ought to be desired and what people actually desire, or how people think the world ought to be versus what people want for themselves.[2] The desired and the desirable do not always overlap. The desirable refers to the general norms of a society and is worded in terms of right or wrong, in absolute terms. The desired is what we want, what we consider important for ourselves. It is what the majority in a country actually do.

There is another paradox: the reflection of the gap between "words" and "deeds," between what people say they do or will do and what they actually do. Values as the desired are closer to deeds than values as the desirable. Because of the gaps between the desirable, the desired, and actual behavior, behavior may not correspond with the desirable, and norms for the desirable can be completely detached from behavior.

We speak of norms as soon as we deal with a collectivity. In the case of the desired, the norm is statistical: It indicates the values actually held by the majority. In the case of the desirable, the norm is absolute, pertaining to what is ethically right. The desired relates more to pragmatic issues, the desirable to ideology. The desired relates to choice, to what is important and preferred; it relates to the "me" and the "you." The desirable relates to what is approved or disapproved, to what is good, right, what one ought to do and what one should agree with; it refers to people in general (see Table 8.1).[3]

The distinction between the desirable and the desired leads to seemingly paradoxical values within one culture. This paradox may even make cultures appear to be similar or to be moving in a similar direction. It may confuse people in the sense that they think cultures are becoming alike. An example is the conclusion that the Japanese are becoming individualistic because of an increased focus on individuality in behavior and communication. In reality, individuality in Japan reflects the need for performance and competitiveness.

Individualism means "doing things your way, going it alone." This is the norm of an individualistic society. Yet companies cannot perform well if all individuals do things their own way. As a result, there is a great deal of focus on teamwork in individualistic societies. Because too much individualism also creates loneliness, the desired or actual behavior is opposed to the desirable: belonging. Belonging is an important American value. In Japan, the opposite is of importance: individuality, or any other value, need, or

TABLE 8.1 *The Desirable Versus the Desired*

The desirable	The desired
The norm, what ought to be	What people want for themselves
Words	Deeds
Approval, disapproval	Choice
What is good, right	What is attractive, preferred
For people in general	For me and for you
Ideology	Pragmatism

want that carries the desire to be different. In a collectivistic society, belonging to the in-group is an implicit part of culture, the desirable. Yet to be an entrepreneur, one has to distinguish oneself from the group. The value related to entrepreneurship is called individuality. It is the desired of Japanese culture: In order to be competitive, the Japanese must be more individualistic. This explains the Japanese focus on individuality. It reflects the decline of extreme subordination of the individual to the group.

The Value Paradox as an Effective Advertising Instrument

In advertising, the opposing values of a culture, although often paradoxical, appear to be effective because they relate to the important aspects of people's lives. Belonging is a ubiquitous value in American advertising, particularly in the sentimental, emotional form. It is included in the concept of "homecoming." It is not a value to use in an appeal in Japanese advertising.

The desired and the desirable are reflected in people's behavior and in how they relate to each other. Both the desired and the desirable are recognized in advertising appeals or claims, but they may be expressed in opposing ways. This makes it even more difficult to understand words and concepts that are labels of values of a culture other than one's own. An example is the concept of sharing in the English language. Superficially, this may imply a nonindividualistic, feminine, caring concept, meaning "not keeping things for oneself." Yet in masculine and individualistic culture it reflects more, it reflects winning, communicating one's success and achievement to others. "One shares only the positive things of oneself, success, one does not share failure." One has to be very cautious with such concepts, as they are ambiguous and when translated into other languages half of the meaning may be lost. If translated, a positive meaning may also change into a negative one.

Paradoxical value statements can be recognized in three ways:

1. Statements contrary to common belief. For example, that the Japanese are individualizing, whereas they actually are collectivistic. As in all increasingly wealthy societies, the Japanese are focusing more on individuality, but their behavior is collectivistic compared with Western societies. What is perceived as individualizing is a changing competitive behavior.
2. Statements that seem contradictory, but that may in fact be true. Seemingly opposing values of one dimension, such as "belonging" and "going it alone" in an individualistic culture.
3. As paradox type 2: Values that seem to be paradoxical within one dimension but can be explained by the configuration with other dimensions. An example is simultaneous "equality" and "large wage differences," a paradox of the configuration low power distance and masculinity.

"Trends," or temporary movements in society, often first adopted by the young, may reflect a reaction to a too strong focus on the desirable. Cocooning (withdrawing from the outside world into the inner world of home and friends) was an example of such a trend in the United States: a counterreaction to too strong individualism and competitiveness in an individualistic and masculine society. Cocooning has not been of great significance in feminine cultures and is absent in collectivistic cultures. Trends or fads in business and management tend to reflect actual culture and, in that culture, the gap between the desirable and the desired. For example, chaos management may be the desired but it conflicts with the desirable: control. There are more examples of paradoxes.

Equality Paradox

Equality is a strong desirable value of U.S. culture. The actual behavior of Americans does not show so much equality. American behavior is related to fairness or that people should get what they deserve if they have the capabilities and work hard. This value results in inequality: If you have worked hard, you have earned the right to be different, to earn more—sometimes excessively more—money then others. CEOs of U.S. companies can earn 40 times as much as an ordinary production worker. In 1994, the biggest increases in income inequalities were in America, Britain, and New Zealand. Wage differences in most of continental Europe changed by much less.[4]

Equality in the United States means the poor have equal rights to become rich. Equality in a large part of Europe means the rich should be equally "poor."

Dependence and Freedom Paradoxes

Another paradox can be found in dependence versus independence, the opposing values related to power distance and individualism. In large power distance and collectivistic cultures children remain dependent on their parents much longer than in small power distance and individualistic cultures, in which children are supposed to go their own way, be self-reliant, and make their own decisions at an early age. This is extreme in the United States. An example is an event in 1996, when a 7-year-old girl, who wanted to set the record as the youngest pilot in the world, crashed and died. Her mother was quoted as saying: "It was her own decision." Independence is a widely used concept or cue in Western advertising, but also in Japan. There, an appeal in advertising is independence as opposed to dependency, which is such a strong part of Japanese culture.

Related to dependency are the opposing values and paradoxes of freedom. In small power distance cultures, freedom means independence. In a collectivistic culture, the opposing values are freedom and harmony. Freedom can mean disharmony, as one ought to conform to the group. Freedom versus belonging can be opposing values for feminine cultures. Because of the affiliation needs in feminine cultures, belonging is an implicit value and is related to conformance, consensus. Yet in order to succeed, one wants to express oneself, be different. This goes against the norm, the desirable. Freedom reflects the desired. In a strong uncertainty avoidance culture, too much freedom may lead toward undesired chaos, which cannot be tolerated, so the opposing value is order. In strong uncertainty avoidance cultures freedom breeds uncertainty, while in weak uncertainty avoidance cultures freedom breeds success. People in strong uncertainty avoidance cultures take calculated risks to avoid failure, in weak uncertainty avoidance cultures people take risks to succeed. Freedom paradoxes vary by culture.

Freedom/Dependence (France)

Freedom/Harmony (Japan)

Freedom/Belonging (the Netherlands)
Freedom/Order (Germany)

Success Paradoxes

The norm, the desirable, in masculine societies is that one wants to shine, to show one's success. Success is communicated, shared, and displayed because it is natural to show off. This is not the norm, the desirable, in feminine societies. Although a universal desire is to be recognized when one achieves something, success cannot be demonstrated directly. Because showing off is against the norm, demonstrating success must be done indirectly. While the British (masculine culture) can say straightforwardly that they are the best, as British Telecom does: "We have the best connections," the Dutch, Danes, and Swedes (feminine) are not likely to do so. The paradox is frequently found in appeals such as, "There is more to it than meets the eye" or "True refinement comes from within" (Volvo, Sweden). Advertising in a masculine culture says: "Show your neighbors," whereas in a feminine culture advertising will say: "Don't show your neighbors." The paradox is in an advertising claim like, "Brilliant in its simpleness" (Omega watches, the Netherlands): on the one hand, one should not show off (the desirable), yet, if successful, one wants to be recognized (the desired). It can also be recognized in pay-offs or taglines that tend to summarize the company's mission statement. An example is the statement by Philips Electronics: "Let's make things better."

> Mazda Miata, United States: "The best selling car in the world."
> Carlsberg, Denmark: "Probably the best beer in the world."
> Swissair, Switzerland: "Best in Business."
> Philips Electronics, the Netherlands: "Let's make things better."

The Innovation Paradox

The paradox traditional/innovative is found in most of Western Europe and the United States. Innovativeness, embracing the new, is something that is implicit in weak uncertainty avoidance cultures. Characteristic of strong uncertainty avoidance is resistance to change, a desire for stability. For strong uncertainty avoidance cultures, accepting the new is the desirable value, but resistance to change is the desired value. Thus, advertising appeals may be paradoxical: *nouveau* or *neu* is an appeal that is as important for the French and the Germans as it is for the British, although the French and Germans are cultures of strong uncertainty avoidance. In France and Germany, innovativeness may represent the desirable, the norm for a society, while the actual behavior of consumers may be conservative, preferring tradition over innovation.[5] Although the cue word *new* is much seen in advertising, actual buying behavior may not be so innovative. The Spanish way of life as reflected in advertising is warm, caring about others, different and original, even if full of unpredictable factors. It reflects the stability/originality paradox. On the one hand, the Spanish feel the desire to be modern and innovative; on the other hand, the desirable is stability, because of the difficulty of coping with ambiguity.

It should be like it used to be.
New is better.

The Tension Paradox

All people will have times of tension, stress; the increased pace of business in particular will cause stress in all societies. In weak uncertainty avoidance societies, however, where people do not show their emotions, tension is not expressed explicitly. So in the perception of members of strong uncertainty avoidance cultures, tension is nonexistent or not easy to recognize. The contrast between the direct and the indirect way of reducing tension is frequently found in advertising. A much-used German advertising appeal is tension or anxiety reduction, expressed explicitly: Airlines, banks, insurance companies, travel agencies, and the like use anxiety reduction in their appeals. An example is, "Ready for the unexpected" (Zürich Insurance Group). This may appeal to anybody, but relatively more to the Germans and the Swiss than to the British and Americans, who may respond by saying, "So what?" The strange and unexpected is far less threatening to them than it is to the Germans and the Swiss. Another example is the headline of a Lufthansa advertisement: "What a day. Lousy weather. A falling stock market. A terrible meeting. A dreadful traffic jam. And then, at last, something to smile about." Although strong uncertainty avoidance cultures build up stress more than weak uncertainty avoidance cultures do, both appreciate relaxation. The way to express this is explicit in the strong uncertainty avoidance cultures and implicit in the weak uncertainty avoidance cultures. Examples are the numerous humorous advertisements of the

British and the "Take a Break" campaign by KitKat. Humor releases tension in an indirect way.

> Ready for the unexpected.
> Take a break.

Examples of Appeals by Dimension

In this section, examples of appeals found in advertising will be described by dimension, as well as activities and interactions between people in television commercials that are often deemed to be "only executional," but that reflect basic cultural values.

Power Distance

Status symbols are more frequently used in large power distance cultures than in small power distance cultures. An example is the use of certain status sports such as golf and related symbols such as golf balls. Power claims can be verbal and direct: "Save your power for the work place" (from an advertisement for the Lexus in Singapore) or as a verbal or visual metaphor: blue blood or yachts, referring to royalty (found in advertising in Portugal). In the execution, power distance can be shown in the way people interrelate or by the type of people shown (older vs. younger). In large power distance cultures, the elder (mother or aunt) advises the younger (daughter or niece), as found in commercials for the P&G brand ACE in Italy and France (Illustrations 8.1 and 8.2). In small power distance cultures, the younger advises the elder (daughter advises mother), as in P&G commercials for Yes in Sweden and Dreft in the Netherlands (Illustration 8.3). A typical Japanese example of large power distance behavior is in a commercial for Sinko Sangyo "Saideria Home" that reflects the custom that, when a group of people share a car, the boss or any higher-placed person must always be brought home first, even if others live closer to the road taken. In this commercial, this custom allows the whole group to admire the nice home of the boss.

Respect for old age in large power distance cultures is reflected by the fact that there are more senior actors in television commercials, and presenters are generally older. A Spanish advertisement for Brandy 103 shows a young man looking with interest and admiration at a much older man. The claim is also related to this: "You know it . . . you will reach 103." In this

Illustrations 8.1–8.4 (From top left to right.)

advertisement, the old man is the one who knows best and the younger one is the learner (Illustration 8.4). The master-learner relationship (*sensei*) is also frequently found in Japanese advertising, for example for Ootsuka curry, where an old man is playing the role of the expert advising a much younger woman.

Independence is an appeal reflecting the desirable in small power distance cultures. In large power distance cultures it reflects the desired. A Japanese ad for Honda uses the word in the copy "I'm independent" in English (Illustration 8.5). In large power distance cultures, children are more protected and are independent at a later age than in small power distance cultures. Showing a young child alone, struggling to enter a building with his bicycle, as done in a Dutch commercial for Blue Band margarine (Illustration 8.6), is not accepted in large power distance cultures. The Dutch will see the boy as an enterprising, independent child, while in other cultures he will be pitied because he is left on his own. Similarly, the baby in a Dutch commercial for Libero diapers, who takes off his grandfather's hairpiece, may be appealing to a small power distance culture, but not to a large power distance culture (Illustration 8.7). An argument can be that "it's only a baby," but it is the advertiser who makes the baby do it. Children's behavior in

Illustrations 8.5–8.7 (From left to right.)

school, if depicted in television commercials, will vary according to the degree of power distance. A Dutch television commercial for KitKat (candy bar) based on the "Take a break, take a KitKat" platform, shows a female schoolteacher who is obviously being driven crazy by her students. A scene like that can only be used in small power distance cultures. Generally, students in large power distance cultures show more respect for their teachers. The commercial would not be appreciated in Germany, either, a culture combining strong uncertainty avoidance with small power distance, where internal discipline would prevent such behavior. The same is true for advertisements referring to the relationship between bosses and subordinates. A Danish advertisement for Lipton tea saying, "Drive your boss mad by making him drink your tea" should not be used in France, Spain, or Italy. Small power distance is reflected in the antiauthoritarian elements of parody and humorous advertising.

The concept of an "empowered consumer" included in a company's claim "Judge for yourself," or more implicitly when a company stresses its role as a facilitator instead of imposing ideas or creating a dependency relationship with the consumer, is part of small power distance cultures.

Individualism/Collectivism

The communication style of individualistic cultures is low-context, the communication style of collectivistic cultures is high-context. Low-context communication is direct and explicit. The public is addressed in a direct and personalized way. Words like *you, we,* and *I* are frequently used. So are imperatives. U.S. examples are: "When you were a kid . . . " (Doublemint gum), "You flip a switch and . . . " (Detroit Edison), "treat yourself right" (Crystal Light), "You have a dream, make a wish . . . " (Reebok). Low-context communication also means that data and facts are important and product merit appeals and rhetoric are frequently used. High-context communication means indirect communication and the use of symbols and entertainment plays a strong role in advertising. These symbols are not easily recognized by people of another culture. An example is a commercial for Lancaster in Spain, where the last bottle is not taken. As in all collectivist cultures, one does not take the last bit of food because that would suggest there was not enough. In collectivistic societies the indirect approach is favored over the direct approach because a direct address would alienate the individuals from the group. The purpose of using well-known presenters or endorsers in collectivistic cultures is that the audience can associate with them, while in individualistic cultures they address the audience more directly.

With respect to time, individualistic cultures are monochronic, and collectivistic cultures are polychronic. The clock as a symbol of efficiency will not be understood in polychronic cultures.

In collectivistic societies people do not like being alone or eating alone, while in individualistic societies people cherish their privacy. In collectivistic cultures, being alone means you have no friends, no identity. If alone, one is outside the group to which one belongs. An article in *Business Week* of September 12, 1994 reads: "While [in the USA] the gritty, independent hipsters in Levi's '501 Blues' TV ads have drawn young customers like a strong magnet, they didn't click for Levi's Hispanic employees and customers. 'Why is that guy walking down the street alone,' they asked. 'Doesn't he have any friends?' "[6] As a result, Levi's changed their advertising for the Hispanic market and downplayed individualism. This difference between showing individuals, loners, or showing people as part of groups can be explicit and presented directly or implicit and presented indirectly. Examples of the explicit approach include Solo soft drinks in Norway, a cyclist alone (Illustration 8.8), and Panasonic bicycles in Japan, showing a group of cyclists (Illustration 8.9). An Egyptian ad for Close Up toothpaste shows a group of young women (Illustration 8.10).

Concepts reflecting collectivism may be more successful across borders than the highly individualistic approach. Marlboro was more successful in Asia than Camel. The Camel man represents the lonely, masculine individual, while the—also very masculine—Marlboro cowboy is implicitly part of a

Illustrations 8.8–8.10 (From top left to right.)

group. He may sometimes be seen alone, but he always returns to the campfire, to his companions. Presenters in advertising in individualistic cultures can be—and often are—alone, while in collectivistic cultures, one often sees more than one presenter. The value paradox belonging/independence can be recognized in Japanese advertising, where on the one hand one sees groups of people in advertising, while celebrities are frequently depicted alone. This reflects the desired, dreaming of another world of individual success as a contrast to conformance to the group.

Appeals in individualistic cultures can refer explicitly to the individualized self, for example the text of a Tampax commercial on MTV is: "Free yourself, to be yourself. Do what you want, wear what you want any day you want." Examples of individualistic claims are: "Designed for the individual" (Mitsubishi commercials, CNN), "Privat concert" for Privat cigarettes (Denmark), "In a world of conformity some things are still made for the individual" (Herblein watch, *Newsweek*), "Go your own way" (Ford Probe, the United States), and, relating to friendship, "Hurry, for the only thing more annoying than an insistent friend is having no friend at all" (Lexus LS 400, the United States). Examples of collectivistic claims are: "Prospering together (Chiyoda bank, Japanese, in *Newsweek,* Illustration 8.11), "Be part of the group" (J&B whisky, Portugal).

A strong example of the different appeals in collectivistic and individualistic societies are the two following appeals: "It is so good, you want to share it with others" (Hermesetas, Portugal) versus "It is so good, you want to keep it for yourself" (Evers, confectionery, Denmark). Philips Electronics in Spain presents the slogan, *"Juntos hacemos tu vida mejor."* They say "together" and show more than one person. This is in contrast with the German advertisement using the overall claim, "Let's make things better" and in which the "working together" aspect is missing. The name "Tchibo Privat Kaffee" reflects individualism, as do such universalistic claims as "Überall auf der Welt" (everywhere in the world), supposing that the feeling will be the same for all people in the world who drink coffee. *Worldwide* and *world* are power words for individualistic societies.

Collectivism can be implicit, within the context: For example, showing a table with three glasses and two cups of coffee with a bottle (Anis Castellana, Illustration 8.12). Or Heineken, expressing the "Friday feeling" by showing four neckties and four glasses of beer, and the word *Viernes* (Friday) (Illustration 8.13). In contrast is the German advertisement showing one man drinking coffee while reading the newspaper (Illustration 8.14) and the lone man with the German beer Jever (Illustration 8.15). Spanish people do not drink alone, and not at home. They go to a bar to be together with their friends, to socialize. Members of collectivistic cultures have a different perception of hospitality than members of individualistic cultures. In collectivistic cultures an unexpected guest will always be served food, so there is always enough food available. A claim like the Dutch one for party snacks, saying "Duyvis, for when there is a party," is not effective for collectivistic cultures where this sort of product should always be available, not just for a party.

In television commercials in collectivistic cultures, an important part of the setting is showing groups of people and extended families. Grandfathers, grandmothers, or both are often part of a family scene, something less frequently found in individualistic cultures. Examples are a shot of the commercial for Fontaneda biscuits, Spain (Illustration 8.16) and Ministrone, Italy (Illustration 8. 17). In Spain, advertisements for cars show the extended family, including grandparents, as opposed to German advertising where a couple is often shown alone in a lonely landscape. A German Mercedes advertisement says, ironically, "Lots of space for your three brothers and your in-laws." For the audience, the suggestion is implicit that there are better ways to use the space—it is for the yuppie and his golf bag.

Some examples present the extreme individualism of some cultures, such as egoism (Chanel, Illustration 8.18) or Doritos, presenting the wild and nonconforming individualistic lifestyle that appeals only to the small groups of individualistic societies (Illustration 8.19). These are the appeals

Illustrations 8.11–8.19 (From top left to right.)

that express extreme individuality within an individualistic society. There is a commercial for Clearasil on MTV Europe in which two girls, who can be thought to be sisters, talk about skin blemishes, and the elder sister advises the younger to use Clearasil. The younger says "Thanks," assuming she can use her sister's; "No," says the other, "get real, buy it yourself."

Masculinity/Femininity

"Winning," a characteristic of masculine cultures, is reflected in U.S. advertising. In particular, the combination of individualism and masculinity (the configuration of the Anglo-German world) leads to the strong need to win, to be successful and show it, combined with the wish to dominate. Examples of wordings are "Being first," "The one and only in the world," and "Be the best." Hyperbole, persuasiveness, and comparative advertising are reflections of masculinity. A claim like, "We'd like to set the record straight on who finished first in Client/Server Applications" (SAP Integrated Software) is typical for a masculine culture and reflects competitiveness. Another example is, "Compete with the document company" (Xerox). Aggressive typology and layout are another reflection of competitiveness. Dreams and great expectations are part of masculine cultures. "A dream come true," "A world without limits" reflect the value "mastery," the idea that anyone can do anything as long as they try hard. This is opposed to dreams in feminine cultures, where dreams are said to be delusions. In masculine cultures, status is important for demonstrating success. To become Man (Woman) of the Year is the ideal for people in masculine cultures because mediocrity is the proof of failure. Pepsi-Cola used this very effectively in one of their U.S. commercials (Illustrations 8.20, 8.21). Old women may show they can have muscle, as in a shot for a U.S. commercial for Dreyer ice cream (Illustration 8.22). Another reflection of masculinity, typical of American culture, is bigness. America is a land of big egos, big cars, the Big Mac, the quarter-pounder or even half-pounder, and the big idea.[7]

Feminine cultures are characterized by favoring caring, softness, and the small. Much of Volvo advertising (Volvo is from Sweden, the most feminine culture in the world) tends to focus on safety, protecting the family. One commercial expresses this in the extreme, showing only baby feet pattering, saying, "The patter that sells Volvo" (Illustration 8.23). Showing off is negative, which means that status is a negative motive. Celebrity endorsement, an advertising form effective in Anglo-Saxon cultures, is less effective in feminine cultures. In the latter, well-known people (rarely used) and presenters downplay the fact that they are well known or they are belittled or even ridiculed. In more extreme cases, the parody style will be utilized. In the Netherlands, a look-alike of Pamela Andersen is used for an optician retail chain called Hans Anders, belittling her body shapes and suggesting

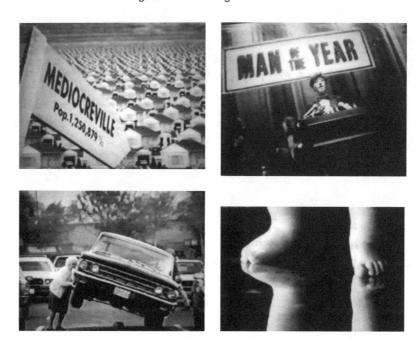

Illustrations 8.20–8.23 (From top left to right.)

that these are as much a prosthesis as eye glasses are. In Spain, a retail chain in opticals uses another "hero" of *Baywatch* running fast and bumping into a shack, for the audience to conclude that he should have worn glasses. The Japanese—Japan is the most masculine culture in the world—love celebrities and use them frequently in advertising. Actors in television commercials are made into celebrities, so-called *talento*.

Strong and weak role differentiation are both reflected in advertising. Italian and German television commercials show bonding between men or between women. In masculine cultures, one sees the combinations of father-son or mother-daughter, while in feminine cultures one also frequently sees the combinations father-daughter and mother-son, as in a commercial showing making cookies for Francine, *farine de blé*. Another example of strong role differentiation is the claim in a Mexican ad for Jethro jeans: "Be his pin-up girl" (Illustration 8.24). A German commercial for Maggi Lasagna (Illustration 8.25) shows a number of housewives cooking together, a scene that would not be accepted in the Netherlands, where couples are shown cooking or cleaning the dishes together. A Dutch advertisement for Pampers shows two young fathers with their babies comparing the diapers (Illustration 8.26).

In Danish advertisements, men can be seen wearing aprons or doing embroidery. Men wearing aprons and playing an active role in family life are also seen in Spanish advertising (Illustrations 8.27 of Caricias, father with baby; Illustration 8.28 of Daewoo, father with baby; and Illustration 8.29 of Edesa, with a man in an apron). Also in France, fathers are seen in ads with their young children (Illustration 8.30, of Lactel, France). Spain is a relatively feminine society. Ads show mothers talking to their sons, not just fathers with sons as in masculine cultures. But French ads also show men in aprons, although then playing the expert cook or a parody on the expert (Illustration 8.31, Vizir). In a Dutch small role differentiation commercial for Dubro, a couple does the washing up together (Illustration 8.32), while in a German commercial for a similar product the man tries, but he plays the stupid guy who burns his hands. It really is the woman's task, and she plays the expert and advises how to use the product (Illustration 8.33).

A masculinity paradox can be found in reverse sexism, meaning that women adopt men's sexist role behavior. It seems to be small role differentiation, but it is a phenomenon of strong role differentiation. In feminine cultures with small role differentiation, men don't mind taking female roles and you find men wearing aprons in advertising. In masculine cultures, women want to take male roles and you either find men in advertising who "help" their wives but not wholeheartedly, or reverse sexism. The "Coca-Cola light break" commercial is an example of such reverse sexism: The young women are openly flirting with the working man. In the Netherlands, a worker in the construction industry filed a complaint against this commercial.

Claims of masculine cultures are more task- or success oriented, whereas claims of feminine cultures will be more affiliation- and relationship oriented. German commercials for detergents tend to argue the effectiveness of the detergent, showing large piles of dirty clothes or many dirty children (Illustrations 8.34 and 8.35, advertising in the Netherlands by the German company Henkel, using a German approach), and the result: large piles of clean clothes or many clean children in brilliant white clothes. The actress is cast in the role of her job of being an effective housewife, not a caring mother. In a feminine culture like the Netherlands, a more affiliation-oriented approach will be more successful, casting the woman in her role of effective mother who has a happy relationship with her children. Clean children are part of her relationship with them. The two are very different approaches. Another opposing concept is that in the German approach of getting more for the same money, reflected in the huge pile of dirty clothes and the small package that can do the job, versus wishing to get equal quality

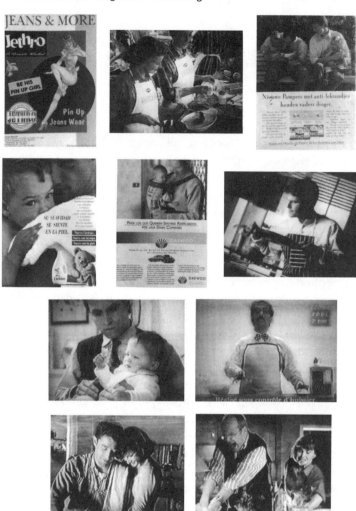

Illustrations 8.24–8.33 (From top left to right.)

for less money, as in the Netherlands, which results in saving. This thrift attitude is reflected in different ways, and a variety of devices are used to show it, from piggy banks (Illustration 8.36, Dreft) to towels with an imprint of a banknote (Illustration 8.37, Sunil).

Modesty is a feminine value and is recognized in the appeals in advertising by Volvo. Underplaying and understatement are elements of feminine cultures, meaning "not showing off." A claim like "There is more to it than meets the eye," is a feminine claim; it reflects the attitude that showing off is "not done." Other examples of feminine claims are: "Brilliant in its

Illustrations 8.34–8.37 (From top left to right.)

simpleness" (Omega watch, the Netherlands, Illustration 8.38), or the understatement in an advertisement for the Audi 100 in the Netherlands: "You have a small house (the visual is a mansion), and a small car, but your neighbors live far enough away, they cannot see it. Moreover, the most important part cannot be seen, it is under the hood" (Illustration 8.39). An opposing claim is by Seat, Italy, showing the car in a garage with a glass door: "It can always be shown, it can always be seen" (Illustration 8.40).

An important difference between masculine and feminine approaches is overstatement versus understatement. A Spanish advertisement for the Audi A4 Avant, an expensive top model of Audi, reads as follows:

> Deceive all of them, saying it's a family car. The new Audi A4 Avant. Never speak about power in public. If, one day, someone mentions something about the 5 valves per cylinder, change the topic, tell him it seems like it's going to rain. 150 hp?—You don't know anything.—Quattro-traction?— What's that? Use the interior space and the variability as a pretext. So that no one thinks that you actually love its design. While traveling with friends make them think that you are bored. Even yawn. Do it and everybody will think that the Audi A4 Avant is only a family car. After all, there are a lot who want to deceive you, saying that they drive a sports car.

Illustrations 8.38–8.40 (From top left to right.)

This text reflects the configuration of collectivism, femininity, and strong uncertainty avoidance. You are not allowed to talk about power in public. You just have it. To avoid confrontations, things should not be said directly. Indirectly, a number of important details are communicated about the technical aspects. This advertisement nicely reflects the femininity paradox: It reflects modesty and harmony, yet it mentions the power of the car.

The configuration of individualism and masculinity explains the hyperbole of American advertising: "All the cosmetics in the world can't do what we can" (Illustration 8.41), "The only plastic wrap with Reynolds strength behind it," and "The greatest of ease" for a white plastic garden chair (Illustration 8.42). Other U.S. examples of hype are: "You'll never find a softer toilet paper than new Northern Ultra," "The pain reliever that hospitals use most," and "The world's number one contact lens" (Acuvue).

A consequence of the configuration masculinity-individualism is the importance of "getting the most out of life," a claim frequently found in U.S. advertising, for example, expressed as "Sacrifice nothing." The desire to get the most out of life is the typical value for masculine-individualistic cultures and reflected in many claims, such as "Now you can lead a fuller life" in

Illustrations 8.41–8.43 (From top left to right.)

advertisements for shampoo, sanitary napkins, and the like, in U.S. media. The claim used by Opel in the Netherlands is paradoxical: "And you thought that you could not have everything in life." Although both the United States and the United Kingdom score high on the masculinity index, there is a difference. The U.S. scores much higher on uncertainty avoidance, which also influences the difference between overstatement and understatement. In the United Kingdom, one also wants to state that one has success, but this is often done "tongue in cheek." Illustration 8.43 shows a shot of a commercial for Persil in the United Kingdom, in which a young man has successfully applied for his—apparently—first job, thanks to his clean shirt. At the end of the commercial, he is seen walking away with his shirttail out of his trousers.

Uncertainty Avoidance

Strong uncertainty avoidance translates into the need for explanations, structure, long copy, testing, and testimonials by experts, but also into high

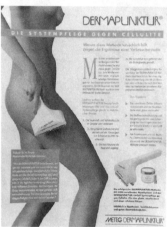

Illustrations 8.44–8.46 (From top left to right.)

regard for technology and design. This is easily recognized in the advertising styles of Germany and Italy. The examples shown are Olivetti (Illustration 8.44) and Lancia (Illustration 8.45). German advertisements are highly structured and detailed. An example of the ultimate, detailed German advertisement is one for Dermapunktur (Illustration 8.46). The competence of the manufacturer must be demonstrated. Showing how a product works, with all the technical details, is important. This is in contrast with weak uncertainty avoidance cultures where the result is more important.

Design is a strong element of German and Italian advertising, though German advertisements tend to focus more on the technological aspect, while the Italians focus more on the outer appearance. The French and the Spanish are more art and fashion oriented.

Testing and test reports are favored in all strong uncertainty avoidance cultures, although the execution tends to be different. Examples of German expressions are: *"Die Besten im Testen"* (The best in the test, Daewoo,

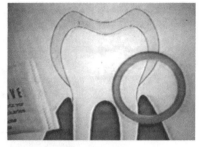

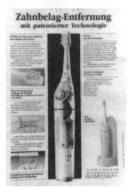

Illustrations 8.47–8.50 (From top left to right.)

Germany) and *"Testsieger"* (Test winner, Sun Micro). Testing can be part of a commercial; see a shot of a commercial for Vernel, a German fabric softener (Illustration 8.47). Technical explanations about the product can be very detailed for all sorts of products, and most for toothpaste and related products. Although much of the advertising for toothpaste tends to focus on how it protects the teeth, this is emphasized even more strongly in strong uncertainty avoidance cultures (Illustrations 8.48, 8.49, and 8.50).

Two other aspects of strong uncertainty avoidance cultures are showing emotions and being well groomed. Showing emotions, or using emotions as an appeal, is common in Italy. In advertisements from the southern European and Germanic countries, people are significantly better dressed than in advertising from the northern European cultures. The difference is the degree of uncertainty avoidance. Two examples of well-groomed people are in ads from Italy, for Happydent (Illustration 8.51) and for Cameo chocolate drink, showing a well-dressed schoolboy (Illustration 8.52); and the opposite, less well-groomed people, are two young women for a Seiko Message Watch in the Netherlands (illustration 8.53), a housewife in a Norwegian ad

Illustrations 8.51–8.55 (From top left to right.)

(Illustration 8.54), and the ultimate understatement of sophistication in an Australian ad for Stella Artois beer (illustration 8.55).

Presenters are experts, the competent professional or the competent boss. The professor or physician type—preferably wearing a white coat—is characteristic for Germany and Italy (Illustrations 8.56 and 8.57, respectively). The professional expert is characteristic for France, Belgium, and Spain (Illustration 8.58, Belgium). They can be anonymous or celebrities. Celebrities, if used, must play the role of the expert or be the expert. In small power distance-weak uncertainty avoidance cultures a parody of the expert is favored, as in Illustration 8.59, a shot from a commercial for Worthington Draught bitter, presenting a parody on the housewife expert testimonial by a man dressed as a woman.

An appeal recognized in advertising in strong uncertainty avoidance cultures is relaxation in the sense of relief from anxiety and tension. This is expressed explicitly, whereas relief from tension is more implicit in weak uncertainty avoidance cultures. An example is the "Take a Break" campaign by KitKat. The platform of that campaign is the "break." It is executed in different ways in different cultures. Most British executions are very humorous and express the sudden moment of relaxation. An example is a couple who try to teach a monkey to act like a human being. After some time, they sit down in a relaxed posture and have a KitKat. The monkey copies their behavior. The moment of relaxation comes when they turn around and see

Illustrations 8.56–8.59 (From top left to right.)

the monkey. Dutch executions are less subtle: The teacher who sits down with her KitKat after having sent all students out of the classroom, or two girls who learn to dive into a swimming pool and take their break. The Netherlands are of higher uncertainty avoidance than the British. Although the Dutch tend to produce humorous advertising, it generally does not have the subtle indirectness of British humor.

Stability is an important value of strong uncertainty avoidance cultures; change is not perceived as favorable. This is expressed in Miele's claim in Spain: *"Miele, Una decisión de pro vida,"* or "a decision for life." In the Netherlands, Miele's claim is: "Miele, there is nothing better." Fear of the new is found in expressions like "no compromises."

Long-Term Orientation

Long-term orientation cultures are debit card or cash cultures, while short-term orientation cultures are credit card cultures. The opposing values are "save for tomorrow" versus "buy now, pay later." Short-term orientation is reflected in the sense of urgency so frequently encountered in U.S. advertising. Examples are: "Hurry," "Don't wait," or "Now at Clyde's, 50% off, no money down, two full years free credit, it's on now!"

Illustrations 8.60–8.62 (From left to right.)

Harmony, with both nature and fellow humans, is an important cultural aspect in Asian advertising. This results in a dislike of hard confrontation and direct address of people. Building trust in the company instead of direct selling is the purpose of advertising. This results in frequent use of the entertainment form and of visuals of any object that pleases the eye, many of which relate to nature: bamboo trees, flowers, autumn leaves, or other representations of the seasons, which are so important and often have a symbolic meaning unknown to foreigners. The wish for longevity and to be in harmony with nature are recognized in advertising all over Asia. Many Westerners do not understand the butterflies in ads for computers or the other nature elements in Asian advertising. The combination of collectivism and long-term orientation demands harmony with nature and thus explains this advertising style, whose objective is to please the customer, not to intrude. Thus the indirect approach, entertainment rather than persuasive communication. Examples of association with nature are in Illustration 8.60 from Malaysia and Illustration 8.61 from Japan. Illustration 8.62 shows an advertisement for Shell in Malaysia, reflecting both association with nature and long-term orientation.

Consequences for Advertising Concepts

Certain configurations of dimensions have significant consequences for the effectiveness of advertising appeals. Appeals or concepts can be presented in two-dimensional maps, showing culture clusters in which the appeal will be effective or not. An example is the use of status, which is influenced by both power distance and masculinity. Status is used to

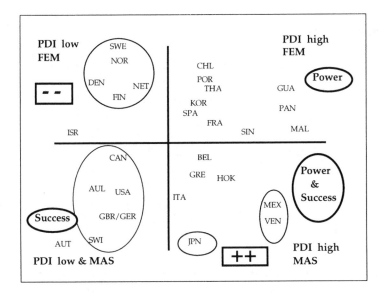

Figure 8.1. The Use of Status as an Appeal
NOTE: AUL = Australia, AUT = Austria, BEL = Belgium, CAN = Canada, CHL = Chile, DEN = Denmark, FIN = Finland, FRA = France, GER = Germany, GBR = Great Britain, GRE = Greece, GUA = Guatemala; HOK = Hong Kong, ISR = Israel, ITA = Italy, JPN = Japan, KOR = Korea, MAL = Malaysia, MEX = Mexico, NET = the Netherlands, NOR = Norway, PAN = Panama, POR = Portugal, SIN = Singapore, SPA = Spain, SWE = Sweden, SWI = Switzerland, THA = Thailand, USA = the United States, VEN = Venezuela.

show power in large power distance cultures and to show success in masculine cultures. In feminine cultures, particularly those of small power distance (Scandinavia and the Netherlands), status is a negative appeal. Feminine cultures are characterized by modesty and jealousy, and so the use of status will be counterproductive. Cultures that score high on both masculinity and power distance will be particularly sensitive to the status motive.

Figure 8.1 shows a two-dimensional map of 30 countries, with culture clusters that will be more or less sensitive to status as an appeal in advertising. In the upper left-hand corner is the Scandinavian and Netherlands cluster, cultures in which the status appeal will not work. In the lower left-hand corner is the Anglo-German cluster, where status will be most appealing if connected with success. The upper right-hand corner shows a mixture of European, Latin American, and Asian cultures in which status is mostly linked with power. The extremes are in the lower right-hand corner, where both power and success are drivers for status brands and appeals in advertising: Mexico, Venezuela, and Japan.

Why Humor Doesn't Travel

In some cultures humor is a much used device in advertising and in others it is scarce. The statement that humor doesn't travel is frequently heard. Why? Because humor is a subversive play with conventions and established ideas; it is based on breaking taboos. Comedy plays with ways of breaking the rules of convention, going against what ought to be, the desired of a culture. Because it uses cultural conventions, it can only be understood by those who share the culture. An example is a fragment in Gogol's play *The Revisor,* where the Revisor's servant is seen lying on a bed. To the Russians of Gogol's time (1836), this was very funny because servants used to sleep on the floor and being on a bed meant being on one's master's bed, which was seen as an unheard of liberty.[8] This fits Russian culture, which was and still is one of the largest power distance cultures in the world. The servant's act would have been impossible to understand by members of small power distance cultures, and thus not be seen as funny. Culture influences the type of humor used. Parody fits small power distance cultures, because it disguises the voice of authority. Much of British humor is based on antiauthoritarianism. Weak uncertainty avoidance cultures, being able to cope with ambiguity, will use the more subtle types of humor, parody and understatement. In strong uncertainty avoidance cultures, the more straightforward type of slapstick humor is used. The admonishing humor of the Germans has to do with their need for perfectionism, which explains their infrequent use of irony.[9] Much of Belgian humor is straightforward. What is recognized is the strong power distance culture. In Belgian humor, the oppressed entrench themselves.[10] A characteristic of humor is incongruity, or the contrast between the expected and the unexpected, the possible/plausible and the impossible/implausible. This element of surprise is an important part of humor: It is often the unexpected turn in a story or event that makes people laugh and that helps them unwind.

Using humor in advertising is a management decision. The reason it is used more in some countries than in others has to do with the cultural values of management; it does not reflect the sense of humor of advertising audiences. Humor in advertising is found particularly in cultures of small power distance and weak to medium uncertainty avoidance, such as the United Kingdom, Denmark, Sweden, and the Netherlands. Obviously, this configuration of dimensions makes managers willing to use humor in advertising, while in strong uncertainty avoidance cultures, management is not likely to do so.

In studies of the use of humor in advertising, a number of different humorous devices are usually distinguished: puns or word games, understatements, jokes, the ludicrous, the "comic" (as in comic strip), comedy, slapstick, satire, parody, irony, and black humor. In contrast to the stereotype of the German lack of humor, German studies (see Hillebrand[11] and Merz[12]) are able to distinguish a similar number of types of humor, with only one difference: in English/American studies, "understatement" is mentioned as a humorous device. This was not specified as a humorous device in the two German studies used in this section. The German studies mentioned *Schadenfreude* (malicious pleasure) as a humorous device, one not mentioned in the Anglo-Saxon studies.

Weinberger and Spotts[13] compared the use of humor as an executional style in the United States and the United Kingdom by content-analysis of television commercials. They distinguished six categories of humor: pun, understatement, joke, the ludicrous, satire, and irony. Findings were that the U.S. advertising style included more of the ludicrous and the United Kingdom's more satire. This can be explained by the different scores on the uncertainty avoidance dimension.

Alden, Hoyer, and Lee[14] compared the use of humor across four countries. They examined the content of humorous television advertising from Korea, Germany, Thailand, and the United States and found one type of humor that worked across all compared countries: incongruity. Almost 60% of the humorous ads in all four nations contained incongruent contrasts, but there were differences among the countries with respect to the degree of contrasts used. Higher proportions of ads with contrasts were found in Germany and Thailand than in the United States and Korea. The Hofstede dimensions were used to explain differences among individual countries. In the collectivistic cultures of Thailand and Korea, humorous appeals involve groups—three or more central characters are included; whereas in the United States and Germany, both individualistic cultures, substantially fewer ads with three or more characters were found. In the large power distance cultures (Thailand and Korea), more humorous ads featured unequal status between main characters than in the two small power distance cultures (Germany and the United States). The majority of the U.S. and German commercials featured characters with equal status.

Hillebrand[15] noted that in Germany's advertising, compared with that of England, the United States, and France, the use of humor is limited, not because German consumers do not have a sense of humor, but because of the risk aversion attitude of the German advertising industry. The characteristics of humor in Germany are incongruity and surprise.

Scheijgrond and Volker[16] conducted a study to compare differences in the liking of humorous television commercials between the Netherlands and Flemish Belgium. Because in the Netherlands and Flanders, the Dutch-speaking part of Belgium, the same language is spoken, many advertisers assume that the people have similar cultural traits. Yet it is the two language areas of Belgium that share basically the same culture, which resembles the French culture more than the Dutch culture. The culture gap between the Netherlands and Flanders is somewhat smaller than between the Netherlands and Walloon, the French-speaking part of Belgium, but it is still very wide. In fact, no two countries with a common border and a common language are so far apart culturally.[17] Holland scores low on power distance, masculinity, and uncertainty avoidance. Belgium scores high on the same three dimensions. This difference became apparent when Dutch and Flemish television commercials were tested among Flemish and Dutch young men and women via in-depth interviews. The types of humor distinguished were (a) uncomplicated, explicit humor, including jokes, anecdotes, and slapstick; (b) linguistic humor, including puns and word games; and (c) complicated humor, including satire, irony, parody, understatements, and absurdism. Findings were that explicit jokes were liked better in Belgium than in the Netherlands, which can be explained by the difference in uncertainty avoidance. Linguistic humor appeared to be liked less by the Flemish than by the Dutch. The anecdote type seemed to be culturally sensitive, because it appears to rely on context, which is related to the country. A typical slapstick commercial appeared to be liked better by the Belgians than by the Dutch. Slapstick usually is at the cost of one of the parties, which is more fitting in masculine cultures than in feminine cultures. In this particular case, one slapstick commercial involved throwing food, which is a no-go item in Dutch culture. Wasting food is "not done" in the thrifty Dutch culture. Understatement fits better in modest feminine cultures while overstatement fits masculine cultures better. Absurdism, parody, and satire, particularly commercials that do not take experts seriously, were not appreciated by the Flemish but were appreciated by the Dutch. Parody in particular is an expression of small power distance: Not wanting to take authority seriously is an implicit value included in parody.

Conclusion

Within each culture there are opposing, seemingly paradoxical, values. The contrast is between the desirable and the desired values of each culture. Those who do not understand the cultural value paradoxes may be tempted to think that the world's values are converging. By perceiving an increased focus on individuality in Japan, for example, it is often concluded that the Japanese culture is becoming more individualistic and thus that the Japanese are Americanizing. This is not the case. Increased individuality will make the Japanese even more competitive than they are now. Each culture has its value paradoxes, and they are different from the value paradoxes of other cultures. They can be understood through the five dimensions.

A culture's opposing values appear to be important for advertising because they are recognized as the most meaningful elements of a culture. Both the desirable and the desired values are used for developing meaningful appeals in advertising. Particularly the value paradoxes of culture appear to be able to trigger people's feelings.

Sometimes a desired value of one culture may seem to be similar to a desirable value of another culture. An example is independence: a desirable American value, a desired Japanese value. Yet there is a world of difference behind the same word. It is not a single concept.

Showing people alone in advertising in collectivistic cultures is interpreted to mean they have no friends. It may go deeper than that, it may mean they have no identity because their identity is in the group. As more than 70% of the world's population is more or less collectivistic, advertisers would be wise to show more people in their advertisements. It doesn't hurt the members of individualistic cultures to see more people in advertising, and it is negative to show solitary people in collectivistic cultures.

Because of the domination of American advertising, there is much more hype in international advertising than members of less masculine cultures appreciate. For example, taking into account that a large number of cultures of the European continent are more or less feminine, international advertisers focusing on Europe might consider using both less hype and less competitive advertising.

Some elements of advertising are typical for one cultural dimension and thus effective for cultures scoring high on that dimension. An example is the use of detail and focus on the process in strong uncertainty avoidance cultures, while a result orientation better fits weak uncertainty avoidance cultures. Combining a process orientation with a result orientation in one advertising campaign means using two contradicting values: strong versus weak uncertainty avoidance. Combining two such opposing values of one dimension in one international campaign may lead to less effective advertising.

Finally, understanding the values of culture helps explain why humor doesn't travel: Humor uses the conventions of culture that cannot be understood by those who do not share the culture.

Notes

1. Wells, W., Burnett, J., & Moriarty, S. (1992). *Advertising: Principles and practice* (2nd ed.). Englewood Cliffs, NJ: Prentice Hall, p. 249.

2. Hofstede, G. H. (1991). *Cultures and organizations: Software of the mind.* New York: McGraw-Hill, p. 9.

3. Hofstede, G. H. (1984). *Culture's consequences: International differences in work-related values.* Beverly Hills, CA: Sage, p. 19.

4. "Inequality: For richer, for poorer." (1994, November 5). *The Economist,* p. 19.

5. Maleville, M. (1993). "How boringly respectable can you get? A study of business slogans in three countries." *Toegepaste Taalwetenschap, 2*(3).

6. Mitchell, R., & Oneal, M. (1994, September 12). "Managing by values." *Business Week,* pp. 38-43.

7. "Land of the big." (1996, December 21). *The Economist,* p. 68.

8. Van den Bergh, H. (1996, November 14). "Lachen als bevrediging." *NRC Handelsblad,* p. 33.

9. Bik, J. M. (1996, November 14). "Variant op ernst." *NRC Handelsblad,* p. 35.

10. Camps, H. (1996, November 14). "Ondertoon van schuld." *NRC Handelsblad,* p. 35.

11. Hillebrand, K. (1992). *Erfolgsvoraussetzungen und Erscheinungsformen des Humors in der Werbung—Dargestellt am Beispiel von Low-Involvement-Produkten.* Prüfungsamt für wirtschaftswissenschaftliche Prüfungen der Westfälischen Wilhelms-Universität Münster. Unpublished.

12. Merz, G. (1989). *Humor in der Werbung.* Freie Wissentschaftliche Arbeit zur Erlangung des akademischen Grades Diplomkaufmann und der Wirtschaftsend Sozialwissenschaftlichen Fakultät der Friedrich-Alexander-Universität Erlangen-Nürnberg, Nürnberg. Unpublished.

13. Weinberger, M. C., & Spotts, H. E. (1989). "Humor in US versus UK TV commercials: A comparison." *Journal of Advertising, 18*(2), 39-44.

14. Alden, D. L., Hoyer, W. D., & Lee, C. (1993, April 1). "Identifying global and culture-specific dimensions of humor in advertising: A multinational analysis." *Journal of Marketing, 57,* 64-75.

15. Hillebrand (1992), *Erfolgsvoraussetzungen und Erscheinungsformen des Humors.*

16. Scheijgrond, L., & Volker, J. (1995). *Zo dichtbij, maar toch ver weg.* Unpublished study for the Hogeschool Eindhoven, studierichting Communicatie.

17. Hofstede (1986), *Culture's consequences,* p. 228.

CHAPTER 9

Cross-Cultural
Advertising Research

How motives can be recognized in an advertising appeal was the subject of Chapter 8. But there are more elements in advertisements that are influenced by culture. Together they make up advertising style, which stands for execution style covering all elements of advertising at three levels. (a) The *appeal* includes values and motivations: Chapter 8 focused on culture's consequences for advertising appeals, including motives that reflect culture. (b) The basic advertising form: Advertising form involves the organization and packaging of the advertising messages.[1] A *basic form* or executional style of advertising is a form used in different executions. Examples of basic advertising forms are "entertainment" and "presentation" or the direct versus the indirect approach. Chapter 10 will focus on basic advertising forms and culture. (c) The *execution* level shows how people behave and what people look like. As we have learned, cultural values can be recognized in behavior. The variation in executional elements is as unlimited as life itself.

Cross-cultural advertising research tends to single out a number of elements of advertisements from one culture and to compare those with similar elements of advertisements from other cultures. Elements can be the three mentioned above: appeal, basic form, and execution; creative strategy, communication style, and execution style or execution details. This chapter is a review of comparative cross-cultural studies of advertising. It includes a summary of findings and it reviews research methods used. A great variety of categorizations are used that are often related to the culture of the researcher. Bias caused by ethnocentrism will be the subject of the next section. Further sections will present findings of selected cross-cultural advertising studies.

Cross-Cultural Advertising Studies

Two types of cross-cultural advertising studies will be topics of discussion: (a) studies of differences in acceptance, liking, and perception of advertising

211

in general in different cultures; and (b) comparative analyses of print advertising and television commercials in two or more different countries.

Studies that attempt to understand cross-cultural differences in advertising tend to be dominated by assumptions, hypotheses, categorizations, and coding methods based on the research customs and marketing philosophy of the home culture of the researchers. This is a natural process. Objectivity is nearly impossible, and only a few scholars have managed to find objective measurement criteria and systems that have also led to meaningful results.[2] Ethnocentrism has to be accepted as part of the research process, and as long as it is recognized as such there should not be a problem. However, because American academics are the leaders in cross-cultural advertising research, the general bias is American ethnocentrism. Within American academia this has not gone unnoticed. Miracle[3] states that

> among major industrialized nations the people of the United States are perhaps unique in their neglect of the study of foreign languages and cultures. . . . It is no wonder, then, that many advertising practitioners and researchers exhibit an incapacity for viewing other cultures dispassionately or emphatically; they view their own society as the center of culture and feel that the rest of the world would do well to imitate their way of life.

Most cross-cultural advertising studies conducted by Americans compare U.S. advertising with advertising of one or more other cultures and are based on ethnocentric assumptions. Elements prone to bias are assumptions and hypotheses, method and sample, categorizations, content criteria, execution criteria, and conclusions.

Assumptions and Hypotheses

Scientific investigation generally starts with a problem and proceeds by solving it. This characterization does not consider that problems may be wrongly formulated, that one may inquire about properties of things and processes that later views declare to be nonexistent.[4]

In cross-cultural research meant to find ways to standardize advertising, the problem is cultural diversity and the solution is identifying the differences and the similarities as compared with the home country's properties. One such property is the assumption that advertising is persuasive by nature or that it should sell. As a result, comparisons tend to focus on the degree of "persuasiveness" or "hard sell," which may not be a property of the cultures studied.

An often-found hypothesis is that cultural differences in advertising are linked with product categories defined as food versus nonfood or durables versus nondurables. In some countries, indeed, specific advertising styles can be found for some product categories, yet it is the culture of the consumer that is more important than the product itself. This product-oriented thinking reflects the defect of marketing, where the role of advertising is often regarded as being determined more by product category than by the culture of the people for whom it is created. And, indeed, some advertising styles appear to be the property of one multinational company and thus reflect the culture of that company, not the culture of the consumer.

An example of an erroneous hypothesis is that there is *a European* culture and that one or two countries can be selected as representative for Europe. Similarly, American advertising is found to be compared with advertising of Eastern cultures, for example with the objective "to compare Japanese with Western advertising." In such cases "Western" stands for American, particularly when it concerns comparing hard sell with soft sell. These criteria are American based and cannot be generalized as Western.

With respect to hypotheses, comparison of American and continental European studies reflects the cultural difference between the two. In strong uncertainty avoidance cultures—most of continental Europe—scholars look for certainty, for theory. They use empirical research to prove their theory. In weak uncertainty avoidance cultures they look more for usable knowledge. Weak uncertainty avoidance makes them willing to run the risk of unpredictable outcomes connected to empirical research. The overemphasis of empiricism and underemphasis of theory is reflected in a lack of theory behind the hypotheses in American studies. Hofstede[5] states that "a lot of energy is wasted in fishing expeditions equipped with powerful computing tools which are doomed to find only trivialities because they do not know what to look for." Hofstede pleads for a marriage between a high UAI concern for theory and a low UAI tolerance for empiricism.

Method

The most studied country is the United States. Samiee and Jeong[6] state that "this trend represents a sort of ethnocentrism that occurs at the expense of acquiring greater knowledge regarding additional cultures." Research is often limited to English-speaking countries, developed countries, and countries close to the United States. Japan is by far the most frequently studied country in Asia. England, alone or combined with one other European country, is sometimes presented as representative for "Europe."

The most used method is content analysis, with a variety of pseudo-etic measurement criteria. Content analysis is designed to produce an objective, measurable, and verifiable account of the manifest content of messages; in other words, what can be seen and coded by a coder. It works through identifying and counting chosen units in a communication system. It works best on a large scale. Content analysis must be nonselective, it must cover the whole message or message system, or a properly constituted sample,[7] yet it often is applied to small, nonrepresentative samples.

The trouble with content analysis is that it tends to leave one asking "so what?" Particularly, the use of content analysis to compare communication systems of different cultures prompts that question. Counting and identifying differences is only useful if conclusions can be drawn from the results, which largely depend on correct hypotheses, problem formulation, criteria, and coding.

Objects of investigation are print advertisements and television commercials. Samiee and Jeong criticize the sample methods generally used. They found an average number of 4.9 magazines or newspapers used for analyzing print advertisements. Samples used for analyzing television commercials are based on convenience. This is caused by the practical difficulties of collecting representative samples on air in different countries.

Other types of bias will play a role when comparing the advertising styles of countries by product category. Certain countries use specific advertising styles for some product categories. An example is advertising for beer in the United Kingdom, which is—more than in other countries and, within the United Kingdom, more than any other product category—characterized by the use of humor and parody. The culture of the advertiser is reflected in product categories in which a few multinational advertisers dominate. Examples are detergents, sanitary napkins/towels, and disposable diapers, which are dominated by Procter & Gamble and a few other large companies. P&G systematically uses the testimonial format throughout Europe. The dominant positions of a few multinationals in the top 10 advertisers of a country can bias the advertising style of that country. Analysis of basic advertising forms in Sweden (Chapter 10, under "Relationship Among Basic Form, Culture, and Product Category: Lesson") discovered that 23% of the television commercials in a 2-week period in 1996 were by international companies using one format for the whole of Europe.

Sample Design

A core question is what makes a representative sample and how it is obtained—if it can be obtained at all. Criteria for representativity can be:

total number of different advertisements in each country, number of local or international advertisers, channel (local, regional, national), number of commercial breaks, product category, seasonality, and time of day. There is an overall guidance criterion that samples should only be taken directly from the channels. Samples taken from agency show reels or organizations such as the Television Register are preselected and not representative of a country's advertising style. Such selections are made for nonrepresentative criteria, such as creativity or presentation of an agency's work to prospective clients. Three criteria for representativity are described below: product category, seasonality, and time of day.

A frequently found hypothesis is that advertising style is related to the product category and that a sample should be an actual representation of the distribution of product categories of countries. This would imply that commercials must be selected by product category and that the number of commercials in each product category should represent the total advertising expenditure for each product category. This presents the problem of defining a product category. Product class definitions differ from one country to another, and they tend to be producer oriented rather than user oriented. Product categories are also increasingly merging, which does not facilitate comparison. Ice cream is often categorized as a dairy product, but new types of ice cream may be better compared with candy bars, thus being confectionery. Moreover, advertising styles may be more related to an international market leader across product categories than to one product category.

Seasonality influences the product types advertised. In winter different products are advertised than in summer. But when it is summer in the northern hemisphere, it is winter in the southern hemisphere. It seems logical that samples should be taken at the same time of the year to be comparable, but the consequence is that product categories will not be equally represented. If the research objective is to draw a representative sample for each product category, one cannot rely on only one season. Advertisers also may change strategy, resulting in a change of form within a given time span.

When collecting commercials from television channels across Europe, the time criterion is complicated: dinner times vary from 18.00 hrs (Germany) to 22.00 hrs (Spain). Children in Spain go to bed much later than children in the Netherlands. Different channels present the news at different times. A method Zandpour et al.[8] used to ensure equivalency of samples was to tape commercials only before, during, and after prime-time national network news programs. In each country, those television networks that did not provide national news programs were excluded from the sample. Selecting only "prime time" in Europe will cause bias toward certain product categories. Each year, M&M Europe publishes a European planning guide that includes an example of an ideal European media plan. The 1995/1996 European planning guide[9] includes a plan targeting "housewives" or "all adult women." Prime time as a percentage of day-parts used varied enormously by country: Belgium-Dutch language area (62%); the Netherlands (60%); Spain (33%); France (36%); Germany (40%); Belgium-French language area (39%); Sweden (50%); and the United Kingdom (37%). Taking media planning criteria into account as criteria for selecting channels, seasons, and times of day may be relevant if a study is related to only one specific product category. Even then, this may not be meaningful because patterns vary and strategies change according to the competitive situation. For example, depending on the clutter of any specific time, advertisers may select different times of day to avoid the competition.

Discussions I have had with practitioners and statisticians have led me to the conclusion that it is impossible to draw a sample of television commercials for the purpose of comparing advertising styles across cultures that meets the representativity criteria product category, seasonality, and time. Those who do so delude themselves. One solution is to take the universe of a short time span and repeat this regularly, such as using all television commercials in a 2-week period in different countries. That exercise will have to be repeated at regular intervals.

Content Analysis Criteria

"Objective criteria" are hard to find and, when presented as such, may actually be biased because of ethnocentric hypotheses and conclusions. Samiee and Jeong[10] note that the majority of cross-cultural advertising studies appear to have adopted the pseudo-etic approach, meaning that emic measures developed and tested in the United States are transferred to other cultures without any modification. An example is measuring length of text or information cues in the text to compare the information content of an advertisement. This ignores the informational elements of visuals.

To operationalize the distinction between informative and noninformative, the Resnik and Stern[11] typology is usually applied. The Resnik and Stern criterion for considering an advertisement informative is "whether the informational cues are relevant enough to assist a typical buyer in making an intelligent choice among alternatives."[12] The assumption that consumers search for information to make "intelligent choices" is doubtful. The assumption that the universal role of advertising is to help consumers make intelligent choices has been disputed both inside and outside the United States. What is informational for members of one culture may not be informational for members of another culture. The list of 14 informational cues used by Resnik and Stern is included in the summary of classifications of advertising forms in Chapter 10. As a result of the lack of scrutiny with respect to the prevailing information cues found in different cultures, the system is not very useful for finding differences in cultural values in advertising.

As the criterion emotional is not well defined, everything that is perceived as noninformational is frequently defined as emotional. This may include different forms such as "erotics," "theatrical," "entertainment," or even the umbrella-style "soft sell" versus "hard sell." As a result, the criterion emotional does not differentiate among cultures.

If there really are objective criteria, they are few and can be exploited only to a limited extent for a limited number of detailed research questions. An example of such a detailed research is the study by Miracle, Taylor, and Chang[13] that measured the time it took before the brand name was shown in American and Japanese advertising. The authors used the method to test an important hypothesis, that the objective of Asian advertising is to develop trust between a company and the consumer rather than to try to sell directly. The intermediate hypothesis was that as a result of the different objectives, advertising in Asia would mention the brand name at a later stage in the commercial than in the Western world. This is indeed an important cultural difference in advertising styles.

The method of using only the few available, purely objectively measurable criteria has its limitations. If one uses purely objective criteria on large samples, one can measure only details. The broader approach is to develop a comprehensive code list with a large number of variables, and to code advertisements or television commercials according to such a list. Statistical analysis of each country may then uncover that country's specific styles. However, in order to capture all possible variations by objective measurement criteria, such a code list must be so extensive that it is hardly possible to do the job for large samples. When small samples are used, each cell will be so small that few conclusions can be drawn. There also are elements one will never be able to capture. For example, how should one measure tone of voice? In decibels?

Categorizations

Comparative cross-cultural studies generally use categorizations based on ethnocentric or pseudo-etic criteria. Various elements of advertising style can be mixed within one categorization. An example of a categorization including the various elements is given by Ray,[14] quoted in Zandpour et al.[15]

Ray categorized television formats in terms of "warmth," "testimony," "refutation," "repetition," and "fear." "Warmth" can be part of the creative strategy or approach, "refutation" can be defined as a strategy, "testimony" is a basic advertising form, "repetition" is execution or strategy, and "fear" is an appeal.

Advertising styles reflect the communication styles of cultures. Cultures vary with respect to the use of verbal and visual styles. Verbal styles tend to include more facts and thus are, according to U.S. "etic" categorizations, characterized as informational as opposed to noninformational, which is then the characteristic of visual style. This is a comparison of noncomparable characteristics. The distinction informational/noninformational is an emic categorization and cannot be used for comparing verbal and visual communication styles.

Execution Criteria

Translations of text, even when back-translations are used, may not uncover the concepts that are culturally meaningful. Words and expressions used in advertising express the core values of a culture, which often cannot be translated. Ethnic coders may be able to discover the values of their own culture. Yet, in order to do a proper comparison, code lists may be too rigid to allow for recognition and expression of their cultural values.

Facial expressions are said to be "the best indicators of emotions." An example is the coding of "frowns and smiles" in advertisements in the United States, Indonesia, and Spain.[16] Cultures particularly vary with respect to showing or not showing facial expressions and in the meanings of these expressions. Experience at BBDO has taught that for their "photo sort" method, which they use to position brands, photographs of facial expressions produced in the United States to represent and be recognized as "mood," could not be transplanted to Europe. The way American actors expressed specific moods could not be recognized by European respondents. The same is true within Europe: No single "photo deck" could be developed for the whole of Europe.[17]

Bias in Conclusions

Rarely are results from content analysis of significance by themselves. To be meaningful, isolated results must be related to other significant findings in the field.[18] In the typical cross-cultural advertising study this is missing. Instead, conclusions are often ethnocentric. Examples of such conclusions are "that longer text will include more information" or "that Japanese advertising is Westernizing because more American words are used." It is a Japanese trait to adopt foreign words. A phonetic system was developed for this: *katakana*. This is nothing new. Dutch words have been included in the Japanese language since the 17th century, but that has not led to Westernization of the Japanese.

Caillat and Mueller[19] compared advertising styles of the United Kingdom and the United States by comparing advertising of one product category only: beer. They found distinctive differences. For example, British beer advertising used humor appeals almost exclusively, while the American sample relied on emotional and sex appeals. The findings for the product category were extended to advertising in general, with the claim that "the results suggest a fundamental difference in each country's approach to creative strategy." This is a major fallacy. Specific product categories—and beer in particular—often are not representative of a country's advertising style.

Laser Vision

Academic advertising research generally has followed research methods used in psychology, which have become increasingly dominated by quantitative studies. Overemphasis on facts as well as easier access to statistical computer programs has resulted in the domination of quantitative statistical analysis in advertising studies and in a decreased focus on insight and broader conceptual analysis. Standard procedures dominate academic research. In order to work correctly within these procedures, the research questions have become extremely detailed and narrow. This "laser vision" combined with the pseudo-etic approach may not be the most constructive way to understand the complex world of cross-cultural communication.[20]

An Argument Against Comparative Etic Studies and for the Emic Approach

A general practice of comparative studies is to compare a "known" framework with an "unknown," incomprehensible one. The incomprehensible framework is replaced by something that looks like the "known" framework. Particularly when comparing Western and Eastern frameworks, the Eastern one is replaced by something that is known and that looks like Western common sense, using a language which cannot represent the elements of the unknown framework.

Because of the bias inherent in comparative studies, the advertising styles of countries may better be described in an absolute way.[21] We should, rather, try to discover the elements, analyze their function, and compare them with other phenomena of the same culture (language, literary style, art) and thus find the underlying worldview that influences the creation of advertising and its perception by the consumer. Part of the method will be comparison, but in a qualitative way. Because culture is a relative phenomenon, one's own cultural values become manifest when exposed to values of another culture. Discussing values in depth between people of opposing cultural values can uncover the core values reflecting advertising styles. An example is how a group of students of mixed cultures at Erasmus University in Rotterdam found a number of core values used in advertising in their own countries.[22] Taylor and Hoy,[23] when analyzing French television commercials, did something similar. They state that

> an alternative way to address the issue of globalization of advertising is to work from a more inductive approach, where each culture is seen as unique and where research begins with an investigation of the core characteristics and then comparisons are made at the next higher level. This approach avoids the pitfalls incurred by taking American values and standards and searching for them in the advertising of other cultures.

Example of a Qualitative Emic Approach

How the core values of culture can be discovered by in-depth analysis of advertising was demonstrated by students participating in an international students' project of a European exchange program at the Erasmus University of Rotterdam, in the Netherlands.[24] The objective was to find culture-specific values of the four cultures represented by the students and to find if they had values in common that could be used for international advertising. The countries represented were England, the Netherlands, Germany, and Spain. The study was done in an inductive manner. To prevent ethnocentrism, no existing structures were used. There was no focus on a set number of predetermined "themes" or "values," to prevent bias in the results. The aim was to look for those aspects that naturally come to the fore and then focus on a small number of values that were most often repeated. The next step was to explain why, exactly, these elements of a commercial made it specific for a culture and set it apart from commercials that can successfully be used across Europe. The method involved group discussion and personal opinion.

A random sample of commercials was collected in the home countries of the students. Each group member individually analyzed the commercials of his or her culture according to the simple likability criteria as used by a consumer, such as "Does it appeal to me?" "Do I like it?" or "Is it repelling?" In other words, they first took the role of the consumer, and only later the role of the researcher, when asking "Why does it attract or repel me?" Commercials expressing values they thought matched their own culture were selected—the way they thought things are and the way they ought to be. Each country's commercials were also watched by another group member. This cross-check gave the group the opportunity to ensure that all commercials were analyzed the same way. The discussion among the group members enabled the individual to gain a clear idea of the underlying value(s) of the commercial.

The discussion and feedback revealed the values and "un-values" (their definition of the values that they found unacceptable for a specific culture) specific to each country and those that cross international borders. They found that some values were often repeated and 5 to 10 of those values were selected per country. These were taken for further in-depth analysis. The core values were described by each individual group member and commercials representing the values were selected for in-depth analysis by discussion with the other team members. The last step was to compare the values in each country and draw conclusions. The aim was to find which values were repeated in all four countries and could thus be used as international values. The only example of such a value was in the appeal to tradition. During the procedure, which involved lengthy discussions, the students showed not only a great ability to express their own values as reflected in the advertising in their own culture, but also the contrast with the values of the culture of their counterpart group member. The results of this study have been used for the descriptions of advertising styles in Chapter 11.

The following sections provide a summary of the findings of the two types of cross-cultural studies found in literature: acceptance and liking of advertising across borders, and comparative cross-cultural advertising studies.

Acceptance, Liking, and Perception of Advertising Across Cultures

Heyder, Musiol, and Peters[25] found differences in the perception and acceptance of advertising in a number of European countries. The British, the French, and the Germans regard advertising as a positive component of everyday life. In most countries, the most cited benefit of advertising was the informational content of advertising. Advertising as entertainment was acknowledged as a benefit only by the French.

A major study by GfK[26] in the United Kingdom, France, and Germany in 1992 discovered that advertising styles varied considerably among the three countries. British consumers describe their advertising as humorous but relatively low on information, understandability, and credibility. The French see their commercials as less humorous and entertaining than the British do, less emotional, but rather high on information. Germans view their commercials as relatively humorless, but as entertaining in an emotional way and as reasonably informative. A study by McCollum Spielman Worldwide[27] found a wide perceptual gulf between Europe and the United States. For example, while Europeans are inclined to have trouble understanding their advertising, they nonetheless view it as entertaining and informative. Americans, on the other hand, have a different view. They have no trouble understanding their advertising, but relatively few Americans consider advertising entertaining or informative.

Research by Y&R[28] in six European countries in 1990 found that advertising is differently perceived and described by different nationalities. These perceptions are presented on two axes: "serious versus entertaining/clever" and "stylish versus informative/honest." Figure 9.1 shows a two-dimensional map with the two axes and the position of the six countries. The findings are consistent with the low- and high-context division within Europe. Germany occupies the extreme end of the "honest-informative" axis, opposite Italy with its aspirations to "aesthetics" and "creativity." The United Kingdom is balanced between "entertainment" and "honesty"; Spain between the "serious" and "stylish" dimensions. There is a distinction between the Latin and Nordic countries. Northern countries tend toward the "informative-honest" pole, Southern countries toward the "creative and aesthetic." The model fits my findings related to the Hofstede dimensions and Hall's distinction between high- and low-context communication.

There is a relationship between economic development and advertising styles or perceptions of advertising. Countries that are in a development stage will ask for a different advertising style than countries with a developed economy and advertising industry. Tian Shuqian[29] observed in 1992 that China was a vast market but still had a high level of illiteracy. As a result, most of Chinese consumers liked visual, straightforward ads and vivid ads with images. Influenced by the tradition of frugality and restricted by the

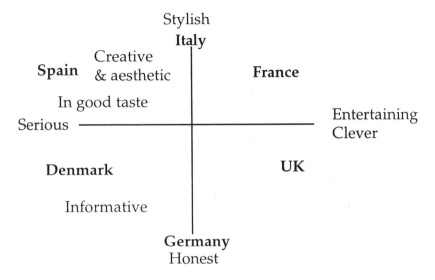

Figure 9.1. Perceptions of advertising in 1990
SOURCE: Françoise Bonnal (1990), *Admap*.

living standard, most Chinese consumers, especially the older ones and housewives, were perceived to be very practical when buying, and to be driven by economic factors. Therefore, advertisements that clearly explained the end uses of the product and that promised solid benefit won their approval. Cheng's[30] later analysis of Chinese magazine advertisement observed a change during a period of rapid development, from the use of utilitarian values toward more symbolic values.

Analysis of basic advertising forms in a South African sample of television commercials (see Chapter 10 under "Relationship Among Basic Form, Culture, and Product Category: Announcement") shows another phenomenon. South African advertising style in 1996 was dominated by straightforward announcements. This is not so much a development matter as a language problem. After the end of apartheid, all advertising must be translated into all languages—which are numerous. The result is many simple statements, because values cannot easily be translated.

Findings of Comparative Studies Between Two Countries

This section presents a summary of comparative studies. The studies generally do not give a cultural explanation of the differences found.

Comparison Between the United States and the United Kingdom

Katz and Lee[31] analyzed differences in forms used in advertising in the United States and in the United Kingdom. They distinguished four forms that they labeled product information, (i.e., explanation of the product's benefits and uses), product image (i.e., symbolic information about the product), personalization (i.e., testimonial), and lifestyle (i.e., connection among person, product, and usage). Lifestyle and personalization were found more in American commercials, whereas product information was found more in British commercials. Television advertisements in the United States seem to be more "people" oriented, showing how the product fits in the viewer's way of life, or how it is the right thing for the "average" viewer. In the United Kingdom, focus is more on what the product or service does. The use of specific formats was found to be linked not only to culture, but also to product categories. Food and drink advertising tended to use the personalized approach, while advertising for cars showed the lifestyle approach.

Spotts, Weinberger, and Parsons[32] found significant differences in creative strategies between the United States and the United Kingdom with respect to advertising for durables. For durable products generally, U.S. ads focused on brand image and more emotional creative strategies. U.K. ads were associated more with USP (Unique Selling Proposition).

Nevett[33] analyzed the sociocultural background of the differences between U.S. and U.K. advertising styles found in literature. The most distinctive differences—hard sell (the United States) and soft sell (the United Kingdom), the use of sentimentality (the United States) and humor (the United Kingdom)—can be understood by analyzing the background of how advertising developed in the two countries, including differences in philosophy. An example is how the hierarchy of effects thinking and the U.S. research style using more quantitative methods have constrained American managers. British advertisers and agencies rely more on qualitative techniques.

France–United States and France–the Netherlands

Biswas, Olsen, and Carlet[34] compared advertising styles of the United States and France. French advertising uses more emotional appeals, more sexual appeals, and more humor than American advertising. American advertising contains more information cues than French advertising. The types of humorous devices used differ: more puns in France and more ludicrousness in the United States.

Taylor and Hoy[35] analyzed French television commercials using a typology of descriptors provided by French advertising professionals. The descriptors used were: *la séduction,* good French advertising should tempt the consumer; *le spectacle,* good French advertising is theater, drama, show; *l'amour* or romance, erotics, desire, display of affection; and *l'humour,* amusing associations, playful use of words, humor. This (exploratory) study found that *le spectacle* and *la séduction* were the dominant themes, followed by *l'humour* and *l'amour.* In comparison with U.S. advertising, the common finding was that French advertising is more emotion laden.

Wassink[36] conducted a comparative content analysis of Dutch and French commercials. Compared with Dutch advertising, French commercials show more attention to a beautiful background in the commercial, frequent comparison or analogy with beautiful women, erotics, softer voice-overs, generally more emotions or a change from "unhappy" to "happy" as a result of product usage. The opposing aspect in Dutch advertising was that women were presented as looking like the average "woman next door" rather than a sensual woman. In Dutch advertising, also, all sorts of devices are employed to reflect thrift, such as piggy banks and towels with imprints of banknotes. Although a variety of entertainment techniques is used, Dutch advertising reflects more everyday life than French advertising does.

Comparison Between the United States and Japan

A relatively large number of studies compare advertising in the United States with advertising in Japan.

Mueller[37] analyzed American and Japanese magazine advertisements to find out whether different styles were used. Her findings were that Japanese advertisements tend to be less direct than American advertising, they appeal more to the emotional level of the consumer, and they build atmosphere. Hard-sell themes are a rarity in Japan. A minimal number of all the Japanese advertisements surveyed contained comparative statements or emphasized the brand's superiority over other products. The role of status in society was reflected in the advertisements almost twice as often as in American advertising. The use of popular American and European words in the copy was linked with highly prestigious products. Product merit appeals are more used than in U.S. advertisements. Veneration of the elderly and respect for the elder generation was an appeal frequently found. With respect to the use of nature, U.S. advertisements focus more on natural as opposed to man-made goods, while the Japanese advertisements emphasize the human relationship with nature.

In a later study, Mueller[38] content-analyzed Japanese and American advertisements from 1978 and 1988 to determine "if Japanese advertising had westernized" (i.e., become Americanized). Results showed that in Japan the soft-sell appeal had increased and the Western appeal of product merit had decreased. American-type hard-sell appeals were a rarity in the Japanese sample. It was concluded that between 1978 and 1988, according to the criteria used, Japanese advertising had become more "Japanese."

Ramaprasad and Hasegawa[39] compared advertising styles of television commercials in Japan and the United States. To find differences in overall strategy, a classification system was used that distinguished between informational and transformational. Informational advertising presents factual information; transformational advertising endows the use of the brand with an emotional experience—it is affect based. The results did not demonstrate a difference in usage of the informational or transformational strategy. However, U.S. advertising style uses more comparative advertising and hyperbole, whereas Japanese advertising style includes the use of nondifferentiating attributes or benefits. Among Japanese consumers, "advertising liking" plays an important role. Consumers transfer the affect toward the advertisement to the product advertised. To develop this affect, Japanese commercials use mood-creating, serene nature symbols.

Miracle et al.[40] analyzed Japanese and U.S. television commercials to determine how soon, how long, and how often the brand, company name, and product are presented. The objective of the study was to identify variables to explain cultural differences between Japanese and American advertising. Cultural variables taken into account were (a) high- versus low-context communication; (b) direct, confrontational behavior versus indirect/harmony-seeking behavior; and (c) individualism versus collectivism. Expectations were that (a) advertisers in the relatively high-context Japanese culture would tend to spend relatively more time setting the stage before they delivered the message; (b) it would take time to build trust in nonconfrontational and indirect ways; and (c) Japanese advertisers would tend to take more of a commercial's time for the development of trust, understanding, and dependency. Only objectively measurable timing and counting variables were used. A conclusion of this important study is that in Japanese commercials the company appears to be more important than the brand. In Japanese commercials the brand is identified later, fewer times, and often only in the last part of the commercial, as compared with U.S. commercials.

Lin[41] analyzed American and Japanese TV commercials. She used the variables informativeness,[42] comparison, testimony, and stylistic characteristics. Her conclusion was that Japanese advertising reflects the high-context Japanese culture in which communication objectives are directed toward achieving consensus and harmony in interpersonal relationships. Compared with American advertising, Japanese commercials less often mention prices, warranties, guarantees, safety, and research findings. Stating prices is considered to be too direct and thus "rude"; claiming scientific proof, backed by company guarantees, is seen as contemptuous of the consumer's intellect and the company's integrity. Japanese ads use the soft-sell approach, including music to set moods.

Sengupta[43] conducted a content analysis of Japanese and U.S. television commercials to determine the influence of culture on the role of women in advertising. Findings from literature that women's and men's roles in Japanese culture overlap even less than they do in American culture appeared to be reflected in advertising. The status of women in both cultures is inferior to that of men and the status of working women in Japan is inferior to the status of working women in the United States. Compared with the U.S. advertising, Japanese advertising presents a stronger endorsement of the attitude that "a woman's place is in the home" among both men and women. Women in U.S. advertising are more likely to be seen in working roles, especially as high-level business executives, while women in working roles in Japanese advertising are more likely to be portrayed as entertainers. When shown in the home, American women are more likely to be shown relaxing, while Japanese women are more likely to be shown cooking, cleaning, and doing other household chores.

Content Analysis of Chinese Advertising

Zhao and Shen[44] report that Chinese attitudes toward advertising are generally pragmatic. The Chinese like advertising for such popular products as television sets and refrigerators, and show less appreciation for advertisements for things they see no chance to buy.

Chan[45] analyzed Chinese television advertising for information content and found that between 1990 and 1995 information content had decreased. Performance and quality were the most commonly featured information cues. A change was found from a product-oriented theme (emphasizing product characteristics) to an audience-centered theme (emphasizing lifestyle and ideal self-image), accompanied by emotional and symbolic appeals to position a product in a particular market segment.

Cheng's[46] content analysis of Chinese advertising shows how Chinese cultural values are reflected in advertising. Comparison between 1982 and

1992 shows three consistent values: "modernity," "quality," and "technology." Between 1982 and 1992, the frequency of "modernity" increased while "quality" decreased and "technology" was fairly stable. Values absent in 1982 but found in 1992 were "courtesy," "magic," "patriotism," "respect for the elderly," "wealth," and "sex." Other values, such as "economic," had decreased. The decreasing values were utilitarian in nature, the increasing values more symbolic and suggestive of human emotions.

Multi-Country Comparisons

Zandpour et al.[47] compared advertising styles in France, Taiwan, and the United States by content analysis of television commercials, and classified them on creative strategy, information content, and advertising form. U.S. commercials directly address the audience, whereas French and Taiwanese commercials use more drama. French commercials try to entertain the public through symbolism, humor, and drama. French commercials rarely use a person to lecture the audience and generally do not present straight, single facts. When information is provided, it is about new ideas around the product, its quality in terms of workmanship, its components. French commercials often play with shapes and names. In French and Taiwanese advertising, when the audience is addressed, it may be with explicit promises of a dream beyond what the product can deliver. This is in contrast with U.S. commercials that use celebrities, credible sources, and users of products to convey the specific benefits of products to consumers. U.S. commercials provide data-based arguments with explicit conclusions of why the consumer should buy the product. The consumer is usually directly addressed, and the product is displayed aggressively. Taiwanese commercials link the product to Chinese values and use symbols and metaphors. Findings are summarized in Table 9.1.

Cutler and Javalgi[48] analyzed the visual components of print advertising in the United States and two countries in the European Union (the United Kingdom and France), suggesting that a comparison was made between the United States and the European Union. Findings were that the following elements in print advertisements differed significantly by country: the size of the visual, the frequency of usage of black-and-white visuals, the frequency of usage of photographic visuals, the size of the product in the visual, the frequency of usage of the product-comparison appeal, the frequency of usage of symbolism (e.g., metaphor), and the frequency of portraying children in the visual. They found that, within Europe, French advertising

TABLE 9.1 *Differences Between Advertising in the United States, France, and Taiwan*

United States	France	Taiwan
Direct address of audience	Less direct address	No direct address
Use of celebrity, testimonial, arguments	Symbolism and minimal copy, drama	
Lecture style	Dramatic events unfold with out apparent attention to the audience	Subtle presentations, drama related to family events
Information: facts	No straight single facts	Straight but unrelated facts
Reason why, explicit conclusions	Avoidance of reasoning or argument; no explicit conclusions	
	Explicit promise of an ideal, a dream	
Aggressive display of product	Play with shapes and names	Chinese values

SOURCE: Zandpour, Chang, & Catalano (1992).

used less comparison than British advertising, and more visuals and more symbolism.

Cutler, Javalgi, and Erramilli[49] conducted a multi-country content analysis, comparing the visual components of print advertising from five countries: the United States, the United Kingdom, France, Korea, and India. They concluded that there are more differences than similarities. U.S. advertising is the greatest user of comparative advertising. Both the United Kingdom and France are large users of symbolic advertising, while the United States is a low user of all types of symbolic approaches. The United States, Korea, and India are heavier users of people in ads than the United Kingdom and France. Children are portrayed most often in Indian ads, while French and U.K. ads contain children the least. Examples of unique aspects of countries were: more children in Indian visuals, the French visual orientation and sensitivity to aesthetics, the price being relatively more often included in Korean advertising, and the frequent use of comparative advertising in the United States.

Appelbaum and Halliburton[50] compared television commercials from France, Germany, Great Britain, and the United States with international advertising by U.S. multinationals. The results with respect to appeals used across the different countries were that "tradition" scored higher in the United Kingdom and the United States, "country of origin" in Germany, and "expressing individuality" in France. International advertising appears to use more hard selling than national advertising. They found that three formats were used most, with little difference between international and national usage: the slice-of-life, the little story around the product, and the character associated with the product.

Maleville[51] analyzed slogans of business-to-business advertisements from the United Kingdom, France, and the Netherlands. She related her findings to the Hofstede dimensions. French slogans showed an abundance of dates, times, and formulas. Although in other studies[52] seriousness was not a style the French found typical of French advertisements, nor a style they would prefer, Maleville concluded that a nonserious advertising style is not found in French business slogans. For business purposes, the high degree of uncertainty avoidance appears to translate into detailed instructions, absolute truths, and preciseness. French advertising showed a relatively high number of "magic" words, while the Dutch advertisements did not show a great variety of such words. "Magic" words are words that are so frequently found in advertising in a country that they have become a sort of "advertising property" in that country. Examples are "new," "best," "world," and "fly" in British advertising. Maleville's explanation for the lack of "magic" words in Dutch advertising is the no-nonsense attitude of the Dutch, explained by the Dutch score on femininity: "the essence of Dutch identity resides in the fact that it is not expressed." In the British advertisements, the most found word was "world," in combinations such as "the world's first global service" or "throughout the world." English advertisements showed more imperatives.

Zandpour et al.[53] conducted one of the most interesting studies to date, combining the Hofstede dimensions with advertising-related variables. The researchers content-analyzed television commercials from eight countries that are culturally very diverse. Research expectations were that differences in creative advertising strategies, in informativeness, and in advertising style would be related to differences in culture and advertising-industry-related factors. The study examined cultures, advertising industry environments, and advertising messages from the United States, Mexico, France, the United Kingdom, Spain, Germany, South Korea, and Taiwan. In order to apply the results, cultural and market-related information was also collected from 15 other countries, including Japan and Canada. The cultural dimensions used were Hofstede's individualism/collectivism, power distance, and uncertainty avoidance and Hall's perception of time: monochronic versus polychronic.

The advertising environment variables were: advertising expenditure per capita, presence of American companies among the top 10 advertisers, the level of government regulation, the existence of commercial breaks during programs, and the degree of advertising personnel shortages. Variables for categorizing the commercials were advertising creative strategy, informativeness, and advertising style. The results showed a number of relationships between culture and advertising variables, a few of which are summarized below.

With respect to advertising creative strategy:

- Information in the sense of unorganized facts without logical reasoning or structure was found most in cultures of weak uncertainty avoidance.
- Argument was found most in individualistic cultures of small power distance and strong uncertainty avoidance. Cultures of higher levels of uncertainty avoidance were more likely to appreciate explicit conclusions in the argument. People of large power distance cultures, placing a greater emphasis on the source of communication as opposed to the evidence and reasoning, were less likely to use the argument strategy.
- Testimonials were found in individualistic cultures.
- Advertising in individualistic cultures was more likely to be informative.

The Hofstede dimension masculinity/femininity was not used, which is unfortunate because it is such an important variable for explaining differences in advertising between American and continental European cultures. It would have been the most distinguishing dimension for finding relationships between the existence of typical American advertising styles found in a country and the presence of American companies. The masculinity dimension is a strong indicator of the use of typical American advertising forms, such as testimonials by celebrities and "argument." From the data in Zandpour et al.'s article it appears that Germany and the United States score highest on the use of "argument" as a creative strategy. As both countries score high on masculinity, this dimension might have been a better discriminator for this strategy. A reason for not using the masculinity dimension may be that U.S. researchers are constrained by the political correctness movement, which makes it difficult to use words like *masculine* and *feminine*.

Comparison of Advertising Appeals

Another most interesting study related to the Hofstede dimensions was conducted by Albers.[54] She related values and advertising appeals to all five dimensions. One of the questions in her doctoral dissertation was whether Hofstede's cultural model offers a tool for anticipating differences in advertising content with respect to cultural values. She conducted a content analysis of advertisements in business publications from 11 countries: the United States, Mexico, Chile, Brazil, Finland, France, South Africa, India, Israel, Taiwan, and Japan. The core question was not whether culture is reflected in advertising, but whether the appeals that are most commonly used actually relate to the values that are most salient in a particular culture. Albers defined a number of relationships between advertising appeals and Hofstede's dimensions. Appeals were collected and hypotheses were formulated with respect to the expected relationships between the appeals and Hofstede's dimensions. The advertisements were content analyzed on the existence or nonexistence of each appeal. Albers connected the following appeals to the five dimensions:

Individualism: Independence: distinctive, freedom, independence

Collectivism: Conformity: popular, succor, family, community, affiliation

Power distance high: Power: ornamental, dear, vain, status, health, sex

Power distance low: Submission: cheap, humility, wisdom, moral, nurturance

Uncertainty avoidance high: Risk aversion: safety, tamed, neat

Uncertainty avoidance low: Risk-prone: casual, adventure, untamed, magic, youth

Masculine: Achievement: effective, durable, convenient, self-respect, productivity

Feminine: Quality of life: relax, enjoy, frail, natural, modest, plain

Long-term orientation high: Long-term orientation: traditional, mature, modern, technological

Long-term orientation low: No advertising appeals measured

The findings of this study are very interesting as they demonstrate the problems in recognizing the expressions of the dimensions and how they are reflected in advertising. In this study, the hypothesis was that a number of appeals would fit specific dimensions. Yet the descriptions of each cluster of appeals include a variety of appeals fitting more than one dimension. Some appeals could be expected to fit better with other dimensions or a configuration of dimensions than the ones hypothesized by Albers. An example is categorizing the safety appeal under strong uncertainty avoidance, while it also can be a function of femininity. One cause of the problems Albers encountered may be the fact that she derived a number of hypotheses with respect to the appeals from American literature in which, for example, femininity values are rarely discussed. This may be the cause of linking affiliation needs mainly to collectivism. Humility in the sense of modesty is a function of femininity. In collectivistic societies it is an implicit part of life, the desirable, and not something to focus on in advertising. Also, the effects of the value paradoxes were not taken into account. This is important with respect to independence and conformity appeals. The distinctive and freedom appeals, linked by Albers to individualism, for example, were found most in Finland. It may be more a function of small power distance. It was not/least found in Japan, which has large power distance and is collectivistic. The conformity/family/affiliation appeals, frequently found in Finland, seem to be related more to femininity than to collectivism. The quality of life appeals, related to femininity, were indeed most found in the feminine cultures. Relaxation, however, found in Finland, may be more related to strong uncertainty avoidance.

The value "traditional" particularly appears to confuse people. It is more a function of short-term orientation than of long-term orientation. What is perceived as "traditional" in long-term orientation cultures is an expression of the rituals related to reverence for elders and ancestors. Pragmatism appears to be overriding the need for tradition. Modern appeals are a function of long-term orientation and are related to pragmatism, the wish to embrace and adapt new things. Short-term orientation was unfortunately not measured separately, although the "instant gratification" appeal is ubiquitous in U.S. advertising.

Conclusion

Academic researchers are increasingly conducting cross-cultural advertising studies. The major problem of such studies is objectivity. Each researcher is a prisoner of his or her culture and thus ethnocentrism in assumptions, hypotheses, and methods is to a certain degree part of all studies. Criteria for comparison tend to be pseudo-etic, and it is extremely difficult to obtain a truly representative sample. Many studies use the content-analysis method and report comparative facts, but rarely try to explain why these facts are meaningful. Conclusions are often biased because of ethnocentrism or lack of experience with other cultures. One fallacy is that the advertising style used for one product category can be representative of the advertising style of the culture in which the advertisements are measured. Another is the bias toward American criteria for comparing advertising among other cultures. This is not only demonstrated by American researchers but also by researchers from other countries. An example is the dichotomy "hard sell/soft sell." Where the hard sell or direct speech is not a part of the culture and its communication style in general, it seems a waste of energy to start looking for it.

Nevertheless, a growing research base is available from cross-cultural advertising research aimed at finding differences and similarities in advertising styles across borders. A number of those studies were summarized and commented on in this chapter. Comments on research methods are not meant as criticism but as a contribution to the development of research methods for finding new paths to developing better global advertising.

A new lead could be the emic approach, trying to explain cultures' communication styles by comparing with other relevant areas, such as literature, art, and journalism, and in that way map the world more generally in order to learn to understand the differences in advertising styles. Advertising style comprises appeals, motive, strategy, and the basic advertising form. Chapter 10 will focus on the basic advertising forms of different cultures.

Notes

1. Zandpour, F., Chang, C., & Catalano, J. (1992, January/February). "Stories, symbols, and straight talk: A comparative analysis of French, Taiwanese, and U.S. TV commercials." *Journal of Advertising Research,* pp. 25-38.

2. Note: The study by Miracle, Chang, and Taylor (see Note 13, below), which is an example of a study using only objectively measurable variables, used an enormous sample of 2,481 television commercials. The results were meaningful because the assumptions and hypotheses were also based on a thorough knowledge of the cultures studied.

3. Miracle, G. E. (1982). "Applying cross-cultural research findings to advertising practice and research." In A. D. Fletcher (Ed.), *Proceedings of the 1982 Conference of the American Advertising Academy.* (Contact Robert King, AAA Executive Secretary, School of Business, University of Richmond, Richmond, VA 23173)

4. Feyerabend, P. (1988). *Against method: Outline of an anarchistic theory of knowledge.* New York: Verso.

5. Hofstede, G. (1984). *Culture's consequences: International differences in work-related values.* Beverly Hills, CA: Sage, pp. 138-139.

6. Samiee, S., & Jeong, I. (1994, Summer). "Cross-cultural research in advertising: An assessment of methodologies." *Journal of the Academy of Marketing Science,* p. 209.

7. Fiske, J. (1990). *Introduction of communication studies* (2nd ed.). New York: Routledge, pp. 136-143.

8. Zandpour, F., Campos, V., Catalano, J., Chang, C., Cho, Y. D., Hoobyar, R., Jiang, S.-F., Lin, M.-C., Madrid, S., Scheideler, H., & Osborn, S. T. (1994,

September/October). "Global reach and local touch: Achieving cultural fitness in TV advertising." *Journal of Advertising Research.*

9. *European planning guide 95-96.* (1995, August). M & M Europe in association with Initiative Media. Media & Marketing Europe.

10. Samiee & Jeong (1994), "Cross-cultural research," p. 213.

11. (1) Resnik, A., & Stern, B. L. (1977). "An analysis of information content in television advertising." *Journal of Marketing, 41,* 50-53. (2) Stern, B. L., & Resnik, A. J. (1991, June/July). "Information content in television advertising: A replication and extension." *Journal of Advertising Research,* pp. 36-46.

12. Stern & Resnik (1991), "Information content in television advertising," p. 36.

13. Miracle, G. E., Taylor, C. R., & Chang, K. Y. (1992). "Culture and advertising executions: A comparison of selected characteristics of Japanese and U.S. television commercials." *Journal of International Consumer Marketing, 4*(4), 89-113.

14. Ray, M. (1982). *Advertising and communications management.* Englewood Cliffs, NJ: Prentice Hall.

15. Zandpour et al. (1994), "Global reach and local touch."

16. Graham, J. L., Kamins, M. A., & Oetomo, D. S. (1993). "Content analysis of German and Japanese advertising in print media from Indonesia, Spain, and the United States." *Journal of Advertising, 22*(2), 5-15.

17. Information from Majorie Dijkstal, advertising researcher at FHV/BBDO, the Netherlands.

18. Samiee & Jeong (1994), "Cross-cultural research," p. 212.

19. Caillat, Z., & Mueller, B. (1996, May-June). "Observations: The influence of culture on American and British advertising: An exploratory comparison of beer advertising." *Journal of Advertising Research,* pp. 79-88.

20. This follows the discussion about how psychological research has become dominated by methodological standards in favor of predictive results, over descriptive and interpretive studies. From: Spiering, H., "Interview with Trudy Dehue, Professor, 'Principles and history of psychology,' University of Groningen, the Netherlands." *NRC Handelsblad,* July 4, 1996.

21. Compare Feyerabend (1988), *Against method,* p. 232.

22. Buijs, F., Biswas, C., Fernandez, M., Roscoe, E., & Wieringa, D. (1996). *Intercultural value research in marketing communication* (Erasmus Universiteit Rotterdam and FHV/BBDO Marketing Communication Services, Unpublished Document IMScEC15. May 10).

23. Taylor, R. E., & Hoy, M. G. (1995). "The presence of la séduction, le spectacle, l'amour and l'humour in French commercials." In S. Madden (Ed.), *Proceedings of the 1995 Conference of the American Academy of Advertising.* pp. 36-42. (Contact Robert King, AAA Executive Secretary, School of Business, University of Richmond, Richmond, VA 23173)

24. I was involved in this project in cooperation with Simone Maas, advertising researcher at FHV/BBDO.

25. Heyder, H., Musiol, K. G., & Peters, K. (1992, March). "Advertising in Europe—Attitudes towards advertising in certain key East and West European countries." *Marketing and Research Today,* pp. 19-23.

26. In "TV Advertising in Europe—Lessons learned from more than 3,000 TV-Spot Tests," in *The Contribution of Advertising Testing to the Development of Effective International Advertising* [Newsletter] (GfK Nuremberg, 1991), pp. 9-17.

27. "Global advertising: Standardized or multicultural." (1992). *Topline* (MSW journal), No. 37.

28. Bonnal, F. (1990, December 1). "Attitudes to advertising in six European countries." *Admap*, pp. 19-23.

29. Tian Shuqian. (1992, September). *China, reform and consumers' changes.* Paper presented at the meetings of the International Advertising Association World Congress, Barcelona.

30. Cheng, H. (1994). "Reflections of cultural values: A content analysis of Chinese magazine advertisements from 1982-1992." *International Journal of Advertising*, No. 13, pp. 167-183.

31. Katz, H., & Lee, W.-N. (1992). "Oceans apart: An initial exploration of social communication differences in US and UK prime-time television advertising." *International Journal of Advertising*, No. 11, pp. 69-82.

32. Spotts, H., Weinberger, M. G., & Parsons, A. (1995). "Creative strategy and execution in international magazine advertising: A US/UK comparison." In S. Madden (Ed.), *Proceedings of the 1995 Conference of the American Academy of Advertising*. New York: American Academy of Advertising, pp. 34-35. (Contact Robert King, AAA Executive Secretary, School of Business, University of Richmond, Richmond, VA 23173)

33. Nevett, T. (1992, December). "Differences between American and British television advertising: Explanations and implications." *Journal of Advertising, 21*(4), 61-71.

34. Biswas, A., Olsen, J. E., & Carlet, V. (1992, December). "A comparison of print advertisements from the United States and France." *Journal of Advertising, 21*(4), 73-81.

35. Taylor & Hoy (1995), "The presence of la séduction."

36. Wassink, C. (1991). *La Douce France versus Nederland. 100 commercials gemeten en vergeleken.* Doctoraalscriptie Communicatiewetenschap, University of Amsterdam. Unpublished.

37. Mueller, B. (1987, June/July). "Reflections of culture: An analysis of Japanese and American advertising appeals." *Journal of Advertising Research*, pp. 51-59.

38. Mueller, B. (1992, January/February). "Standardization vs. specialization: An examination of Westernization in Japanese advertising." *Journal of Advertising Research*, pp. 15-24.

39. Ramaprasad, J., & Hasegawa, K. (1992, January/February). "Creative strategies in American and Japanese TV commercials: A comparison." *Journal of Advertising Research*, pp. 59-67.

40. Miracle, Taylor, & Chang (1992), "Culture and advertising executions."

41. Lin, C. A. (1993, July/August). "Cultural differences in message strategies: A comparison between American and Japanese TV commercials." *Journal of Advertising Research*, pp. 40-47.

42. Resnik & Stern (1977), "An analysis of information content."

43. Sengupta, S. (1995). "The influence of culture on portrayals of women in television commercials: A comparison between the United States and Japan." *International Journal of Advertising, 14,* 314-333.

44. Zhao, X., & Shen, F. (1995). "Audience reaction to commercial advertising in China in the 1980s." *International Journal of Advertising, 14,* 374-390.

45. Chan, K. K. W. (1995). "Information content of television advertising in China." *International Journal of Advertising, 14,* 365-373.

46. Cheng (1994), "Reflections of cultural values."

47. Zandpour, Chang, & Catalano (1992), "Stories, symbols, and straight talk."

48. Cutler, B. D., & Javalgi, R. G. (1992, January/February). "A cross-cultural analysis of the visual components of print advertising: The United States and the European Community." *Journal of Advertising Research,* pp. 71-80.

49. Cutler, B. D., Javalgi, R. G., & Erramilli, M. K. (1992, January). "The visual components of print advertising: A five-country cross-cultural analysis." *European Journal of Marketing,* 26(4).

50. Appelbaum, U., & Halliburton, C. (1993). "How to develop international advertising campaigns that work: The example of the European food and beverage sector." *International Journal of Advertising, 12,* 223-241.

51. Maleville, M. (1993). "How boringly respectable can you get? A study of business slogans in three countries." *Toegepaste Taalwetenschap,* 2(3).

52. For example, Bonnal (1990), "Attitudes to advertising in six European countries."

53. Zandpour et al. (1994), "Global reach and local touch."

54. Albers, N. D. (1994). *Relating Hofstede's dimensions of culture to international variations in print advertisements: A comparison of appeals.* A doctoral dissertation presented to the Faculty of the College of Business Administration, University of Houston, May.

CHAPTER 10

Executional Style and Culture

The appeals, motives, and basic forms used in advertising vary by culture. Basic forms or executional styles represent contexts for the advertising message conveyed by a commercial.[1] A number of basic advertising forms that are used in different executional variations can be distinguished. Major international advertisers have used a single form indiscriminately across cultures. An example is the testimonial form used worldwide by Procter & Gamble. That does not mean that these formats are a first choice of all cultures. The "comparison" form is controversial. The "testimonial" form is a very direct form of communication that is not equally appealing to people of all cultures. The "drama" form is more indirect and may fit in more cultures. Certain forms have proved to be effective in one culture but not in others. An example is the entertainment form, effective in Japan but not in the United States. Some cultures may use basic forms that are not found in others. For international advertising, it is necessary to determine which basic forms are universal and which are not. There is little knowledge about the existence of universal forms that can be used equally well across cultures or of the relative effectiveness of forms of one culture for others. The purpose of this chapter is to review basic advertising forms, both potentially universal ones and culturally defined basic advertising forms. Classifications of advertising style will be reviewed and one will be described comprehensively. A few research problems will be presented, with questions and hypotheses for further research.

Classifications of Advertising Style

For the purpose of comparing advertising styles, all sorts of classification systems are used. They can be very comprehensive, covering all aspects of advertising style, or they can cover only a few aspects. This section reviews systems for classifying the various aspects of an advertisement or a television commercial: creative strategy, content, theme, and form. The summary refers to studies described in Chapter 9 for which the classifications were used.

The classification informational-transformational was used by Laskey[2,3] to categorize creative strategies in television commercials. Moriarty[4] mentions them as main message strategies. Informational advertising covers explicit messages; transformational advertising covers images.

Kroeber-Riel's[5] classification distinguishes between functional (what the product does) and emotional elements.

To operationalize the distinction between informative and noninformative, Resnik and Stern[6] developed a typology of 14 informational cues. These represent the factors that can be used by consumers in making an intelligent choice among alternatives: price or value, quality, performance, components or contents, availability, special offers, taste, nutrition, packaging or shape, guarantees or warranties, safety, independent research, company research, and new ideas.

The division soft sell/product merit/hard sell was used by Mueller[7] to analyze change in Japanese advertising. A soft sell was described as a primary emphasis on creating a mood or an atmosphere. Product merit is a primary focus on the product and its characteristics. A hard sell was described as having its primary emphasis on distinguishing the product from the competition.

Well's categorization[8,9,10] of drama, lecture, and lecture-drama provides a simple distinction of advertising forms for the United States. According to Wells, a drama is a form of indirect address, like a movie or a play, because in a drama the characters speak to each other, not to the audience. A lecture is a form of direct address; the speaker addresses the audience from the television screen or the written page. In a lecture, the speaker presents evidence (data) and employs techniques such as arguments to persuade the audience.

The advertising format typology by Leiss, Kline, and Jhally[11] has four forms: product information, product image, personalization, and lifestyle. It was used by Katz and Lee[12] to compare advertising forms in the United States and the United Kingdom. In product information, the emphasis is on the product itself, its benefits and usage, or a "rational" sell. The product image format includes symbolic information with respect to product and context. Both product and setting help the consumer "interpret" the message. Personalization advertisements feature people talking about the product. The lifestyle format shows a connection between the product, the person, and usage, combining entertaining or active scenes with (ordinary) people. This format focuses on the consumption experience itself.

Appelbaum and Halliburton[13] categorized tone and form of advertising. They identified five dimensions in their analysis of the tone of the commercial: the use of humor; argumentative (direct address of viewer) versus narrative (indirect address); competitive (any reference to the competition) versus noncompetitive (no reference to competition); hard sell (sales orientation is emphasized) versus soft sell (mood and atmosphere); and direct approach (information about the product is conveyed through words) versus indirect approach (information is conveyed through images). An advertisement's form is defined as how it is presented, structured, and delivered. The following forms are distinguished: slice-of-life; little story around the product; testimonial (from experts, stars, or "average" people); talking heads; characters associated with the product; demonstration; product in action; cartoon; international/national; other (all other formats not classified above).

Cutler and Javalgi[14] analyzed visuals in advertising and distinguished four types of advertising forms: description (what the brand looks like), comparative (naming competitors), association (lifestyle or situation), and symbolic (metaphor, storytelling, and aesthetic).

Taylor and Hoy[15] use a classification of descriptors provided by French advertising professionals: *la Séduction* or temptation, French advertising tempts the consumer with its offering; *le Spectacle,* French advertising is theater, drama, show; *l'Amour* or romance, erotics, desire, display of affection; and *l'Humour,* amusing associations, playful use of words, humor.

Shimp[16] developed a categorization based on the general nature of the execution employed. He identified four basic commercial styles, distinguished by whether the commercial focused on an individual, a story, a product, or a technique. Each basic style had several alternative executions, leading to an 11-category typology. Laskey, Fox, and Crask[17] used this category to investigate the impact of executional style on television commercial effectiveness in the United States.

Moriarty[18] distinguishes among basic appeals, creative strategy, and execution forms. She lists 14 types of commonly used execution forms in the United States: (a) News announcement; (b) Problem solution; (c) Product as hero; (d) Demonstration; (e) Torture test; (f) Song-and-dance spectacular; (g) Special effect; (h) Before-and-after and side-by-side comparison; (i) Competitive comparison; (j) Announcer; (k) Dialogue/interview/conversation; (l) Slice-of-life; (m) Spokesperson; and (n) Vignette. She elaborates on the six of these that seem to cover most of U.S. advertising forms: comparative advertising, announcer, dialogue/conversation, slice-of-life, testimonials, and vignettes.

Franzen's Classification System of Basic Advertising Forms

The classification system for comparing advertising forms across cultures that is presented in this chapter is my adaptation of a classification model by Franzen.[19] Franzen used this model to analyze the characteristics of advertising that influence effectiveness and found that a limited number of basic forms and executions accounted for differences in effectiveness. Although this classification system may be biased by the Dutch culture of its producers (Franzen and myself), Franzen's categorization was based on literature and a lifelong advertising experience in Europe. It was tested by a content analysis of Dutch advertising using a comprehensive code list of 112 variables, and by statistical analysis. My adaptation is based on analysis of television commercials of more than 11 different cultures. The model consists of eight groups and a number of subgroups. The eight main groups are: announcement, display, association transfer, lesson, drama, pure entertainment, imagination, and special effects.

Eight Basic Advertising Forms Worldwide

In order to develop the application of Hofstede's 5-D model to advertising, I have analyzed print advertisements from more than 20 different countries[20] and more than 5,000 television commercials from 13 countries.[21] I have found that Franzen's eight basic forms do exist in all cultures, although the distribution and the way they are executed will vary. An adapted version of Franzen's model is presented in this section (see also Table 10.1). Each basic form is described, and hypotheses are added regarding how culture may influence usage of the basic form or cause the need for variations in execution. There are eight groups, and each group has a number of subdivisions. The basic forms are not mutually exclusive, so a commercial or advertisement may represent more than one main form or subcategory. The forms can be recognized in layers: there may be a dominant form, while the underlying tone of the advertisement may represent another form. Some combinations are found more often than others.

1. Announcement

Announcements are presentations of facts, with no use of people. The facts or visuals are assumed to speak for themselves. This is the most basic type of advertisement: the product and information about the product.

TABLE 10.1 *Eight Basic Advertising Forms*

Basic Forms	Subcategories
1. Announcement	1.1. Pure presentation 1.2. Factual explanation 1.3. Product message 1.4. Corporate presentation, documentary
2. Display	
3. Association Transfer	3.1. Lifestyle 3.2. Metaphor 3.3. Metonymy 3.4. Celebrity transfer
4. Lesson	4.1. Presenter 4.2. Testimonial/endorsement 4.3. Demonstration 4.4. Comparison 4.5. Analogy 4.6. "How to" 4.7. Dramatized lesson
5. Drama	5.1. Slice-of-life 5.2. Problem-solution 5.3. Vignettes 5.4. Theater
6. Entertainment	6.1. Humor 6.2. Play or act around product
7. Imagination	7.1. Cartoons 7.2. Film properties in action 7.3. Other, unrealistic acts
8. Special Effects	8.1. Product in action, animation 8.2. Film, video techniques, artistic stimuli

1.1. Pure Presentation. This can be a pure display of the product or a presentation of facts. Low-context cultures are more verbally oriented, high-context cultures are more visually oriented. Examples of this form are found in retail advertising: presentation of CDs, computer games, perfumes, and luxury alcoholic drinks. Subtle elements may reflect culture, such as displaying a bottle with one glass (individualism) or with a number of glasses (collectivism).

1.2. Factual Explanation. This form is based on an explanation of facts about or around the product or brand. It is found most often in low-context cultures because factual, logical explanation is a characteristic of individualistic, low-context cultures. This form is typical for new products or services, cameras, business-to-business products, printers, copiers, computers, and innovations.

1.3. Product Message. These are statements rather than explanations and are usually verbal. Messages can be about ingredients or availability of the product, news about products and services, discounts, sales, locations, films, and more.

1.4. Corporate Presentation. This form is most often seen in corporate advertising, but also in commercials for high-involvement products or services. It is frequently found in international corporate advertising. It can be compared with a documentary and concerns the presentation of the company or product by visuals, sometimes including people in relation to the company or product to illustrate its activities. In an international commercial, people from all parts of the world may be shown. The visuals are related to the company's stakeholders, its product, or both. The company's message may be presented in a voice-over or a song. This is a form that can easily be internationalized by translating the voice-over. The voice-over presents facts. The amount of facts is culture-bound: more in low-context cultures and less in high-context cultures. In 1996, I found the form used by—among others—General Electric, Mobil, Volvo, Baxter.

2. Pure Display

Pure displays include all forms that are based primarily on a product's appearance, rather like a product in a shop window or showroom. The product is the hero. This is a relatively culture-free form and may be useful for international advertising. It is found in advertising for fashion items, jewelry, and perfume.

3. Association Transfer

In association transfers, the product is combined with another object, a person or situation, or an environment. Associations with the objects or persons are meant to be transferred to the brand. Subforms include lifestyle, metaphor, metonymy, and celebrity transfer.

3.1. Lifestyle. The lifestyle concept is meant to transfer an association with people (young, successful, etc.). The type of lifestyle is culture-bound.

 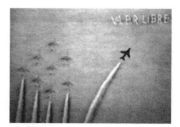

Illustrations 10.1–10.3 (From top left to right.)

Masculine cultures prefer to associate with the successful, the rich; feminine cultures will want to associate with nice, friendly people. As people are often depicted interacting with other people, the execution of the form is culture-bound.

3.2. Metaphor. A metaphor can be used to transfer the characteristics of an object or an animal (concrete) or an idea (abstract) to the brand by drawing a parallel. Metaphors are much used in advertising for all product categories. They are both verbal and visual, concrete and abstract. Visual metaphors are used more in high-context cultures and verbal metaphors more in low-context cultures.

Illustration 10.1 gives an example of a concrete metaphor, comparing a car with a wolf in an Italian commercial for the Nissan NX Almera. Illustration 10.2 shows a more abstract metaphor in a Spanish commercial: Sidra Lagar *"va por libre,"* expressing freedom or nonconformity by showing one aeroplane deviating from a number of other airplanes flying in formation. Illustration 10.3 depicts "a small world" for Thai Airlines.

3.3. Metonymy. Metonymy transfers the meaning of the original object to the brand—for example, a flower turning into a perfume, or a piece of fruit turning into a syrup, or a strawberry turning into jam (Hero). This is a form that can cross borders. It is purely product oriented and does not include values. Because it is an indirect and visual way of explaining, it will be more appealing to high-context cultures than to low-context cultures.

3.4. Celebrity Transfer. This subform covers advertising in which a celebrity is shown or in which a celebrity acts with other persons without demonstrating or endorsing or giving a testimonial. The only objective of showing the celebrity is so that the target group can associate the product with the celebrity. Examples are showing Michael Johnson with Nike or Gatorade, or an elegant actress who puts on a fashionable watch and engages happily in a party. The image of the sports star is transferred to the sports shoes or the sports drink; the image of the actress, or "elegance," is transferred to the watch. An actress playing the role of a housewife and referring to a refrigerator is viewed as an endorsement, not as pure association, because there is no transfer of "elegance" to a fridge.[22] If in a commercial for Martini in Italy, the model Naomi Campbell appears at the end and says no more than "Martini, it's a party," that is an association with a celebrity or celebrity transfer rather than an endorsement by a celebrity. Individualistic, low-context cultures need more facts and thus will use more endorsements than association transfers, which are a more indirect form fit for collectivistic cultures.

4. Lesson

Lessons are direct communications, presentations of facts and arguments, meant to lecture the audience. They state, explain, show, try to convince or to persuade. There may be presenters or voice-overs telling or explaining something to the audience, demonstrating something, or comparing, often with the help of visuals. The audience can be addressed in the "we-style" or the "you-style" and imperatives can be used. Examples from the United States are: "Meet the all new Ford 150," "Take control with Nicotrol," "The only good wrinkle is the wrinkle you never get" (Oil of Olay), "Any time you need us, anywhere you need us" (Wells Fargo), "You are over 50 and have not lost your edge . . . " (Centrum Silver nutritional supplements). There is little or no interaction or dialogue. This category fits best in individualistic, low-context cultures.

Illustration 10.4

4.1. Presenter. Presenters are persons with a dominant presence, speaking into the camera, and conveying the main message. They can give a demonstration, make a comment only, or interview or be interviewed with or without the interviewer being shown. The role of the presenter and the way he or she behaves will vary by culture. In high power distance cultures, presenters will be older. A single dominant presenter is characteristic of individualistic cultures. More than one presenter will be seen in collectivistic cultures. An example is given in illustration 10.4, a shot from a Japanese commercial for Panasonic. In cultures scoring high on masculinity, the presenter will be a "personality." In cultures of the configuration masculinity-individualism, presenters use a more persuasive style that is perceived as "pushy" and irritating by members of feminine cultures. Feminine cultures do not like dominant people, so there the presenter and the approach will be more softly voiced. Presenters in cultures of strong uncertainty avoidance must convey competence related to the product or service.

4.2. Endorsement and Testimonial. In this subform, a presenter or spokesperson suggests that he or she is a user of the product (testimonial) or has an opinion about it and therefore endorses the product (endorsement). Pure user-testimonials are used in low-context cultures and particularly by American companies. Procter & Gamble uses this form worldwide for a number of brands in the category of disposable products (diapers, sanitary napkins/towels). Endorsements include celebrities or experts who, because of their role in society or expertise, are supposed to have an opinion, are credible, can convince. An important element of the testimonial is its credibility, which is an important element for cultures occupied with seeking the truth. Credibility is less of a requirement for Asian cultures.

The testimonial form is used in various cultures, but the roles of the presenters in both endorsements and testimonials vary. In masculine cultures, presenters tend to be high profile—celebrities, stars, or known people. If ordinary people give testimonials, they are identified, their name is mentioned, and sometimes their signature is added. In feminine cultures they are usually anonymous. P&G follows a single American strategy but selects local women who give endorsements. In feminine societies more used to anonymous presenters, giving the name of an endorser who is not a celebrity makes people wonder "Who is she?" Masculine cultures appreciate stars and celebrities, "heroes." In a collectivistic and masculine culture, such as Japan, segments or age groups have their own stars. A characteristic of Japanese advertising is the many famous people who appear in commercials. They support the brand indirectly and may say a few words, such as "tastes good." Many so-called *talento* are professional models who became famous by first appearing in commercials and then, on the basis of popularity attained through these commercials, started their own singing and/or acting careers.[23]

Western cultures combining masculinity and strong uncertainty avoidance show high-profile presenters who are also experts: competent experts who must provide credibility. This is the type found in countries like Germany and Italy. Feminine cultures don't take their heroes seriously, or else downplay their importance. The presenter is preferably anonymous; person and message are low profile. Big egos are not appreciated. A testimonial by a celebrity is therefore not a format that fits feminine cultures. The Dutch, for example, may use well-known people, but these do not present themselves in a serious way, resulting in a parody on the testimonial. The Spanish show a similar approach to testimonials in advertising. They also tend to understate the importance of the endorser. In the United Kingdom, a masculine culture that is low on power distance and uncertainty avoidance, people do not like authority, which also results in the parody style.

The roles of presenters can be summarized according to four culture clusters, as illustrated in Figure 10.1 for 30 countries:

1. In the upper left-hand quadrant is the culture-cluster masculinity-weak uncertainty avoidance. Members of these cultures will appreciate a high-profile public person or personality. Illustration 10.5 shows the endorsement of Sun Chips by Ray Charles. Illustration 10.6 presents an example of an identified presenter for an English commercial for Oil of Ulay.

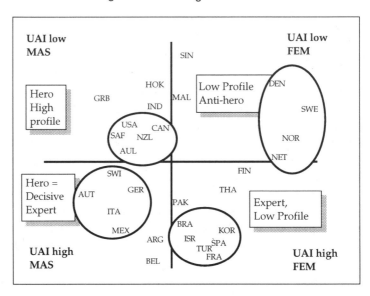

Figure 10.1 Testimonials: Roles of Presenters

NOTE: ARG = Argentina, AUL = Australia, AUT = Austria, BEL = Belgium, BRA = Brazil, CAN = Canada, DEN = Denmark, FIN = Finland, FRA = France, GER = Germany, GRB = Great Britain, HOK = Hong Kong, IND = India, ISR = Israel, ITA = Italy, KOR = Korea, MAL = Malaysia, MEX = Mexico, NET = the Netherlands, NOR = Norway, NZL = New Zealand, PAK = Pakistan, SAF = South Africa, SIN = Singapore, SPA = Spain, SWE = Sweden, SWI = Switzerland, THA = Thailand, TUR = Turkey, USA = the United States.

2. The upper right-hand quadrant shows the cluster femininity-weak uncertainty avoidance. Feminine cultures will prefer low-profile presenters. Mothers testifying for products used for their children will tend to play the role of a caring person rather than the role of an expert. Examples are shown in Illustrations 10.7 and 10.8, both from Dutch advertising. In the Nissan advertisement, the babies are the advisors. A commercial for low fat milk shows a presenter who ridicules the expert. He is giving a "scientific" comparison of low fat milk in which a cow interferes by switching the two glasses in the test.

3. The lower right-hand quadrant shows the combination femininity-strong uncertainty avoidance. Here, a low profile will be combined with the role of the expert, but underplayed. The specialist is the expert professional, the craftsman. Illustration 10.9 shows an advertisement for Aspirina (Spain) with a violin player who cannot afford to have a headache. Illustration 10.10 shows the owner of a bar and the cleanser he uses (Estrella gel, Spain). Illustration 10.11 shows a Spanish commercial for Queso de Burgos (cheese) endorsed by a local farmer. He talks in understatements about the product, relating it to people who are "not salty" (*soso*), which also means boring.

Illustrations 10.5–10.6 (From left to right.)

Illustrations 10.7–10.8 (From left to right.)

Illustrations 10.9–10.11 (From left to right.)

4. The lower left-hand quadrant shows the combination masculinity-strong uncertainty avoidance. In these cultures the high-profile competent

Illustrations 10.12–10.14 (From left to right.)

or expert presenter is preferred. Endorsers must be legitimate, must show they know what they are talking about. Examples are specialists, doctors and professors or people wearing white coats, suggesting they are experts or CEOs of companies. Mothers will be depicted more in the role of the efficient, professional housewife than in the role of a caring, loving mother who has a good relationship with her children. Illustrations 10.12 and 10.13 show a female dentist and a woman in a white coat endorsing toothpaste (Perlweiss and Blend-a-dent, respectively, Germany), the white coat suggesting her expertise. Illustration 10.14 shows an advertisement for window frames, endorsed by the director of the factory where they are produced.

4.3. Demonstration. The advertisement shows how (well) the product works. Product attributes and benefits may be shown, or the situation before and after use. A presenter may demonstrate how the product works. Demonstration of how a product works is a particularly good form for low-context cultures, yet the amount of information, details, and instruction will depend on the degree of uncertainty avoidance. Strong uncertainty avoidance cultures, for example, show more detailed information than weak uncertainty avoidance cultures. Focus can be on the attributes and benefits of the product, before and after using the product, and testing. Description of the attributes of the product and the direct benefits to the user is usually factual and is attractive to low-context cultures. The message can be conveyed verbally and visually.

Before and after use is a result-oriented approach. More focus on the result, the effect of usage on the user, will be appealing to masculine cultures. Cultures of the combination masculinity and strong uncertainty avoidance will want to add the details of how the product works, showing the process.

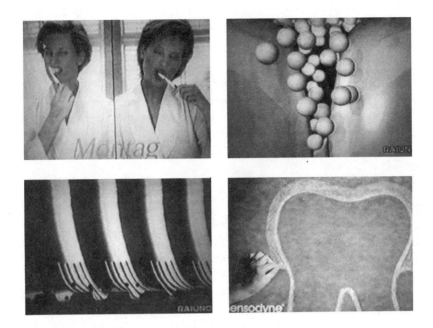

Illustrations 10.15–10.18 (From top left to right.)

That is what you see in Germany, while in the United Kingdom focus is more on the benefit to the person. Advertising for Colgate Total toothbrushes in the United Kingdom focuses on the result, on white teeth, and adds: "Brushing that works." Advertising for German dental care products usually adds the details of how they work. Illustration 10.15 shows a shot of a German commercial for toothpaste, showing the results after a number of days' usage, but focus is more on the process. On top of that, all sorts of details are added to demonstrate how it actually works. Testing is often part of demonstrations and is a particularly strong element of German advertising. Many German advertisements advise testing it yourself in the shop where the expert is available. Illustrations 10.16 and 10.17 show examples of details in demonstrations for Mentadent toothpaste and Vileda brushes in Italy. The picture of the details of the Mentadent commercial is also found in commercials for Pepsodent in Sweden and in a commercial for Signal in France. Illustration 10.18 shows a shot of a commercial for Sensodyne toothpaste in Spain. In that commercial, apart from the explicit illustration of how the toothpaste works, the presenter scratches her diamond ring across glass as an analogy of what happens if you scratch unprotected teeth.

4.4. Comparison. Four types of comparative advertising can be distinguished:

- Competitive comparison: the brand is compared with another, identified brand
- The brand is compared with an unidentified product, not named, called "Brand X," "the other brand leader," or a "conventional" product, often presented in the form of side-by-side comparison
- The brand is said to be better than "other products in the category"
- "The best" or "the best in the world"

The appreciation of comparative advertising is culture-bound. It is a typical form for the United States. It fits best in cultures of the configuration individualism-masculinity-weak to medium uncertainty avoidance. It is not appreciated in most other cultures. Acceptance and nonacceptance can best be explained by the varying configurations of individualism/collectivism and masculinity. Figure 10.2 shows four culture clusters. In three of them, the form is not acceptable.

1. The upper left-hand quadrant shows the combination collectivism-femininity, with both Asian and Latin American cultures. In collectivistic cultures, comparison with the competition is not acceptable because it makes the other party lose face. Using comparative advertising means trying to make the other party lose face, and it will backfire: You are the one who loses face, as it is not proper. More than two thirds of the world population are more or less collectivistic, which may explain the relatively low use of comparative advertising. It is not perceived as an attractive form in feminine cultures, either, because it is considered too aggressive. Also, modesty makes people feel that it is not proper to demonstrate how good you are.

2. The upper right-hand quadrant shows the combination collectivism-masculinity. Masculine cultures, characterized by their interest in winning and fighting, are basically in favor of competitive comparative advertising. Although these cultures may want to express the fact that they are good, the combination with collectivism makes avoiding a loss of face for others overriding. If comparison is used, the comparison is with another product of the same company to show, for example, that an innovative new product is better than an old product from that company. Japan is the typical example of such a culture, but a number of Latin American cultures are also in this cluster.

3. The lower right-hand quadrant shows the combination masculinity-individualism. In cultures of this combination, people tend to focus on their

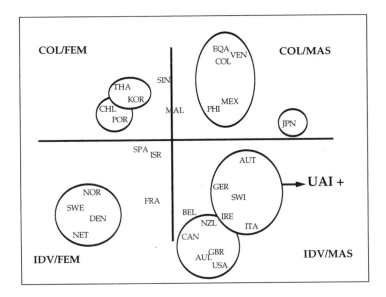

Figure 10.2. Comparative Advertising
NOTE: AUL = Australia, AUT = Austria, BEL = Belgium, CAN = Canada, CHL = Chile, COL = Colombia, DEN = Denmark, EQA = Equador, FRA = France, GER = Germany, GBR = Great Britain, IRE = Ireland, ISR = Israel, ITA = Italy, JPN = Japan, KOR = Korea, MAL = Malaysia, MEX = Mexico, NET = the Netherlands, NOR = Norway, NZL = New Zealand, PHI = Philippines, POR = Portugal, SIN = Singapore, SPA = Spain, SWE = Sweden, SWI = Switzerland, THA = Thailand, USA = the United States, VEN = Venezuela.

rights. As a result, Anglo-Saxon cultures, and in particular the U.S. culture, tend to see comparative advertising as informational, offering the consumer "the right to choose." Only the Anglo-Saxon cultures like the hard confrontation as represented by the "cola wars." Germany, Austria, and Switzerland may also like it, but are inhibited by their strong uncertainty avoidance, which makes it difficult to cope with the related ambiguities—such as having to prove the correctness of the claims. Various types of competitive comparison are used in the United States. Examples include side-by-side comparisons, demonstrations with competitor's name mentioned, or pictures of packages of competitors' brands with a cross through them. An example of the indirect style is comparison with "the other leading brand." U.S. examples of "the best" are: "America's best service at Michigan's best retail store," "We make the world's best mattresses" (Serta), "The most innovative staffing company in the world" (Interim personnel).

4. The lower left-hand quadrant shows cultures of the configuration individualistic-feminine. This is the Scandinavian-Dutch cluster. Feminine cultures, because of affiliation needs, are more in favor of the soft approach.

Illustration 10.19

They do not like the confrontation included in direct comparison. Being the best is OK, but saying so is not: "Probably the best beer in the world" (Carlsberg, Denmark).

Illustration 10.19 presents an example of the most used type of comparison: The brand Always compared with a conventional sanitary napkin/towel (the United Kingdom brand). This is part of an international campaign in Europe (1996) based on testimonials by users of the product and on side-by-side comparison. The location is the same in the commercials for the different countries, but local women give the testimonials.

4.5. Analogy. Use is made of a similarity or resemblance to other items or events in order to make the attributes or effects of a product clear. An unexpected connection between two phenomena is involved, such as comparing the effect of toothpaste with the smoothness of a clean dish.

4.6. "How to . . . ". Use of the product and the result achieved are explained or demonstrated. All recipe advertising is covered by this form. Another example is demonstrating how to use technical products. Illustration 10.20 gives an example of how to use the Braun Super Volume Twist to style one's hair.

4.7. Dramatized Lesson. This subform is a combination of lesson and drama, like Well's lecture-drama form, but the lesson is dominant. Drama illustrates the lesson. There is no dialogue as in the category "drama." The strong verbal message dominates, can be factual or instructive, by voice-over

Illustration 10.20

or song. There may be a "mute" dialogue; people interact to illustrate occasions, moods, and moments. The argumentation is in the voice-over. Examples are stories around people, such as in a U.S. commercial for Jack in the Box fast food restaurants, a narration about Jack and how he guards the quality of his business. In 1996, the form was used by DHL and UPS. A European example is a commercial for Werthers Echte (Germany), showing the relationship between grandfather and grandson and the sharing of the candy. There is a full story demonstrating moods and moments, but no dialogue. Because people do not speak and the message and product information are in the voice-over, this form can be used internationally provided the people and situations are not culturally defined.

5. Drama

Drama entails the interplay between two or more people. There is a continuity of action, a beginning, middle, and "happy ending." The performers deliver the message. Although drama is intended to convey a product message, it is a more indirect way than the lesson form. It originated in the United States and was blown across the ocean with soap operas. Small stories and plots are included; people experience things, interact and react to situations, and relate to each other. Unlike in the lesson forms, viewers are not addressed directly, they are observers. They are assumed to watch how other people interact and to draw their own conclusions. Subforms are slice-of-life, problem-solution, vignettes, and theater. The indirectness of the form may make it useful for high-context cultures. Yet we should keep in mind that the form is based on the typical "solution" or "happy ending" orientation of the United States.

5.1. Slice-of-Life. Slice-of-life advertisements have dramatized dialogue dealing with everyday events and "true-to-life" situations. The product is pivotal to the story. There is usually an emotional reward for using the product. A slice-of-life from one culture cannot be implanted in another culture without adaptation. The adaptation will concern not only how people look, but also how they relate to each other. For example, in Italy, France, and Spain the elder will advise the younger, whereas in the Netherlands, Germany, the United Kingdom, and Scandinavia the younger person will advise the elder. Related to this is the choice of depicting people alone or in groups, a family consisting only of parents and two children or an extended family including grandparents, showing older or younger people. Another important choice is whether to show people inside or outside the home. In southern Europe, the social context of many products is outside the home, while in northern Europe the social context is inside the home.

What people regard as rewards varies by culture because rewards are related to peoples' values. There are basic differences in how products deliver emotional rewards to consumers, which can be pointed out by using the Hofstede dimensions. A first distinction is between two types of emotional reward: task orientation or relationship orientation. Individualistic cultures are task oriented, collectivistic cultures are relationship oriented. A second distinction is between ego needs and affiliation needs. Masculine societies are characterized by ego needs while feminine societies are characterized by affiliation needs. These characteristics can be recognized in commercials. The role of the housewife in German commercials is task- and ego oriented. The results shown can be lots of dirty clothes and then lots of clean, white clothes. In more feminine cultures, the emotional reward will be the relationship between mother and children. This topic is also discussed in Chapter 8, under "Masculinity/Femininity."

5.2. Problem-Solution. This is an easily recognized advertising form in Western society. It is related to cause-effect thinking. The problem is dirt, the detergent cleans. The problem is dandruff, the solution is Head & Shoulders. It can also be demonstrated in a slice-of-life format with a story around a problem and the product offering a solution. An example is a commercial for Wash & Go shampoo (used in a number of countries in Europe). Two young women backpackers want to have a drink in the bar of a hotel, but their hair looks terrible. They wash their hair at the village pump and look so nice that they can enter the hotel. Wash & Go solves the problem. A German example is Toppits baking forms. Baked Christmas decorations are damaged, Toppits helps produce new ones.

5.3. Vignettes. Vignettes are a series of independent sketches or visual situations with no continuity in the action. The product plays a part in each vignette. Vignettes are characterized by interaction between people. There may not always be a dialogue, but instead a voice-over or song suggesting the relationship between the product and visualized activities.

5.4. Theater. This subform is a story that is *not* "true-to-life" acted as in a theater. People might interact in an exaggerated way or there might be an unusual story around the product. Interaction takes place as part of a show, sketch, play, or any other piece of drama conveying "occasions," "moods," and "moments" meant to illustrate the main message about the product. This form is relatively frequently found in France and Italy. An example is a French commercial for Volvo, in which the car plays a role in a sort of thriller.

6. Entertainment

A characteristic of entertainment is that it is indirect. Entertainment can be in the form of musicals, shows, comedies, slapstick humor, horror, or satire. It is meant to please the audience rather than to sell. The form outshines the content of the advertising. Pure entertainment does not fit in the persuasive communication model. It is, however, a typical form for Japan and other collectivistic cultures. It is effective because it builds relationships and trust between consumers and companies. According to Dentsu: "Japanese people don't want to be lectured, they want to be entertained."

What makes advertising entertaining can be judged only by the people of the culture in which it is meant to entertain. Entertainment is also relative: In countries where advertising generally uses much direct selling, even the slightest deviation from the direct address may be perceived as entertaining. Much of Japanese advertising may be perceived by the Japanese as a clear message to the consumer, while to Western eyes it may seem to be purely entertaining. To low-context cultures, all high-context advertising may seem to be meant to entertain, yet much information is actually perceived by members of the culture for which it is produced. Subforms are humor and plays or acts about the product.

Illustration 10.21

6.1. Humor. Humor is anything that makes an audience laugh. There are various types of humor, which were described in Chapter 8 under "Why Humor Doesn't Travel," where I also explain that humor doesn't travel because humor reflects culture: One often laughs about the most characteristic aspects of one's own culture. The type of humor that is said to travel is incongruity, the unexpected thing happening. Humor in advertising is most often encountered in cultures of weak uncertainty avoidance. England, Denmark, Norway, the Netherlands, South Africa, and Australia have produced award-winning humorous television commercials.

6.2. Play or Act Around the Product. All nonhumorous entertaining commercials fit this subform. A Japanese example shows mimes forming a bridge, a tunnel, a park for a construction company (Illustration 10.21). Another example is the use of famous actors like Alan Bates and Ben Kingsley reciting their poems for the Union Bank Switzerland; or "Tales of the Black Horse," relating to a pleasant story from the past, by Lloyds Bank (the United Kingdom). Recent technology makes it possible to produce pieces of art, based mainly on video techniques, that can be viewed as pure entertainment.

7. Imagination

The imagination format covers cartoons or film and video techniques that depict events experienced as nonrealistic—presentations of a make-believe world. The form is often used for children's products or to avoid a too-literal interpretation when conveying messages for sensitive products,

Illustration 10.22

such as sanitary products. An international application is the promotion of film properties, such as characters in Disney films. These can cross borders. Subforms include cartoons, film properties in action, or other unrealistic acts. Examples of film properties are the clowns used by Henkel, the monkeys used for OMO in France, and the little men used for CIF or JIF, a household cleaning product.

8. Special Effects

The special effects format covers all sorts of artistic elements, animation, cartoons, camera effects, recording and video techniques, music, and tunes. Modern techniques offer a new range of artistic resources for developing creative advertising that can be adapted to the stimuli of particular target groups. This is a popular form for advertising on channels for the young, such as MTV. The use of artistic stimuli is found in some cultures more than in others; for example, more in Spain than in Germany. Showing the "product in action" through animation is a visual that can cross borders, provided there is no value included. Illustration 10.22 shows an example of a product in action, a shot of a German commercial for Smarties.

A Global Classification System of Basic Advertising Forms

Assuming that global advertisers will benefit from knowing which forms are used most in which countries, developing a global classification system of advertising forms appealed to me. It should to be a system that (a) helps the practitioner see the differences in basic forms used in different countries; (b) distinguishes between forms that are specific for any local culture and forms that are implanted by the large companies and thus reflect the culture of the country of the company (e.g., P&G-style advertising); and (c) recognizes the truly global forms, if such forms do exist.

A rough classification system may be useful when developing an international advertising strategy. Such a system has to be simple and flexible enough to be used on a regular basis, because the advertising world is not static. New forms may emerge and companies may change their strategy, including their basic advertising form.

I found that Franzen's eight main categories, because they are a synthesis of the categorizations found in literature, could well be used as such a simple system. They are broad enough to embrace a number of subforms that, to different degrees, can be found in all countries of the world. The question, then, was whether the eight main forms actually exist worldwide and to what extent each of them is used. As a first step to finding out, I used a convenience sample of television commercials from 11 countries, which I had collected and analyzed to develop the application of the Hofstede model to advertising.

A number of students, teachers, and practitioners in different countries helped me. In this pilot project, I focused only on the basic forms, not on other content elements of advertising. I formulated the following questions:

1. Do the eight forms occur in all countries reviewed?
2. Does the extent to which each form is used vary by country?
3. Can the differences be explained by culture or are they more a function of product category?
4. What is the influence of large multinationals on the forms used in a country?

Because of the variety of samples available, the results from the various countries could not be statistically compared, so only Question 1 could be answered sufficiently. Indeed, all eight basic forms and their subforms do exist in all of the countries reviewed, but in different executions. An example is the difference between the direct versus the indirect execution style found in the lesson form. A statistically sound study is necessary to answer Questions 2, 3, and 4. Nevertheless, this exploratory study provided enough information to draw a few tentative conclusions that can stimulate researchers to follow up on this study. A few observations will be described.

Franzen's system had already been tested by three of his students. Dingerdis[24] verified Franzen's categorization by analyzing 100 Dutch television commercials using an extensive code list of 112 variables. Raspan[25] used Franzen's categorization to compare French, German, and English television commercials from the "Television Register" in London, which collects selected creative commercials from many countries around the world. She found that the dominant form in the United Kingdom was the lesson, followed by drama and special effects. The dominant form in France was drama, followed by lesson and association transfer. In Germany, association transfer and imagination both scored highest, followed by drama. Franzen used preselected commercials for her samples, so the results may not be representative.

Examples of problems with respect to coding were provided by Wassink,[26] who compared French and Dutch television commercials. She used Dingerdis's code list of 112 variables. Her question was whether a code list developed for one culture could be used to code the commercials of another culture. She took a sample of 50 Dutch and 50 French commercials that she said were representative. Over a period of 20 days, she videotaped commercials at random from the Dutch and French channels. Duplicate commercials were removed and each second commercial was selected from the Dutch and French videotapes for a total of 50 for each country. She reported on the typical elements that seemed to distinguish French from Dutch advertising but that could not be measured by the code list. Analogy and association were difficult to capture by pure coding because they are often very subtle. Tone of voice can convey specific meanings and cannot be easily coded. An example is the "velvet voice" frequently used in French advertising, but used in Dutch advertising only for some products that are associated with softness. In general, judgment of tone of voice, such as "velvet," "soft," or "aggressive," is subjective and based on the perspective of the coder. Another example of a feature that could not be captured by the code list was the frequent association in French advertising with beauty by showing all or part of a woman's body. Coding is one of the problems when categorizing advertising forms. A number of other research problems were discussed in Chapter 9.

A Review of Basic Forms Across Eleven Countries

A review of basic forms across cultures was conducted by analyzing 3,409 television commercials. All were taken off the air from national channels in the first half of 1996 in the following countries: the Netherlands (595), Belgium (157), France (193), Sweden (191), Germany (327), Italy (382), Spain (475), the United Kingdom (301), the United States (387), South Africa (150), and Japan (251).[27] The commercials were categorized according to the eight basic forms and their subforms and the following product categories: cars and car products, food and beverages, beer and alcoholic beverages, household products, personal care products and cosmetics, confectionery and ice cream, dental care, pharmaceuticals, computers and telecommunication, retail, travel, finance, household appliances, media, disposables, pet food, and miscellaneous. The following observations were made.

Television Commercials Are Combinations of Forms and Subforms

Because the basic forms are not mutually exclusive, many commercials represent a combination of forms. One form usually dominates and another is secondary. In the case of one dominant and one underlying form, the following combinations were found most often:

- Lesson can be accompanied by metaphor, entertainment, imagination, and special effects
- Drama can be accompanied by entertainment, imagination, and special effects; many of the drama-entertainment forms later appeared to fit better in the newly added subform theater
- Forms that were frequently found combined at the same level were: entertainment-imagination, entertainment-special effects, special effects-imagination, display-announcement, display-special effects, and announcement-special effects.

Additional Subforms

The descriptions of the basic forms in this chapter include forms added to Franzen's original model. This section explains why. Whatever categorization one makes, there will always be forms that cannot be captured because any system is biased by the culture of the maker. Thus, during the process of reviewing the commercials, some commercials in certain countries could not be classified. One example was the type of commercial coded with the combination of drama and entertainment that appeared to be specific to France and Italy. These were commercials in which the drama was not a depiction of real life, but represented a theatrical play around the product. Because all elements of drama were present, it was decided to add the subform theater. A similar phenomenon was encountered with respect to the use of celebrities. Celebrities can give a testimonial, which is a form used by

American, British, and German advertisers. In Japan the testimonial is either very indirect or the form tends toward association with a celebrity. Certain commercials that were coded both as testimonial by celebrity and as lifestyle were later pulled together under a new subform, celebrity transfer—the success of the celebrity rubs off onto the product. This was usually found in masculine cultures: the United States, Japan, and Italy. The other subforms that were added were corporate presentation and dramatized lesson. The corporate presentation subform appeared to cover a type of illustrated announcement that is often used in corporate advertising by multinationals. Dramatized lesson included a clear message but illustrated it by showing people interacting without dialogue.

Coding

Coder reliability can be assumed to be related to the degree of objectivity of the criteria and to the complexity of the study. The less complicated the categorization system, the stronger the coder reliability. I assumed that coding only well-described basic forms should not pose the strong reliability problems that coding cultural aspects would. Generally, students could recognize the eight main forms but had problems with a number of subforms, particularly those containing cultural values. There were few coding differences between the students and myself with respect to the eight main forms, but there were variations with respect to a number of subforms.

Because the culture of the coder influences perception, it is argued that only ethnic coders can do the job properly. This is certainly the case when typical cultural aspects must be found. Native inhabitants of the country whose culture must be analyzed will be best able to do this, provided they are given the proper instruments. In some cases, being too much a part of a culture may also cause selective perception. An example is how an American student did not code U.S. commercials as comparative when, according to the definition, they were definitely comparative. This may have been caused by the generally more competitive advertising environment he was used to in the United States. If so many strong forms are found, the softer ones are not seen as significant. An example is a commercial for eyedrops that says, "Unlike the other leading clear eyedrop, reduces . . . " and so on, which was not coded as comparative. Similarly, much Japanese advertising may be perceived by Westerners as entertaining, while for the Japanese this type of advertising is part of their high-context environment and only a small part will be perceived as entertaining.

The following subforms could easily be recognized: lifestyle, metaphor, testimonial, demonstration, comparison, dramatized lesson, slice-of-life, and problem-solution.

Relationship Among Basic Form, Culture, and Product Category

A few observations can be made with respect to the basic forms related to culture and product category.

One observation is that basic forms are less related to the product category than they are to a market leader across product categories. There is one P&G style used for advertising detergents, fabric softeners, bar soap, disposable diapers, and sanitary napkins/towels. Henkel, the German detergent manufacturer, follows one concept for much of its advertising for detergents and fabric softeners across European countries. Nestlé has its own style, as does Beiersdorf, the company selling the global brand Nivea.

It appears that the basic form is decided by the culture of the advertiser or by the international development phase of a company. While some companies have completed the cycle of standardization-adaptation-localization, other international companies are still in a standardization phase. There is a sort of international style used by French companies selling their cosmetics worldwide. L'Oréal, for example, uses the announcement style everywhere in Europe, showing the same visuals to illustrate the presentation and explanation of their products. In 1996, a number of new Asian entrants into European markets used a simple announcement style. Examples include Korean companies such as Daewoo and Hyundai. German styles, French styles, British styles, Dutch, Swedish, and Danish styles can be recognized in the approaches and basic forms used by the international companies from those cultures. As a result, it may be more the presence of a few large multinationals in a country than the product category that has to be taken into account when analyzing advertising styles of countries. Both P&G and Unilever cover a number of product categories, from perfumes and cosmetics to detergents and sanitary napkins/towels. The basic forms used for their brands of different product categories may have more in common with the culture of the company than with the product category. Further observations are given for a few basic forms.

Announcement

The announcement form was strong in the samples from the Netherlands, Spain, and South Africa. The announcement form is linked to a few product categories: retail, media (CDs, videos, films, magazines, and newspapers), children's toys, and travel. For the Netherlands, the relatively high representation of retail, travel, and media may be the explanation. The Spanish sample of commercials was dominated by a large number of advertisements for children's products, standardized international cosmetics, and personal care brands using the announcement form. The large presence of the announcement form in South Africa was explained by the fact that, since the end of apartheid, all advertising has to be translated into the numerous local languages. As a result, messages are short and simple and cannot easily convey values or other elements that carry a deeper meaning.

Display

There were few commercials in each country that could be classified as display. This frequently overlapped with the pure presentation form of announcement.

Association Transfer

Association transfer is a basic form that spread over all product categories in all countries. It was more frequently found in France, Spain, and Italy. This may be the influence of culture: All three countries reflect cultures that use more symbolic communication.

Lesson

The lesson form is typical for low-context cultures, and it particularly fits the American preoccupation with facts. Wells, Burnett, and Moriarty[28] state that it is the dominant commercial message form (in the United States). Advantages of the lecture form are that it costs less to produce and is compact and efficient. A lecture can deliver a dozen selling points in seconds, if need be. Indeed, in the U.S. sample of 387 TV commercials, a total of 213 of the various lesson subforms was found.

In Europe, the lesson basic form was strong in Germany, Belgium, the Netherlands, and Sweden. This fits the cultures of these countries: All are individualistic and low-context. Yet its presence in the Swedish sample may also be due to the large representation of imported commercials. The Swedish sample (which was a universe of 2 weeks of advertising) included 23% "imported" commercials. This is not surprising because Sweden is a small market, which may not justify the production of many local commercials.

Because of the assumed influence of a few large companies using the testimonial form and comparative advertising, these two subforms were further scrutinised.

Testimonial

As described earlier in this chapter, the testimonial form fits best in cultures with the individualistic-masculine combination, which represents the Anglo-Saxon world and Germany. Although the lesson form is much used in the United States, most often it is used as voice-overs. Of the 213 lessons found, 71 were done by a presenter in the form of a testimonial or endorsement. The non-U.S. samples were also analyzed. In the German sample, 11 out of 35 testimonial forms were in international commercials. In the Netherlands, 29 out of a total of 47 testimonials were in commercials by Anglo-Saxon advertisers. In Belgium all of the testimonials were by non-Belgian advertisers. In Sweden, 18 out of 31 were in non-Swedish commercials. In Spain, 16 out of 23 could be recognized as non-indigenous Spanish advertising. In the Italian sample, 9 out of 17 testimonials were found in international commercials. In France, 10 out of 12 were in non-French advertising.

Celebrity endorsement is very popular in Japan. The coders in Japan recognized a fairly large number of celebrity testimonials as a form of lesson, although they acknowledged that this was not the Western type of lesson. In a high-context society like Japan, things are said indirectly and implicitly, for example, saying "It is good for me" or "They say it is good" (vs. saying "It is good for you"), without the explicit argumentation and product merit found in U.S. testimonials. A typical Japanese testimonial, therefore, is an implicit recommendation by a familiar talent. A large number of these were found in the Japanese sample.

Comparative Advertising

In the U.S. sample of 387 commercials, 16 examples of direct comparison (a brand compared with one or more identified, competitive brands) were found. Another 16 included indirect comparisons. Only one commercial with a direct comparison was found in the 301 U.K. commercials, and none in the samples of commercials from continental Europe. Of the 251 Japanese commercials, 3 were coded as indirect comparison; one of these was for a Nippon Lever brand. One commercial was coded as "The best in the category." In Europe, comparison with "Brand X" or "a conventional product" or "the other leader in the field" was not frequently found. Those that were found were usually part of a non-indigenous, international commercial. In the German sample, 10 out of 12 were non-German. Of the 12 found in the Netherlands, 10 were non-Dutch ads. Of the five found in Belgium, four were non-Belgian. In Spain, all seven found were by non-Spanish advertisers. In Italy, comparative advertising was not found at all. In France, four out of six were by non-French advertisers.

My findings suggest that the comparison form is not a European form, but exported by U.S. companies to cultures where it does not belong.

The "Procter & Gamble Effect"

The P&G effect can be demonstrated in the testimonial and comparison subforms. Around two thirds of the observations regarding testimonials and comparison in France, Belgium, Spain, the Netherlands, and Sweden were due to commercials for Anglo-American or German brands using fixed forms for all of Europe, in the categories of sanitary products (e.g., Always, Evex, Ausonia Seda, Carefree, Tampax), cosmetics (e.g., Max Factor, Oil of Ulay/Olay/Olaz), detergents and other cleaning products (e.g., Ariel, Dash, Vizir, Calgon, Dreft, Yes, Fairy, Fleuril, Sunil, Dove), diapers (e.g., Pampers, Liberos, Dototis), pet food (e.g., Whiskas, Pedigree Pal), and other brands such as Head & Shoulders or Clearasil shampoos, American Express, Listerine, and Stimorol (chewing gum).

Drama

Separate analysis of the representation of the different drama forms in the samples showed that this form was found most often in France and Belgium, followed by Italy and Sweden. The slice-of-life form was most often found in Sweden and Italy, but also in the Netherlands. The theater form was found most in France and Belgium.

Entertainment

Entertainment was most often encountered in Sweden, followed by the Netherlands and Japan. This is not really surprising because entertainment is an indirect form and therefore expected in Japan, but it also is a soft form, to be found in feminine cultures.

Imagination

Imagination was most often found in art-loving Spain, followed by the United Kingdom.

Special Effects

Special effects were most often found in England, followed closely by South Africa and Spain.

Conclusion

Eight basic advertising forms can be distinguished that are used worldwide. Their distribution varies, however, and appears to be related to culture. The lesson style is part of Anglo-German culture and exported to many other cultures where one might wonder if it is equally effective. Comparative advertising fits only individualistic-masculine-weak uncertainty avoidance cultures—only the Anglo-Saxon world. Those companies that try to extend the home country comparative advertising ideas to their subsidiaries in other cultures would do well to think twice before they do so. It will be counterproductive. There appear to be different types of drama: the typical "soap opera" based on real-life drama, so much a part of the United States, the United Kingdom, and Germany, and the theatrical type of drama, part of southern European countries. Basic forms appear not to be connected to product categories, but rather have become representative for some companies—they have become corporate forms. There may be more P&G, Unilever, and Henkel forms than forms linked with product categories.

Further research is needed to confirm tentative conclusions presented in this chapter and to determine whether a culture's most used basic forms are also the most effective for that culture. Although large multinationals like Procter & Gamble have been successful in using one basic form across cultures and adapting it to cultural differences in a meaningful way, they might be even more successful if they were to use other forms for those cultures in which the international form is not really culture-fit. A literature review confirms a number of my observations. Additional research should be encouraged to discover culture-specific basic forms in different countries. It is hoped that professionals and academic researchers will follow up on this. I will be pleased to cooperate.

Notes

1. Laskey, H. A., Fox, R. J., & Crask, M. R. (1994, November/December). "Investigating the impact of executional style on television commercial effectiveness." *Journal of Advertising Research,* pp. 9-16.

2. Laskey, H. A. (1988). *Television commercial effectiveness as a function of main messages and commercial structure.* Unpublished doctoral dissertation, University of Georgia, Athens, GA, cited in Jyotika Ramaprasad & Kazumi Hasegawa, "Creative strategies in American and Japanese TV commercials: A comparison," *Journal of Advertising Research,* January/February 1992.

3. This form is also used by Puto, C. P., & Wells, W. D. (1984). "Informational and transformational advertising: The differential effects of time." *Advances in Consumer Research, 11,* 638-643.

4. Moriarty, S. E. (1991). *Creative advertising: Theory and practice* (2nd ed.). Englewood Cliffs, NJ: Prentice Hall, p. 82.

5. Kroeber-Riel, W. (1990). *Strategie und Technik der Werbung: Verhaltenswissenschäftliche Ansatze.* Kohlhammer, Edition Marketing, 2. Aflage. Stuttgart, cited in U. Appelbaum & C. Halliburton (1993), "How to develop international advertising campaigns that work: The example of the European food and beverage sector," *International Journal of Advertising,* No. 12, pp. 223-241.

6. Stern, B. L., & Resnik, A. J. (1991, June/July). "Information content in television advertising: A replication and extension." *Journal of Advertising Research,* pp. 36-46.

7. Mueller, B. (1992, January/February). "Standardization vs. specialization: An examination of Westernization in Japanese advertising." *Journal of Advertising Research,* pp. 15-24.

8. Wells, W., Burnett, J., & Moriarty, S. (1992). *Advertising principles and practice.* Englewood Cliffs, NJ: Prentice Hall, pp. 398-400.

9. Used in cross-cultural analysis by Zandpour et al. (1994, September/October). "Global reach and local touch: Achieving cultural fitness in TV advertising." *Journal of Advertising Research,* pp. 35-63.

10. Wells, W. D. (1988). "Lectures and dramas." In P. Cafferata & A. Tybout (Eds.), *Cognitive and affective responses to advertising.* Lexington, MA: D. C. Heath.

11. Leiss, W., Kline, S., & Jhally, S. (1986). *Social communication in advertising.* London: Methuen.

12. Katz, H., & Lee, W.-N. (1992). "Oceans apart: An initial exploration of social communication differences in US and UK prime-time television advertising." *International Journal of Advertising,* No. 11, pp. 69-82.

13. Appelbaum, U., & Halliburton, C. (1993). "How to develop international advertising campaigns that work: The example of the European food and beverage sector." *International Journal of Advertising,* No. 12, pp. 223-241.

14. Cutler, B. D., & Javalgi, R. G. (1992, January/February). "A cross-cultural analysis of the visual components of print advertising: The United States and the European Community." *Journal of Advertising Research,* pp. 71-80.

15. Taylor, R. E., & Hoy, M. G. (1995). "The presence of la séduction, le spectacle, l'amour and l'humour in French commercials." In S. Madden (Ed.), *Proceedings of the 1995 Conference of the American Academy of Advertising.*

(Contact Robert King, AAA Executive Secretary, School of Business, University of Richmond, Richmond, VA 23173)

16. See Laskey et al. (1994), "Investigating the impact of executional style," pp. 9-16.

17. Laskey et al. (1994), "Investigating the impact of executional style," p. 10.

18. Moriarty (1991), *Creative advertising*, pp. 89-91.

19. Franzen, G. (1994). *Advertising effectiveness*. Henley-on-Thames, Oxfordshire, UK: NTC Business Publications.

20. Norway, Sweden, Finland, Denmark, Germany, Poland, the Netherlands, the United Kingdom, Belgium, France, Italy, Spain, Portugal, Egypt, Malaysia, Singapore, Japan, Mexico, Peru, Chile, the United States, and South Africa.

21. Sweden, Denmark, the Netherlands, the United Kingdom, Germany, Poland, Belgium, France, Italy, Spain, South Africa, Japan, and the United States.

22. Information from Hiroe Suzuki, Dentsu Inc., Tokyo, Japan.

23. Information from Carlo Praet, Kobe University, Japan.

24. Dingerdis, H. (1993). *Grondvormen in de reclame. Analyse van 100 commercials*. Universiteit van Amsterdam. Stageverslag.

25. Raspan, C. (1994). *Internationale Reclame: Mogelijkheden van een paneuropese campagne bij verschillende reclameculturen*. Scriptie Communicatiewetenschap. University of Amsterdam, #8811601, July.

26. Wassink, C. (1995). *La Douce France versus Nederland*. Doctoraalscriptie Communicatiewetenschap. University of Amsterdam, #8815399, August.

27. The following people helped by collecting television commercials, by coding the commercials of their own country, and/or by checking my own coding. I am very grateful for their help. Theunis Pelser, Lecturer, Department of Management Studies at Potchefstroomse Universiteit, South Africa collected 150 commercials, coded them according to my instructions, and sent me his tape. Eva Larsson, Nina Söderström-Thoor, and Carin Wilkås, students at Lund University, Sweden collected 191 television commercials, coded according to my instructions, and sent me their tape. Anna Simonetti of ISR in Milan taped the Italian commercials for me. Paul Grol, Senior Consultant at ITIM, taped the French and Belgian commercials for me. Hiroe Suzuki, Deputy Director, Information Technology Center, Dentsu, Tokyo, collected a sample of 100 Japanese commercials and coded them. Carlo Praet, doctoral candidate at Kobe University, Japan, collected 151 commercials, coded them according to my instructions, and sent me the tape. Seth Romine, student at Michigan State University, analyzed 50 U.S. commercials, reported on his findings, and sent me his tape. Further tapes were assembled by Sonja Kleijne and Sage publications. Leonie Radder, Wilma van Riel, Bastiaan Vroonland, Danielle Campo Mimoent Elhachioui, Sandor Vrij, and Friedo van Gelder, all students at the Hogeschool van Utrecht, the Netherlands, coded samples of Dutch (140), French (120), and German (105) commercials.

28. Wells et al. (1992), *Advertising principles and practice*, p. 398.

Advertising Styles

The advertising style of a country reflects the culture of that country. The previous chapters have discussed the separate parts—appeal, basic forms, and execution—because by understanding the separate elements one may be better able to understand the total influence of culture on advertising. Advertising is made by practitioners, however, not by academics who try to tackle the separate details of advertising. So for the benefit of the practitioner, this chapter presents more holistic descriptions of the advertising styles of a number of countries.

Characteristics of Advertising Styles of Selected Countries

As we have learned in the previous chapters, the configurations of the five dimensions of a specific country can help us understand its advertising style. Yet each country has its own way of presenting its cultural values. When developing international campaigns, knowledge of the rough characteristics of the advertising styles of different cultures will provide confidence in judging proposals by local agencies. For example, knowledge of the fact that French advertising style includes much sensuality may prevent judgment of a proposal including sensuality as an individual art director's aberration. This chapter sums up a number of characteristics of advertising styles of selected countries. Advertising styles are summarized for the United States, a number of countries in Europe, and a few in East Asia. A few of the research findings summarized in Chapter 9 are used, as well as information from: Taylor, Miracle, and Wilson[1] and Miracle, Chang, and Taylor[2] on Korean advertising; Johansson[3] on the "seemingly nonsensical" Japanese advertising; Graham, Kamins, and Oetomo[4] on the influences of home-country culture on a firm's marketing strategies and tactics in foreign markets; and Go and Bours,[5] who found characteristics of English, German, French, and Dutch advertising by interviewing copywriters in international advertising agencies. To this are added my own observations based on the consequences of Hofstede's dimensions as reflected in advertising, and work by students in various countries.[6, 7, 8]

The American Advertising Style

The American advertising style reflects the assertiveness of its culture. It is characterized by the direct approach and competitiveness, which can be explained by the configuration masculinity-individualism. The lecture or lesson format is popular, with data-based arguments and explicit conclusions why the consumer should buy the product. The direct address is often personalized. The words *you, we,* and *I* are frequently used, as in "You are over 50 and you have not lost your edge." Television advertising is very verbal, as if it were illustrated radio advertising. It uses rhetoric, argumentation, narratives, literary language, and imperatives. U.S. advertising has to make a point, thus taglines or pay-offs are used frequently, or short statements that play with words or little rhymes. Examples are: "UPS, moving at the speed of business"; "Detroit Edison, turning energy into solutions"; "Cotton: The fabric of your life"; "Trident chewing gum: Taking taste to a whole new place"; "Johnson & Johnson, the power to heal." Sometimes moral messages are included. Advertisers tend to tell people "how good their life is" and that the advertiser contributes to that good life. Tradition and patriotism are important values, and sentimentality is a key ingredient of American advertising.

Overstatement and hyperbole are characteristic of the American advertising style. Hard selling is used to distinguish the product from the competition. Power words such as *new, improved, a miracle, the best,* and *now* are part of the U.S. advertising style. "The best in the world" or any other reference to "worldwide" is another power expression—for example, "A world car for your world, Ford Contour."

The product merit appeal is much used. Explicit language is used, and there is a need to substantiate claims, to argue and to use rhetoric. Persuasive communication is the core philosophy of how advertising works. Facts and "reason-why" arguments are a part of the persuasion process, accompanied by information on product characteristics and by logical, scientific data. U.S. commercials often feature a celebrity who serves as an endorser or user of the product, or a credible source to convey specific benefits of the product. Comparisons and recommendations are commonplace. Direct comparison, in particular, is encountered in a way not found in any other culture. Competitive brands are mentioned by name or shown crossed out. Arguments can be that competitive brands' labels do not say what the label of "our" brand says. Indirect comparison is also frequently found, comparing the brand with "the other leading brand" or a "conventional product."

The British Advertising Style

British advertising[9] reflects a highly individualistic society. Advertisements show individuals or couples. Commercials depicting large groups of people are rare. Commercials not only reflect individualism, but appear to sell both individualism and masculinity. The promise seems to be that if you buy a product, it will make you stand out from the crowd. "Do your own thing" and "Be an individual" are recognizable appeals in British advertising. The focus is on depicting young people. This fits a small power distance culture, in which the young have as much authority and knowledge as their elders. In this culture, the young daughter teaches her mother which detergent produces the best result. Youth are independent and individualistic.

The United Kingdom is the only European country in which class differences are recognized in advertising. Some commercials are especially designed for the lower classes. They do not appear to be making a "hard sell." They show real people telling the viewer how inexpensive the product is, yet how it also meets the best standards. These commercials are not stylish or edited or cut at a fast pace. In contrast are the advertisements directed at the upper classes, whose buying power is targeted for trend-setting images, style, and brand names. These possibly reflect the other half of society in which competition, striving for individualism, and style are all important.

U.K. advertising relies heavily on direct communication, using persuasiveness and trend-setting images. Appeals to the ego and to personal success are popular advertising approaches. This goes with a direct approach using presenters and comparisons. The British are a masculine culture with strong role differentiation. Related to this is the trend of reverse sexism: Females dominating or manipulating males with their sexuality. Humor and parody are used for two reasons: to put important messages across to a public that will basically not accept authority, and to allow people who are not used to showing their feelings to release tension. Humor and parody are important elements of British advertising.

The lesson is an important advertising form, including the use of presenters, endorsements, and testimonials. There is much direct address of the public: "We offer," "We will," "You will," and so on. Testimonials are personalized and given by identified or well-known people. Focus is more on how the product will benefit the user than on explaining how it works.

When the slice-of-life form is used, ordinary people are generally depicted, and the drama generally is not made into "theater."

The Americans and the British share many cultural characteristics, but their advertising styles are different. The British style is more subtle. Although explicit language is a characteristic, it is more tongue-in-cheek. It is also more entertainment based: long copy, puns and word games, intelligent humor, understatement, daring. Modern typecasting in U.K. television commercials can lead to parodies of real life.

The German Advertising Style

The German advertising style[10] is characterized by the need for structure and explicit language to avoid ambiguity. Strong uncertainty avoidance, which makes management want to avoid ambiguity, is one of the explanations for the fact that German advertising uses so little humor as compared with British advertising. German advertisements show a strong information orientation; they are direct and factual. The lesson form is much used, with testimonials and presenters giving demonstrations and providing data and test reports. Germans downplay imagination and favor orderly, logical presentations. Their style is clean, rational, straightforward, and serious. Quality, technology, and design are important appeals. Both the product's benefit to the user and the technical details of how the product works are important items in the messages. The competence of the manufacturer is demonstrated. Competence can be embodied in the form of experts or experienced persons, and often the independent testing organization *Stiftung Warentest* is referred to. Endorsements are made by experts, scientists with academic titles, researchers, or by the CEOs of companies. There is great attention to details, particularly technical details, as well as tests. Commercials for toothpaste, shampoo, laundry detergents, diapers, hygienic articles, and dishwashing liquids tend to show in detail how the product works and emphasize trust in technology and science more than the benefit to the user. History and tradition are important appeals and can be found in advertising for coffee and beer, stating that the history and tradition of the brewery guarantee a high quality process, and thus high quality products. Purity and cleanliness are important appeals. So is value for money, yet more in the sense of efficiency than savings. Quality is more important than price. "More quality for the same money" is more attractive to Germans than "equal quality for less money." Winning is important, especially winning with respect to competence: "Testsieger" (test winner) or "the best in the test" illustrate this sort of appeal.

Although Germany is of small power distance and individualistic, freedom as such does not appear to be an important claim. There is high regard for authority, and excessive freedom is not accepted because it could lead to disorder.

The Italian Advertising Style

What the Italians share with the Germans is their love of technology, design, and quality, explained by a similar configuration of masculinity and strong uncertainty avoidance. The difference between the Germans and Italians is that the Germans are of small power distance and the Italians of large power distance.

The configuration of large power distance-strong uncertainty avoidance explains conceptual thinking, a focus on strong characteristic design, big ideas, and a propensity to be theatrical. There is drama and theater in Italian advertising. Although the northern, more affluent part of Italy, where most of the advertising campaigns are made, is individualistic, Italy south of Bologna is more collectivistic. This is reflected in advertising. Respect for elders and educators, for example, is evident in Italian advertising. This observation proves that mass media advertising targets the (less affluent) masses and as a result reflects more collectivistic values. Key words are *emozione* and *passione* and, as in France, sensuality plays a role in advertising. Extended families are evident and children play an important role.

Strong role differentiation is reflected in depictions of males and females socializing separately and of mothers with daughters, (grand)fathers with (grand)sons. Craftsmanship and art are used in advertising, as are metaphors. The presentation is important, and execution receives detailed attention. An example is a metaphor for a burning throat for throat lozenges, where a face is created out of colored matches that are then set afire. Products are presented as pieces of art. Songs, tunes, or little acts to make things look nice add to this. The association form is frequently used: lifestyle, metaphor, metonymy, and celebrity transfer. Nature is used to convey purity.

The Spanish Advertising Style

Spanish advertising[11] is less direct than the advertising style of the northern European countries, probably because Spain's culture is more collectivistic. Visual metaphors are much used, both concrete and abstract. Appeals are design- and art oriented. The feminine aspect of culture can be recognized in the softer approaches and relatively low use of celebrity endorsement. The Spanish way of life, as reflected in advertising, is warm, mutually caring, different, and original, even if full of unpredictable factors. It reflects the innovation/stability paradox. On the one hand, the Spanish feel that being modern and innovative is desirable, yet on the other hand, tradition is an important element of culture and the desired is stability, because of the difficulty of coping with ambiguity. This desire for the new and modern may be the reason why so much advertising is full of young people, although older and experienced people are still regarded as those who hold the truth. This can be found in sentences like ". . . your mother did not tell you . . ." (*"no te dijo tu madre . . ."*). Obedience and respect remain important, so younger people do not make fun of or disregard the advice of their elders. They cooperate, help, and have fun at the same time. Relations between individuals are based mainly on friendship and family ties, the desirable of a collectivistic culture. Yet the desired individuality and a growing reluctance to accept authority makes individualistic claims, such as "doing things your own way," accepted. An example is an international Hugo Boss television commercial expressing this by saying, "It is not a style, it is my style. It is not doing things, it is doing them in my own way." (*"No es un estilo, es mi estilo. No es hacer cosas, es hacerlas a mi manera"*).

Spain is a collectivistic culture. People usually appear in groups. Belonging to a group brings stability and identity to the individual. A person's role in society is determined by the group he or she belongs to, and the family is the most relevant group and is self-defining. The family gives the individual a sense of identity and stability. Self-confidence is group confidence, and group consciousness defines the individual's life: *"mi barrio"*—my neighborhood, *"mi gente"*—my people. Affiliation with certain groups determines the way a person behaves. This is reflected in the importance of a person's manner of dressing: a certain way of dressing determines that the person belongs to a certain group. Belonging to a group is essential for having a place in society, so individuals will take care how they dress and act in order not to lose their place in society. This need for the correct manner of dressing is the reason why some dubbed commercials could never work in Spain. On the other hand, a growing number of individuals shown in Spanish advertising express modernity and fashion. Although there is not a strong role differentiation, the woman has the role of the expert and is the one who provides unity in the family. The feminine dimension is related to the quality of life, the enjoyable things in life, as included in the word *placer.* The beauty and warm feelings reflected in advertising are an expression of strong uncertainty avoidance. Beauty and warmth are the safety valves for anxiety and stress. Another expression of anxiety reduction is taking care of oneself, being proud of oneself. When one takes care of one's body, one is at the same time taking care of one's soul. This is not similar to Anglo-Saxon perfectionism, which is stressful and competitive. This is not a matter of being perfect, but of feeling good and being proud of oneself. Dignity and pride are very important in Spanish culture, they are expressed by the phrase *tomar en serio* (to be taken seriously). Although the Spanish can express themselves humorously and can laugh at themselves, they are not inclined to ridicule the imperfect as the British do. Humor in Spanish commercials is not complicated.

In Spanish advertising, strong uncertainty avoidance is expressed not so much through technology and design as it is in German and Italian advertising, but more by association with art, color, and beauty. *Placer* is a pivotal concept in Spanish advertising, an expression of "the good life" (*la vida buena*). It is strongly connected with food and eating in Spanish culture. Eating is not only a biological necessity, but a way for people to show how they care about others. Eating not only means taking care of your body, but also of your soul. In food advertising in particular, the *placer* concept is important; for example, a Danone ad talks about *placeres de escandalo* (scandalous pleasures). Another expression of uncertainty avoidance is that ideals and dreams are an important part of life. Dreams, aims, and the main objectives in life are idealized. This is related to comforting one's soul and avoiding the uncertainty of the unknown future. Ideals and values are more important than material wealth.

Another characteristic of Spanish culture reflected in advertising is an external locus of control. Success is not based on hard work—as in cultures with an internal locus of control, such as the Anglo-Saxon ones—but is a result of random coincidences and "secret formulas," which makes creativity the best tool for attaining it. This is reflected in the use of "magic," "dreams" presented by means of special effects. Creativity does not involve sophisticated solutions, merely original ones.

The French Advertising Style

What makes French culture unique is its configuration of high power distance and individualism, a configuration the French share with the Belgians. This configuration makes people "want to do their own thing," on the one hand yet feel dependent, on the other hand. This results in the need to be different, which is reflected in French advertising. A propensity for the theatrical and the bizarre is part of French advertising style. Commercials are more likely to be dramatic and less likely to address the audience directly with a lecture. The French *joie de vivre* is reflected in an orientation toward image, fantasy, and theater. The saying *la vie est pleine* may express the feeling that life must be lived to the full, don't let yourself be limited by the small problems of life. This enjoyment and pleasure orientation, as well as the need to show emotions, are reflected in many of the drama-like acts in television commercials. It is also reflected in a "theatrical" type of presentation: stories, film acts, imaginary situations, people acting in an exaggerated manner, or the plainly emotional such as people tearing photographs to pieces to emphasize emotion. The message is incorporated in the story. *Savoir faire* is another expression of French culture found in advertising, meaning that people should know their place in life and act accordingly; in other words, know the right way to behave and dress, and eat at the right moments in life with the "right" people.

Addressing or "lecturing" the audience directly about the product is often done in the form of a song, with music and word games. An example is *"Vizir—pour le mieux et surtout pour le pire"* ("Vizir, for better, but for worse"). Their focus is on engineering and craftsmanship, often featuring new ideas and the advantages of new ideas. Commercials that do address the audience are likely to promise a dream that cannot be readily delivered by the product. A great deal of symbolism is used with relatively little copy. If products are distinguished from the competitor, the distinction is based on evaluation of workmanship, engineering, durability, and excellence of materials. Entertainment through symbolism, humor, and drama is an important aspect of French advertising style. In pursuit of being entertaining or funny, French commercials tend to play with shapes and names. Popular appeals are beauty, sensuality, erotics, or using beautiful women as metaphors for beauty and aesthetics (what may be called a "sexist use of women" by Americans), image, style, and extravagance. Metaphors are frequently found. Erotics, showing a female body as a metaphor for beauty, or little scenes of man and woman touching, glancing at each other, and the like are an integral part of French advertising. Little gimmicks, magic, symbols, imaginary beings, cartoons, and advertising properties are often included. Presenters are generally older, and elders tend to advise the younger: mother, grandmother, or aunt advises daughter or niece.

Though consumer advertising may seem implicit, or high-context, rhetoric is also found in French advertising. Business-to-business advertising uses symbols and metaphors combined with explicit language and data, although metaphors are frequently found.

A Few Remarks on Belgium

The Belgian advertising style has much in common with French advertising style. Belgian advertising uses direct address more often: Presenters and testimonials are often in combination with a demonstration. In the sample used for comparing basic forms, Belgian advertising showed the highest use of demonstration. Professional experts are favored as endorser, not an academic or professorial type, but the craftsman, the professional specialist. Testing is important.

The Dutch Advertising Style

Characteristic of Dutch culture[12] is the configuration of low power distance, individualism, and femininity as well as—for a Western culture—a relatively high score on long-term orientation. Hype is not appreciated, nor are pushy presenters, who cause discomfort to the audience. Pushy presenters are perceived as authoritarian, as is showing uniforms, experts, doctor's titles, and loud speech in commercials. A direct presentation style gives the Dutch viewer the feeling of being regarded as foolish, not equipped with enough decision power, not equal in status, or both. Testimonial and comparison forms do not fit the Dutch culture and, when used, are principally from Anglo-German advertisers. If testimonials or endorsements are used, the presenters should neither take themselves too seriously nor play the role of the expert, as this is not appropriate to the feminine cultural values of modesty combined with disrespect for authorities and experts. Presenters are often typecast as a parody on the presenter.

A Dutch value paradox is conformity versus adventure. The desirable is conformity as part of the leveling attitude, which leads to boredom. The reaction to this boredom, the desired, is adventure, but the adventure cannot be too big. Neither can big "dreams" be part of the advertising message: There is a saying in the Dutch language: "Dreams are deceptive, a delusion." · Dutch advertising uses relatively few power or magic words, another reflection of the leveling value.

Small role differentiation is reflected in advertising, as well as a people-oriented attitude rather than a result-oriented attitude.

A pivotal concept is thrift or saving money, which can be expressed directly but also in parody to underline its importance. There is an enormous variety of executions, such as piggy bank symbols, coins, towels with imprints of banknotes, and frequent use of the word *gratis* (free).

Modesty leads to infrequent expressions of "being the best." Success can be shown only in understatements. A reflection of small power distance is the fact that young children are shown as independent, taking care of their own lives at an early age. Small children and even babies are presented as speaking in voice-overs with disrespect to their elders or to the audience. For example, a baby making wise remarks at the expense of someone else's mother would be inappropriate in countries of large power distance, such as Spain.

Another pivotal concept in Dutch advertising is the concept of *gezelligheid*, which is one of those concepts that are untranslatable or that translate only into the languages of similar cultures such as Danish, Norwegian, and Swedish. To the Dutch, *gezelligheid* brings an instantaneous recognition of care, warmth, intimacy, and being together with friends and loved ones, and is often linked with specific situations and moments of product usage. It describes the combined feelings of coziness and comfort, of enjoying oneself in the company of close friends.

The entertainment form is increasingly used because it is softer than the direct-lesson form. Humor, as an element or even as the principal factor of entertaining commercials, often serves as an important illustration of disrespect for authority.

A Few Remarks on Advertising in Sweden

Sweden scores very low on masculinity, thus is a very feminine culture, which is reflected by the fact that men are shown doing the work in the home. They are obviously so used to this that they can be shown doing it in their own style, even turning it into fun. This is very different from the way males doing housework are depicted in German advertising, where they only "try to help" and then tend to fail. Entertainment is a frequently used Swedish advertising form but, as in the Netherlands and Germany, imagination is not an important value. Disrespect for authority is shown in many ways, particularly in entertaining, humorous commercials. The "togetherness" value so typical of Dutch and Scandinavian cultures is expressed by the word *kafferep,* which means something like "getting together for a cup of coffee." In all sorts of organizations and private groups, people tend to get together for meetings in which coffee is always served. These can be private meetings or work meetings, and for all sorts of reasons.

A Few Remarks on Advertising in Poland

As in the other Eastern European countries, a characteristic advertising style is being developed in Poland. Polish culture is reflected in a respect for elders and in strong family values in both adapted international and indigenous advertising. I have found large family groups in television commercials. Polish people are individualistic, but not extreme. There is strong role differentiation. An example is a commercial for Bulka Tarta (packaged dried bread crumbs), in which a man wears an apron, suggesting that he does the cooking, but he only does the heavy work: grinding stale bread in an old-fashioned, hand-cranked meat grinder to demonstrate preference for the Bulka Tarta product. Poland's below average score on uncertainty avoidance is reflected in the use of both demonstration and result orientation. But humor is also found in Polish advertising. The need for the traditional, for roots, is reflected in the frequent use of folklore, nostalgia, and historical drama.

The Japanese Advertising Style

Japanese advertising reflects Confucian and collectivistic values. Concepts of face and harmony lead to an indirect communication style. Clearly stating a point of view in TV commercials makes people uncomfortable. The direct approach can be perceived as an "insult" to the consumer's intelligence. The Japanese style is, rather, to apologize for the intrusion, the imposition on the viewer's time. The goal of Japanese advertising is to make friends with consumers and get them to trust and rely on the seller, to win their respect. This goal may be achieved by telling a story or by entertaining the audience. Identification of the brand, company name, or product in a commercial is less important than pleasing the consumer. Japanese advertisers tend to take more of a commercial's time for developing trust, understanding, and dependency. The soft-sell approach is meant to induce the consumer to be kind enough to take a close look at the product in the store, where "Thank you for coming to the store" is the paradigm, rather than the more intrusive "May I help you" approach. The result is overall mood, advertising that is entertaining, has fantasy appeals, and is low on facts. Thus advertising does not explicitly provide the product benefits, and "advertising liking" plays an important role. Japanese commercials use serene, mood-creating nature symbols. The importance of the seasons is reflected in advertising. The tone of voice is indirect, subtle, with much symbolism. Business-to-business advertising is also characterized by the indirect approach, by the use of symbols, and rarely by direct address.

Competitive or comparative advertising is confrontational and thus is perceived to denigrate competitors, which is against the Asian value of harmony. The style and manner of presentation is an important part of the presentation. A beautiful scene, story, or verse can be an important part of the advertisement. Values and appeals found in advertising are veneration of the elderly, showing respect to elders, and status. Dependency is the desirable value, independence the desired as expressed in advertising. There is a focus on man's relationship with nature, oneness with nature.

The Japanese are fond of celebrities. A product is frequently associated with a celebrity, who often represents the target group. If Western models, celebrities, or settings are used, they are used to convey the symbol of prestige or status and not meant to represent Western values. Television commercials are much more a part of popular culture in Japan than elsewhere in the world and are also much more intertwined with the world of entertainment. Advertising songs are sung in karaoke bars. Songs are often launched via commercials and composed especially for use in commercials. As a result, the celebrities, so-called *talento,* are professional models who become famous by appearing in commercials first and, based on the popularity gained through the commercials, start their singing or acting careers.[13]

Advertising in Chinese Societies

There is only a short history of the use of modern advertising techniques in China, but a rapidly developing advertising industry seems to lead toward a Chinese advertising style representative of Chinese culture. Generally, advertising in developing markets focuses on product attributes, and only when a market is developed do more sophisticated approaches emerge. According to Chan's[14] findings, a more characteristic advertising style is developing on mainland China, with less direct product-selling approaches.

Below, a few assumptions based on the Hofstede model are added to the little research available. Although the mainland Chinese have the same ethnic origin as those of the Chinese diaspora, they do not show the same characteristics because of their different history and environment. The Taiwanese, for example, show the influence of their Japanese heritage due to occupation by the Japanese. An important difference from the other Chinese cultures is strong uncertainty avoidance.

The Hofstede dimensions for Chinese cultures in China, Taiwan, Hong Kong, and Singapore show similar scores for the dimensions power distance (large) and individualism (low); none are strongly masculine or feminine. Generally, Chinese culture is of weak uncertainty avoidance. Only the Taiwanese score high on that dimension. Uncertainty avoidance is not a fundamental dimension for Asian cultures, and there is a wide variety among countries in Asia. The long-term orientation dimension is a more fundamental variable. All score high on long-term orientation except the Singaporeans, who score below average but higher than most Western cultures. The scores on the dimensions may predict similar values and appeals in advertising.

An advertising style befitting Chinese culture will include the indirect approach, a general characteristic of collectivistic cultures. The values found in Chinese advertising will be based on long-term orientation and collectivism. Specific values of Chinese advertising are modernity, quality, technology, courtesy, respect for the elderly, "magic," prosperity, wealth, economy, "neatness," social status, and tradition in the sense of respect for customs and conventions. My own observations of September 1996 include the use of nature symbols such as skies and clouds, which are perceived as auspicious. Television commercials make frequent use of special effects, graphics, and computer animation, and they play with words, characters, and sounds.

Taiwanese advertisements provide a subtle presentation linking the product to a place, event, person, or symbol. The sales pitch is implicit and there is little product visibility. Taiwanese commercials generally link the product to the consumer's traditional Chinese values, such as family relations and respect for authority. They deal with the abstract and lack specific consumer orientation. They promise an ideal that may be reached through the use of the product. Such ideas, however, are seldom linked to attributes of the product. They tend not to provide any reasoning or explicit conclusions, indicating a use of the indirect approach.

An example of how family values are reflected in a Hong Kong campaign for Ericsson is a commercial in which a well-meaning son buys his father a remote-control TV set and a microwave oven, but declines to stay for dinner. On reflection, the son changes his mind and chooses to spend the time with his father rather than his friends. The tagline is "Communication is caring."[15]

A Few Remarks on Advertising in Korea

Korean advertising style shares a characteristic of Japanese advertising style in that it gives more importance to the company than to the brand. Miracle et al.[16] found that almost all Korean commercials identify the company in the commercial, as compared with only 56% of U.S. commercials. Korean advertising also is a reflection of a collectivistic culture, with a focus on the indirect approach and symbolism. Confrontation is avoided and harmony sought. Koreans are different from the Japanese with respect to two dimensions: They are more collectivistic and more feminine. This means that the need for harmony will be stronger than it is for the Japanese. Koreans will also favor affiliation over competitiveness in their communication styles, but will also be more direct, a characteristic of feminine cultures.

Conclusion

The advertising styles of countries reflect the cultural values of those countries, but there is more to it than that. Because advertising is an expression of culture, the symbols and rituals used may even reinforce cultural values, hence the strong characteristics of indigenous advertising styles, such as sentiment along with assertiveness and hype in American advertising versus the strong focus on humor in British advertising. The sensual and erotic style of French advertising would not work in Germany, whose advertising style reflects the need for structure, directness, and facts. Italian advertising style reflects a collectivistic culture, which was a particularly interesting finding, as the Hofstede IBM data on the North of Italy indicated individualism. Likewise, Spanish advertising reflects a collectivistic society, with both the desirable and the desired reflected, taking into account the individualistic claims. The Spanish try hard to behave as individualists but prefer the stability resulting from strong family values. Dutch advertising style strongly reflects the leveling attitude of the Dutch induced by their feminine culture. Yet this also leads toward a softer, more entertaining type of advertising. Japanese advertising style strongly reflects masculinity in its frequent use of celebrities. Celebrities are even created by advertising. Nowhere else in the world are people so involved in advertising. Yet symbolism and indirectness are also a strong part of Japanese advertising style. The advertising industry of China seems to be developing a characteristic Chinese advertising style, reflecting collectivistic and Confucian values, but it cannot be compared with the styles of other Chinese societies such as Hong Kong, Singapore, and Taiwan, as their advertising industries have developed separately.

Notes

1. Taylor, C. R., Miracle, G. E., & Wilson, D. (1994). "Culture's consequences in advertising: The impact of information level strategies on the effectiveness of Korean vs. U.S. television commercials." In K. Whitehall King (Ed.), *Proceedings of the 1994 Conference of the American Academy of Advertising*. (Contact Robert King, AAA Executive Secretary, School of Business, University of Richmond, Richmond, VA 23173)

2. Miracle, G. E., Chang, K. Y., & Taylor, C. R. (1992). "Culture and advertising executions: A comparison of selected characteristics of Korean and U.S. television commercials." *International Marketing Review, 9*(4), 5-17.

3. Johansson, J. K. (1994, March). "The sense of 'nonsense': Japanese TV advertising." *Journal of Advertising, 23*(1), 17-26.

4. Graham, J. L., Kamins, M. A., & Oetomo, D. S. (1993, June). "Content analysis of German and Japanese advertising in print media from Indonesia, Spain and the United States." *Journal of Advertising,* 22(2), 5-15.

5. Go, J., & Bours, L. (1992). *Analyseren van Advertenties* [Unpublished internal project, FHV/BBDO].

6. Buijs, F., Biswas, C., Fernandez, M., Roscoe, E., & Wieringa, D. (1996). *Intercultural value research in marketing communication,* Erasmus Universiteit Rotterdam and FHV/BBDO Marketing Communication Services. Document IM-ScEC15. May 10. This was an international students' project as part of a European exchange program at the Erasmus University of Rotterdam. Unpublished.

7. Larsson, E., Söderström-Thoor, N., & Wilkås, C. (1996). *Categorisation of Swedish Television Commercials,* Lund University, Sweden, May/June.

8. Spanish and German students' work at the University of Navarre, Spain, May 1996.

9. This summary is based on my own observations and experience and on the text by Elizabeth Roscoe, in the report on the Intercultural Value Research in Marketing Communication at the Erasmus University of Rotterdam, May 1996 (see Note 6, above).

10. This summary is based on my own observations and experience and on text by Chanchal Biswas and Dirk Wieringa, in the report on the Intercultural Value Research in Marketing Communication at the Erasmus University of Rotterdam, May 1996 (see Note 6, above).

11. This summary used the text by Myriam Fernandez in the report on the Intercultural Value Research in Marketing Communication at the Erasmus University of Rotterdam, May 1996 (see Note 6, above). Findings were reinforced by my own experience with students' projects when teaching at the University of Navarre, Spain.

12. This summary includes statements by Frank Buijs, from the report on the Intercultural Value Research in Marketing Communication at the Erasmus University of Rotterdam, May 1996 (see Note 6, above).

13. Information provided by Carlo Praet, doctoral candidate at Kobe University, Japan.

14. Chan, K. K. W. (1995). "Information content of television advertising in China." *International Journal of Advertising,* 14, 365-373.

15. "Ericsson pitches family values." (1996, December). *Asian Advertising & Marketing,* 10(24), 15.

16. Miracle et al. (1992), "Culture and advertising executions," pp. 5-17.

CHAPTER 12

From Value Paradox to Strategy

Understanding global value paradoxes may help to modify one's assumptions and will be most fruitful if added to practical experience. Those who know the pitfalls of global marketing and advertising will recognize the application of the 5-D model to marketing and advertising as a tool for comparing one or more known cultures with other, unknown cultures. It is a tool for analyzing the product use, needs, and motives of one culture and extending that knowledge to other similar cultures. Thus—if one agrees with the assumption that marketing will only be successful if the values of consumers match the marketing mix of the product or brand—strategies successful in one culture can be extended to other cultures with similar relevant values, though not necessarily in the same geographical area.

The 5-D model will be most useful to those who have learned to cope with ethnocentrism and are able to shed their own cultural blinders as far as that is possible. The most difficult thing to get rid of is one's cultural bias. Another difficulty is to drop the very commonly expressed assumption that modernization leads to universal values worldwide, that some target groups such as modern youth are similar worldwide because they adopt a few similar habits.

Modernization

Increasingly, it is being recognized that culture is a strong power in the making of an economic society.[1] Approaching the 21st century, social and political scientists tend to agree that there will be no global culture or converging values, and certainly the world is not Westernizing. Huntington[2] attacks the common assumption that modernization is Westernization and states that "modernization is producing neither a universal civilization in any meaningful sense nor the Westernization of non-Western societies," and adds, "The spread of Western consumption patterns and popular culture around the world is not creating a universal civilization." The assumption that there will be one global culture is based on Western universalism and the wishful thinking of global companies, reinforced by American marketing and management philosophies. The opposite is the case: People may desire to think globally but as a result of globalization actually become more aware of their specific local values. As we have seen in Chapter 5 under "Value Shift," urbanization does not necessarily lead to increased individualism. In Europe, there is no relationship between individualism and type of household. There is no significant correlation between people living in one- or two-person households and individualism or between people living in households of six or more persons and collectivism.[3] How people shape their environment does reflect their cultural values, but, urbanization will not by definition change collectivistic values into individualistic values. Focus on family values is increasing in Asian cultures rather than diminishing as a result of modernization and urbanization. It is the form of a value that changes, not its content. In Japan, modernization has shifted the family value system from the extended family to the company, and pragmatism may find yet another form if the company system should change. In Singapore, it is the government that forces the people to look after their elders.

People increasingly identify with their local or regional communities. I have yet to hear anyone from a European country say to me, "I am from Europe"; they always state their nationality. I have also found that Americans increasingly mention the state they live in rather than saying, "I am American." Even to me, from "Europe" they tend to say they are from Minnesota, Connecticut, Virginia, or wherever in the United States they live.

Global Target Groups

In global marketing and advertising, a common assumption is that there are a few global, homogenous target groups. Those most often mentioned are businesspeople and youth. Motives of businesspeople vary just as much by culture as consumers' motives do. However, the ubiquitous business school education has changed ways of management worldwide, or at least the gap between the desirable and the desired. French managers, who may demonstrate large power distance behavior in their family life, may behave as modern managers according to the prevailing fashion. Likewise, managers of high-context cultures may change behavior according to the context.

Even if it is accepted that peoples' values worldwide are not the same, and will not converge, either, a common misperception remains that the values of youth worldwide are basically the same, that everywhere the young rebel against their elders as a universal aspect of adolescence. The way the young develop their identity, the way they relate to their elders, the way they behave in school, varies enormously across cultures because of the values with which they are raised. Children's value patterns are settled before they are 10 years old. Adolescence is the step from childhood to adulthood that, in individualistic cultures, may be the step to developing one's identity—differentiating oneself from others. This is so much a part of Western thinking that even Huntington[4] generalizes as follows: "In social psychology, distinctiveness theory holds that people define themselves by what makes them different from others in a particular context." We have now learned that this process is different in collectivistic cultures. Although Western images may induce Japanese youth to strive for more autonomy and independence, this striving for independence is at an upper, more superficial level. The basic, traditional issues of dependency, achievement, and fear of failure are much more deeply rooted.[5] Indian adolescents shows much less conflict than the adolescents of traditional American youth, who are involved in self-creation and integrating an identity. In traditional Indian society, adolescence is not the separate psychological state that it is in U.S. culture.[6]

If young people adopt what is called "a global popular culture," such as music and fashion, they tend to adapt it to their own values. Students worldwide wear jeans, but the type of jeans they wear and their personal grooming are very different. Spanish students will not wear torn jeans like Dutch students do. They prefer designer jeans and combine them with a fashionable jacket, not a faded T-shirt. Spanish students look very well dressed compared with Dutch students, but this sort of difference is relative. I once asked a student from El Salvador studying in Spain if she found the Spanish students different from those in El Salvador, and she answered, "Spanish students are so badly dressed." Both Spain and El Salvador are strong uncertainty avoidance cultures, but El Salvador scores much higher than Spain. Students from El Salvador may even, writ large, iron their jeans to look properly groomed.

Consumer Behavior

Knowing whether and how consumer behavior is influenced by culture is of great importance when developing a cross-cultural marketing strategy. However, the first question to ask is still whether there are other influences, the most important one, naturally, being income. Throughout this book, examples are given of how the various aspects of consumer behavior are related to culture, irrespective of economic variables. One example was the influence of uncertainty avoidance on buying new or second-hand cars (see Chapter 6, "Needs"). I have heard other reasons, like no second-hand car market (not a cause, but an effect) or new cars being relatively cheap, the level of wealth of a country, or a strong local car industry. Indeed, Italy and Japan hardly have a second-hand car market though they both have a car industry, but so have the United Kingdom and Sweden, and both have second-hand car markets and relative wealth.

Another example is how culture influences the type of camera people prefer. As discussed in Chapter 6 (see "Needs"), there is a negative correlation between autofocus camera buyers and uncertainty avoidance, because competence can be demonstrated by manipulating the camera. The level of uncertainty avoidance will also affect the money value of compact cameras bought. More expensive cameras can be assumed to be more reliable and thus more attractive to members of strong uncertainty avoidance cultures. This is correct, and a significant correlation is found for 13 European countries with respondents of similar levels of income. There is, however, no significant correlation when comparing respondents of different income levels. EMS 95 data show the correlation between uncertainty avoidance and low-value compact cameras owned for 13 countries, after the high-income Swiss and lower-income Greeks and Portuguese were removed from the sample (see Figure 12.1).

Another example of an influence on buying behavior overriding culture is the relationship between a car's engine size and whether the car is company owned or privately owned. Engine power is an attribute found in car advertising in masculine cultures, because it is a power and status motive. Yet I could not find a correlation between masculinity and engine size of the main car in the 16 European countries in the EMS 95 survey. There was, however, a correlation between engine size and company ownership of the main car.[7] Thus, leased or company-owned main cars tend to have more engine power. Interestingly, whether the main car was a company car or privately owned did not affect the correlation between the influence of the partner on the choice of make and type of car and the MAS index as described in Chapter 6 under "Groups and Reference Group."

Why people prefer one sport over another can sometimes be explained by Hofstede's dimensions, but other, historical influences often have to be found to explain such a preference. From the EMS 95 survey I discovered a multiple correlation ($R = .47^*$) among interest in motor sports, masculinity,

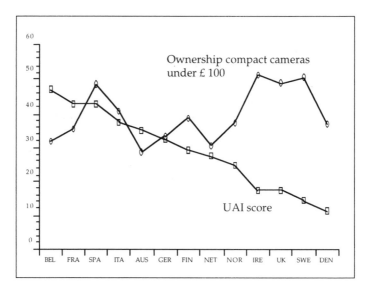

Figure 12.1 Correlation Between UAI and Value of Compact Cameras in 13 Countries.
SOURCE: Data EMS (1995). Copyright © Inter/View.
NOTE: rho = 0.43*

and strong uncertainty avoidance—understandable, as motor sports seem to be a masculine activity and one that helps release stress. But so far I cannot explain why, in Europe, the Italians, Dutch, and Portuguese show such a high interest in volleyball. In some cases, history or tradition can explain specific market behavior that may be caused by situational factors and may change if the behavior is not culture-bound. An example is a traditional coffee culture like Turkey that changed into a tea-drinking culture. In developing markets, a foreign product or brand is important because it provides status. That tends to change when markets become developed.

The difference between the desirable and the desired helps explain paradoxical behavior. The Dutch and the Danes, on the one hand, love their freedom, want adventure; on the other hand they like the coziness (*gezelligheid* and *hyggelighet*, Dutch and Danish, respectively) of home. This paradox explains the relatively high ownership of caravans (trailers in the United States) for holiday use. In the Reader's Digest Eurodata Survey, a significant, negative correlation (rho = −.57**) is found between ownership of caravans and the MAS dimension. Caravans provide the freedom to go, but at the same time to take your own, cozy home with you, preferably to a camping place where friends also have their caravans.

Product/Market Development

Marketing teaches that a low-penetration market should be regarded as a potential growth market. I remember the anecdote I was brought up with in marketing education to make me understand the concept of a market. It was about the shoe salesman traveling in an African country and phoning back to his boss, "People wear no shoes here, there is no shoe market," while a couple of weeks later his colleague phoned from the same country, "This is a great shoe market, nobody has shoes yet." I never liked the example, because climate and low income were expected to be prohibitive for developing such a market. If the reason for low penetration is culturally defined, other products should be developed that better fit that culture. Life insurance is a product for individualistic cultures; entering a market with a collectivistic culture asks for different products. New product-market combinations must be developed for markets with new cultural configurations. An example could be offering parent-related pension insurance to the Singapore yuppies whose new mobile lifestyles make it more difficult to fulfil their obligations of looking after their parents, a strong element of their collectivistic and Confucian values. Another example is the penetration of home computers into collectivistic cultures. In Japan, where business is a social phenomenon, work is done in the office, not at home, and there is such a strong role differentiation that the home is the wife's career. There is no real place for the husband. So home computing is not an option for Japanese men. It might be for their wives, however, to help educate the children in the competitive Japanese educational environment. Home computers are not expected to achieve a similar penetration in Japan as they have in, for example, Sweden where flexibility is highly treasured and small role differentiation makes husband and wife equally involved in the housework, thus spending more time at home—for work, as well.

Well-defined cultural differences can help in the development of more appropriate products or product adaptations for different cultures. Voice mail will be more appropriate for high-context cultures, e-mail more appropriate for low-context cultures where people like the written word. Software for high-context cultures will have to be different from software for low-context cultures. If it appears that certain do-it-yourself products do not sell as well in strong uncertainty avoidance cultures as in weak uncertainty avoidance cultures, adapt the product to the need for competence. Add instructions, offer training, whatever helps the market to feel more competent.

Similarly, electronic appliances such as remote control devices should be easy to use for weak uncertainty avoidance cultures, but may have complicated details for strong uncertainty avoidance cultures.

The future of global marketing strategy will be differentiation between cultural and economic or other noncultural factors, and the development of relevant product-market combinations for cultures with different configurations on the dimensions.

Global Brand Strategy

Differences in consumer expectations have important consequences for brand strategies. Relationships between consumers and brands and the function of brands vary across cultures, depending on the type of self-concept. In cultures in which people do not attach importance to differentiating themselves from others, concepts of product differentiation and brand positioning may be difficult to grasp.

It is common practice to describe the brand's attributes as personality attributes in terms of warmth or humanness. This sort of description may mean different things to people of different cultures.[8] The wish to develop a consistent brand image leads toward labeling the brand personality with concepts that may mean different things in different languages/cultures. Instead, a better option may be to find what is meaningful to the different culture clusters with respect to the brand and its role in people's lives and to load the brand with different core values, even though the product may be the same worldwide. International brands succeed when consumers in each market believe they are being spoken to by somebody who understands them, somebody who knows their needs and who talks and feels just as they do.[9]

In cultures in which trust in the company and long-term relationships between consumers and companies are more important than strong product-brand personalities, a focus on the company brand will be a more effective strategy than developing strong product brands. Indeed, most successful Asian brands are company brands, whereas U.S. brands rarely carry the name of the company. Corporate branding and endorsement strategies will be more effective in Asian markets than a product-brand approach of strongly positioned brand personalities. The very least that should be added to product brands in Asian advertising is the company's name, as I have seen done by P&G in China, adding a P&G signature to, for example, Head & Shoulders in TV commercials, and by Nippon Lever in Japan. On the other hand, now that Asian products are increasingly entering Western markets, Asian companies may do better in Western markets by developing more differentiated product brands.

Global Communication Strategy

Communication strategy development is based on an assumption of how advertising works. Should advertising be persuasive or should it be liked? Researchers and academics have heated discussions about what is right. Maybe everyone is, and it is not a case of either-or but that advertising must be liked in one culture and it must be persuasive in another culture. Moreover, the degree to which people like or dislike, approve or disapprove of advertising in general is also related to their culture. Notoriously, the Dutch and the Scandinavians have a critical attitude toward advertising, while the Americans, British, and Japanese have made it a part of their daily lives. This is related to culture. In the Reader's Digest Eurodata Survey, the question of whether one had "a great deal of confidence in the advertising industry" was answered very differently across 16 European countries. A significant correlation was found between confidence in the advertising industry and both the MAS and the UAI dimension, as illustrated in Figures 12.2 and 12.3. The multiple correlation among confidence in the advertising industry, MAS, and UAI is even more significant ($R = .66$***). In the figures, Portugal seems to be extreme in the MAS graph, which is due to its also having a high score on UAI; in the UAI chart, Switzerland shows a peak, due to its relatively high score on MAS. A similar significant multiple correlation ($R = .61$**) was found in EMS 95, in the "strongly agree" answers to the statement "I often enjoy advertising on TV."

What does this multiple correlation mean? First, a characteristic of feminine cultures is a critical attitude, so people will not readily say they like something. On the other hand, the most feminine of the cultures of the 16 countries represent relatively small markets that may have been relatively swamped by advertising reflecting other cultures' values, advertising not made for their culture and thus not liked. The masculine markets, the United Kingdom and Germany, also are markets with more indigenous advertising. It is particularly the combination FEM-weak UAI that makes people dislike advertising, whereas the combinations MAS-weak UAI and FEM-strong UAI show more confidence in advertising. The configuration MAS-strong UAI shows most confidence in the advertising industry. Extending this finding to different countries, both outside and within Europe, explains the difference between how people relate to advertising as such. Look at Japan: There is

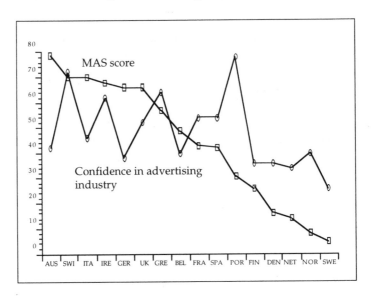

Figure 12.2 Correlation Between MAS and Confidence in the Advertising Industry

SOURCE: Data reproduced from Reader's Digest Eurodata—A Consumer Survey of 17 European Countries, sponsored by The Reader's Digest Association, Inc.

NOTE: rho = 0.53*

no country in the world where people have made advertising so much a part of their lives as Japan, which also scores very high on both MAS and UAI. The opposite is how the Dutch tend to view advertising—as an irritating intrusion into their lives. The Netherlands score more or less the opposite on the MAS-UAI dimensions as the Japanese. Thus, certain value configurations may make some people generally more receptive to advertising as a phenomenon than others, which must be taken into account when comparing advertising effectiveness across borders.

Another conclusion is that the advertising industry in each country gets what it deserves. Where it develops advertising that fits peoples' values, advertising is liked and people have confidence. Where much advertising is imported or based on imported values, it is not liked and probably does not work as well, either. Advertising, to be effective, must reflect the values of the audience.

If a core concept reflects the values of the home country, it can travel to only a limited number of other countries. The international advertising world is full of examples of concepts that cannot travel, one of them being British Telecom using the concept "Freedom of Choice." Literal translation into Dutch (*Vrijheid om te kiezen*) doesn't give the Dutch a similar warm feeling.

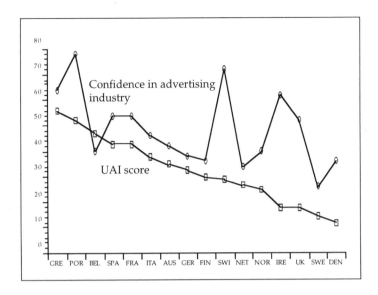

Figure 12.3 Correlation Between UAI and Confidence in the Advertising Industry
SOURCE: Data reproduced from Reader's Digest Eurodata—A Consumer Survey of 17 European Countries, sponsored by The Reader's Digest Association, Inc.
NOTE: rho = 0.52*

Motives don't travel, either. If asked which factor is most important in choosing one's car, most people will give priority to safety (EMS 95). But safety is a hygienic factor, modern cars are all more or less safe, and it is the desirable thing to say. As we learned in Chapter 5 under "Value Structure Maps," there is a variety of motives for choosing cars, and safety is found to be most favored in feminine cultures. For decades, Volvo's advertising has reflected this home-country value worldwide. Volvo is slowly focusing on other values in nonfeminine markets, such as comparative advertising with BMW in the United States.[10]

Developing effective global advertising requires mapping needs, motives, and values according to culture clusters and including them in one's advertising. In the 1990s, many international advertisements have reflected the home values of the advertiser, not the values of a globally diverse audience. In *Business Week* of September 23, 1996, the home country's values of the advertiser could be recognized in 14 advertisements. An advertisement by Korean Air reflects the need for status by calling its business class "prestige class" and by showing a golf course; the advertisement for Pirelli reflects the Italian design orientation; Deutsche Telekom's ad is highly structured and reflects the German technology orientation; BMW's pay-off,

"The ultimate driving machine," also reflects a technology orientation; the advertisements for the French/Swiss watch brands Breitling and Breguet reflect tradition, precision, and craftsmanship; the German Siemens Nixdorf talks about "avoiding the threat"; Air France uses an abstract metaphor; Swissair uses the typical masculine statement, "Best in Business"; *Business Week* reflects its home country's values by stating "In any country, success has a price: US $90"; the U.S. company Tyco wants to make "shareholders happy"; an advertisement by Japanese Selex (copy machines and plotters) reflects long-term orientation plus the value harmony with nature by showing a thick, centuries-old tree; the advertisement from Philips Electronics of the Netherlands uses the long-term orientation statement, "The future belongs to anyone who'll listen," combined with the feminine understatement "Let's make things better"; the Dutch ING bank wants to feel "At home in Emerging and Capital markets." If these advertisers all keep targeting their home-culture audiences with their home culture's values, why are they using a cross-border medium?

Global Advertising Strategy

After what has been said about values and global advertising, a number of strategies can be distinguished. Each strategy uses a different combination of basic forms and execution. Global advertising eventually boils down to six different strategies.

1. Fully Standardized: One Product or Brand, Display, No Values

There is one product or brand that is sold across borders. The product is the message. There will be a song, background music, but little or no copy or pure descriptive or narrative text. It will be in one language. This strategy is used in umbrella campaigns, additional to local advertising, as for example by Levi's, for perfumes and alcoholic beverages. Examples are Bacardi and Martini. It is also recognized in corporate advertising. This strategy cannot differentiate the product by specific values. If it does, it will run into cultural problems. If the campaign focuses on product attributes it can be a successful strategy as long as a product can distinguish itself from the competition. In a world of growing parity in products and brands such a strategy is rarely effective at long term.

2. Semi-Standardized: One Brand, One Advertising Form, and Standard Execution (Voice-Over and/or Lip-Sync)

The advertising form may be a combination of basic forms such as the combination of announcement or lesson with life-style or metaphor or entertainment. Visuals are central to the advertisement. In some countries the original language is used (often English); in others a voice-over is necessary. As not all countries are used to lip-sync, showing a person's lips while talking is not advisable as it shows too clearly that the advertising is "imported." In most cultures this irritates consumers. This strategy is used for internationally sold personal care brands and confectionery brands. Using only a voice over and not showing real interaction with dialogue between people allows for cross-border usage. This is the strategy used for Gillette, Nivea, Mars, and Snickers. It also is the strategy for brands that thrive on a USP or distinct product attributes. Gillette's Sensor Excel, for example, is such a high-quality product that after it was launched, even without advertising, demand exceeded production.

3. One Brand, One Form, Varying Standard Executional Elements

This strategy uses one advertising form including a number of executional elements which can be used in different configurations. The executional elements reflect different values. Focus on values may vary by culture, for example expressed by variations of "benefit to the user," "demonstration of how the product works" or "focus on detailed product attributes." This is a strategy combining opposing values in one advertisement although focus on values can vary by culture. The cultural specifics are compromised. The combination of appeals may not be as effective as each separate appeal would have been in the countries where it fits. Examples of such combinations of appeals in pan-European campaigns are campaigns for shampoo, toothpaste, and household products.

Advertising for toothpaste used to be very different in the UK and Germany. In the UK, focus used to be on self-confidence, showing the product benefit, the result: effect of the white teeth or good looking teeth to the user. The typical German appeal would be to protect the teeth, showing all the details of how the toothpaste works on the teeth. Focus was on anxiety reduction. Similar approaches were found with respect to shampoo: either showing a woman being admired for her beautiful hair, or details of how the shampoo works. Pan-European campaigns focus on both: details of how the shampoo works on the hair as well as the shiny hair as a result. An example is the campaign for Pantene Pro V which started at the end of 1995. Between the different countries the focus was either stronger on the one element (in the UK the result: shining hair during party time) or more focus on the details (Germany: longer time focus on the details).

4. One or Different Brandnames, One Advertising Form, Different Executions

This is the P&G strategy, advertising similar products with different brand names using one consistent basic advertising form such as comparison, testimonial, or drama, but adapting to people, languages and culture. It is used for sanitary napkins and detergents or cleaning liquids (Dreft, Fairy, Ace). P&G has been very successful with this strategy. Within one form, different commercials are made for each country and the execution reflects cultural values. An example is how in large power distance cultures the elders advise the younger and in small power distance cultures the other way round. Another household products company, Henkel, uses one problem-solution concept (dirty-clean) all over Europe in different forms, many locally made. Yet, they all reflect a typical German value: ergiebig. There are two distinct money concepts in advertising for household products: "more value for equal money" and "equal value for less money."

The former is the German approach (the word "ergiebig" expresses it), the latter is the Dutch approach. In Dutch advertising it is expressed by showing coins, piggy banks, or even towels with bank note imprints and bank directors. The word "gratis" (free) is frequently included. The German approach is expressed by showing many dirty clothes and after washing, many clean clothes. Many children, many dirty cooks, long clotheslines with many sheets, large washing machines, etc. The function of the detergent is to deliver in an efficient way. The function of the Dutch approach is to save money. Some pan-European advertisers combine the two: they use the "ergiebig" appeal and combine it with the piggy bank. They must have noticed the difference but have not understood how culturally distinct the two approaches are.

5. One or Different Brandnames, One Platform, Different Executions

One abstract platform or idea is the basis for different local executions. Examples are campaigns for KitKat candy bar, Knorr sauces, and Sara Lee/DE coffee. The platform for KitKat's campaign is "take a break, take a KitKat." Knorr's platform is "professional cooking." Sara Lee/DE's platform is "togetherness, enjoying coffee in the home." There will be recognizable elements such as the brand name and package, the pay-off (KitKat), music (Sara Lee/DE), a symbol (professional cook—Knorr). Different executions based on the platform can be developed in different countries and adopted by others of similar cultures. The advantage of this strategy is the combination of local values and a centrally recognizable idea. Actual ads may be used globally, regionally, or locally depending on the need for cultural adaptation.

6. Multi-Local: Act Global, Think Local—Endorsement

This is the opposite of the "think global—act local" paradigm. It means reaping all the benefits of globalization in production, sourcing, distribution, marketing, and the connected benefits of economies of scale in production and organization, but accepting that mental images cannot be standardized. This is the global strategy of those companies who have learned to understand that they will only thrive on respect for and exploitation of local cultural values. These companies build relationships with consumers and their advertising's objective is to build trust. The company's name is used as endorsement. This is Nestlé's strategy, it can be recognized in Volkswagen's strategy and in strategies of many Japanese companies.

Further Research

I have focused more on Europe than on other parts of the world for the practical examples in this book, both because most of my personal experience is in Europe and because Europe has a head start in pan-European campaigns and research. Further research must be extended to regions such as Asia, Latin America, and Africa. Within the United States, too, the application of the Hofstede model can be helpful for differentiating campaigns for ethnic populations. I am confident that my application of Hofstede's model to advertising in Europe, the United States, and a few countries in Asia will be equally successful in other areas. Hofstede's own application to management has also proven itself just as effective in Asian cultures as in European ones.

Large global companies, such as P&G, Unilever, and Nestlé, have understood that Anglo-Saxon strategies are not necessarily fit for all other cultures and have invested enormously in research to determine what is. Many other international companies have not done as much proprietary research. The incorporation of Hofstede's model in the EMS database will be of future assistance to those companies that do not have similar large research budgets, that is, for Europe. Add to that the increasing pan-regional research in other areas, and it will be possible to discover culture-bound and culture-free motives worldwide by empirical research and to map them meaningfully into culture clusters for all sorts of product and service categories.

The application may also help academic researchers to shed their ethnocentrism and stimulate them to do more cross-cultural advertising research, particularly in countries that have not been covered to date.

This book may stimulate educators outside the United States/United Kingdom to do research to adapt U.S. experience and theory to their own cultures in order to teach their students to develop more effective marketing and advertising strategies. U.S. books are usually written for the U.S. market's culture—for U.S. students and not for students of other cultures.

Finally, I was raised in a medium uncertainty avoidance culture, following the continental European school in which theory is emphasized. The theory developed in this book is based on more than 30 years of experience in advertising practice and education and is illustrated by empirical findings that validate the theory. The book reflects two academic cultures: the continental European academic culture with its focus on theory, and the Anglo-Saxon empirical one. For those who think that theory is overemphasized, this may be an incentive to prove it all empirically.

The Future of Global Advertising

Advertising, to be effective, must reflect the values of its audience. Hofstede's 5-D model appears to be an instrument that can help us recognize the values of different cultures. It can help to predict what reflects culture and what fits with a particular culture. It can show go and no-go areas for specific appeals, motives, and concepts, which is what global advertisers need for developing effective global advertising. Understanding how culture is reflected and should be reflected in advertising may not lead to the largest cost-saving in the production of advertising. It will lead to more effective advertising appeals and concepts; that is, more cost-effective advertising. Decision makers have to decide whether (a) they want the easy-to-calculate savings of standardization, leading to bland less-effective messages that lack culture fit but are easy to calculate in terms of money and are aimed at short-term accountability; (b) or they will choose non-standardized, culture appropriate, effective advertising without short-term savings but generating long-term sales effects.

Conclusion

Global advertisers will increasingly have to deal with a cluttered environment for their advertising messages. One standard message may reduce costs because of economies of scale. Consistency in presentation is another frequently heard argument for standardization. These arguments may be conflicting. On the one hand, the need to stand out from the crowd means differentiating one's advertising; on the other hand, there are limitations to the receptiveness of consumers. Strong differentiation from the competition may increase short-term awareness, but consumer understanding and acceptance may decrease. A standard approach cannot carry values, yet advertisers know they can only build leadership brands by differentiating them vis-à-vis the competition.

New technology enables advertisers to develop beautiful, arty advertising that easily crosses borders, the type of advertising that is based on visual metaphors and characterized by fast and frequently changing visuals and pop music. Yet this type of advertising does not differentiate. Thus, advertising for cars becomes similar to advertising for ice cream. This was the trend at the moment of finishing this book's manuscript. Such a trend makes U.K. commercials for Volvo cars similar to advertising for Persil detergents and ice cream brands such as Solero/Soledo and Calippo. These commercials may have in common that they are made by the same agency or that they advertise brands owned by the same company, but also that they do not make a brand meaningful to the consumer.

Another trend is increased sensitivity to cultural diversity and its consequences for developing global advertising. A consistent corporate identity and a consistency in presentation can go together with cultural sensitivity. Global companies increasingly develop one corporate platform that allows for meaningful local extensions. This will be the future of global advertising.

Finally, the importance of building relationships and trust between company and consumers may bring companies to develop their own cross-border advertising styles. These should be advertising styles that do not alienate consumers and can be meaningfully adapted to local cultures.

Notes

1. Fukuyama, F. (1995). *Trust, the social virtues and the creation of prosperity.* New York: Free Press.

2. Huntington, S. P. (1996). *The clash of civilizations and the remaking of world order.* New York: Simon & Schuster, pp. 20, 58.

3. Data reproduced from Reader's Digest Eurodata—A Consumer Survey of 17 European Countries, sponsored by The Reader's Digest Association, Inc.

4. Huntington (1996), *The clash of civilizations,* p. 67.

5. Roland, A. (1988). *In search of self in India and Japan.* Princeton, NJ: Princeton University Press, p. 136.

6. Roland (1988), *In search of self in India and Japan,* p. 236.

7. A significant correlation of .48* was found between size of engine and company car in the EMS 95 data. With respect to the same relationship, a significant correlation of .44* was found in the data of the Reader's Digest Eurodata Survey of 1991.

8. Anholt, S. (1996). "Making a brand travel." *The Journal of Brand Management, 3*(6), 360.

9. Anholt (1996), "Making a brand travel," p. 361.

10. McGinn, D. (1997, January 13). "Whoa! Was that a Volvo. It is no longer your father's square station wagon." *Newsweek,* p. 34.

Index

About the Author

Marieke de Mooij is president of her own consultancy, Cross Cultural Communications Company, the Netherlands, and is a consultant to companies for international communications strategy development. CCCC is affiliated with ITIM, the Institute for Training in Intercultural Management, and with the research company Inter/View, both located in the Netherlands and working worldwide. She is Associate Professor at the University of Navarre in Spain. She has lectured on cross-cultural communications and advertising in many European countries, in Asia, and in the United States. Marieke de Mooij draws from 30 years of experience in both advertising practice and education, with an international textile company, in an advertising agency, and as a director of the Dutch Foundation for Education in Advertising and Marketing. She has been involved in international advertising education since 1980, both for the International Advertising Association and as Managing Director of BBDO College. She is author of *Advertising Worldwide* (2nd edition), the leading textbook on international advertising.